POSTCARD HISTORY SERIES

South Carolina Postcards

Volume VI

Newberry County

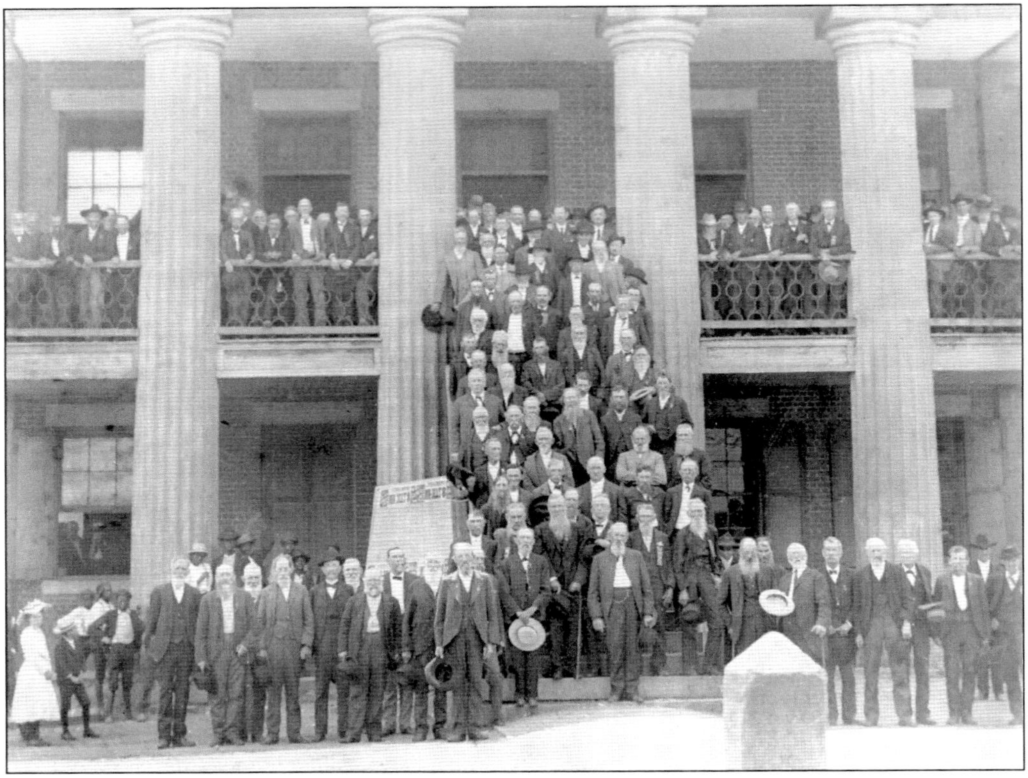

[REUNION OF CONFEDERATE VETERANS, c. 1907.] Reunions were annual events that attracted every healthy veteran in the county. Developed by the James D. Nance Camp and organized in 1893 by the Confederate Veterans of Newberry, the officers were Capt. J.W. Gary, commander; Dr. R.C. Carlisle, lieutenant commander; and J.F.J. Caldwell, 2nd lieutenant commander. In 1907 O.L. Schumpert was the adjutant of Camp J.D. Nance, one of the largest in the state. The Drayton Rutherford Chapter of the Daughters of the Confederacy prepared an elaborate program and dinner for 200 to 300 veterans, which they served in the Old Courthouse. Dixie was sung by the D.A. Dickert Chapter as veterans marched in to the meal and program.

FRONT COVER:
[HORSE AND BUGGY ON THE SQUARE, c. 1923.] *This image of Newberry's city square at the turn of the century was likely taken after a Main Street parade. The Commercial Bank officials of 1923 are seated in the buggy in front of their new bank building (right center) on the northwest corner of Boyce and Caldwell Streets. The Commercial Bank is beside the Bank of Newberry building, built in 1853 (left center).*

BACK COVER:
[C.E. HUTCHISON AND SNELGROVE GROCERY STORE, c. 1910.] *This grocery store was located on the east corner of the 1000 block of Main Street at McKibben Street and faced the lower end of the Public Square. Presumably the owners stand in front of their grocery store along with what appears to be a peanut-roasting machine. This grocery was listed in Newberry's 1932 City Directory.*

POSTCARD HISTORY SERIES

South Carolina Postcards

Volume VI

Newberry County

Howard Woody

ARCADIA PUBLISHING

ISBN 978-0-7385-1391-1

Published by Arcadia Publishing
Charleston, South Carolina

Printed in the United States of America

Library of Congress Catalog Card Number: 2001093948

For all general information contact Arcadia Publishing at:
Telephone 843-853-2070
Fax 843-853-0044
E-mail sales@arcadiapublishing.com
For customer service and orders:
Toll-Free 1-888-313-2665

Visit us on the Internet at www.arcadiapublishing.com

DEDICATION

In memory of Annie L. Reed, Helen R. Reed, and Edward C. Reed Jr. for your thoughtful support. –HW

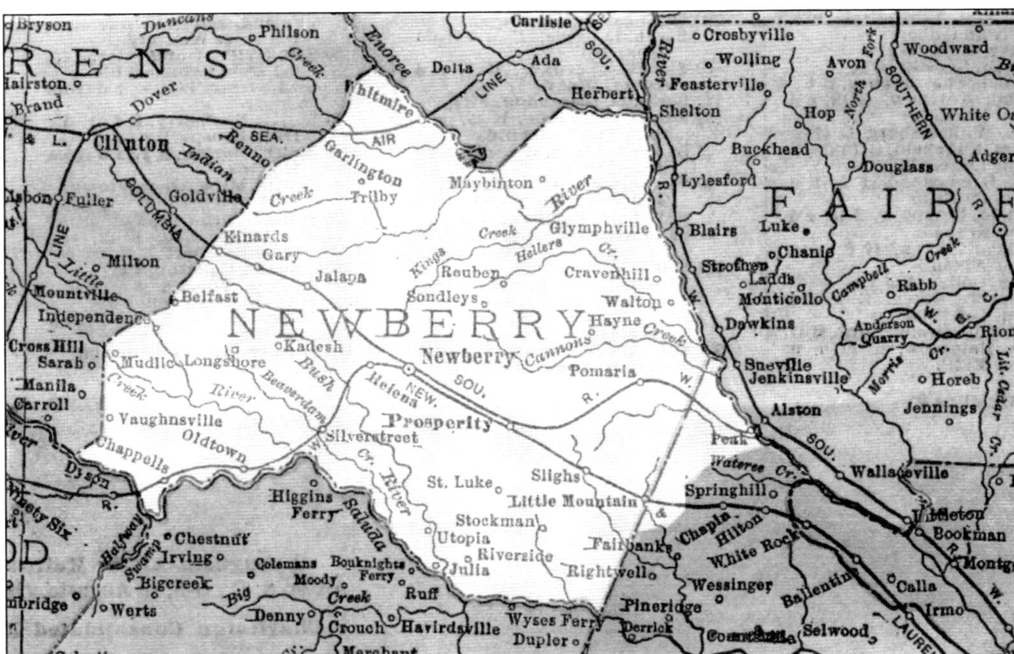

[NEWBERRY COUNTY MAP, 1911.] This map includes the 1911 boundaries along with an annexed area that included Little Mountain (1902) and Peak (1920). Lake Murray, which was created in 1928, is not on this map.

CONTENTS

INTRODUCTION

The pathway of this *Postcard History Series* journey documenting South Carolina culture through turn-of-the-century postcards began in the Charleston area; shifted south to Southern Carolina in volume two; continued on to Aiken and West Central Carolina in volume three; and then reached the Midlands with Lexington County in volume four and Richland County in volume five. Newberry County, volume six, continues the search for the visual images that reflect the previous but not forgotten daily lifestyles of the counties making up the section known as the Midlands. Volume six covers the county on the northern side of Lake Murray and the remainder of the Dutch Fork area and extends to the Laurens line and the Sumter National Forest during the period of the 1890s to 1930s. Newberry County is 25 miles northwest of Columbia and consists of 623 square miles.

Newberry County is located in the lower Piedmont region of South Carolina. Its northern border faces Union County and is partially defined by sections of the Enoree, Tyger, and Broad Rivers. Its eastern boundary with Fairfield County is determined by the Broad River and small sections of Richland and Lexington Counties. The southern line is formed by a portion of the upper shore of Lake Murray, the Saluda River, and Saluda and Greenwood Counties, while the western border faces Laurens County. The Indians initially living in Newberry County were the Shawnees, Catawbas, and Cherokees.

The earliest European settlers were mainly the German, English, and Scotch-Irish families who used the 735-mile Great Philadelphia Wagon Road down the Shenandoah Valley from Pennsylvania and Virginia in an attempt to escape the French and Indian War in the North. They passed near Danville, Virginia, went on to Charlotte, continued south to the Catawba River at Nations Ford, over to the Broad River at Fish Dam Ford, and on into Newberry County. They found that the soil was good and the eastern and southern sections produced abundant crops of corn, peas, beans, apples, and peaches. Cotton later became the county's major cash crop.

Newberry began as an isolated agrarian county with a scattering of villages and communities. The major force for commercial development was the early railroad service (whose need for numerous fuel and water stops related to their wood-burning steam engines) that took an indirect path passing through villages and the county seat on its route between Greenville and Columbia. The incorporation of these villages often came after the railroad established depots, and the flow of freight and passenger service both in and out of these communities created the economic base.

With the flow of commerce from the world beyond, education became a more significant social concern. In 1869 J.K. Jillson, state superintendent of education, noted four problems that needed to be corrected: (1) lack of qualified teachers; (2) inefficiency of school officials; (3) apathy of the general public; (4) inadequacy of school funds. Many of the initial rural schools were created and funded by a local church with children of all ages and levels taught in a one-room structure. In the first year of Newberry County's public schools, 1869, the school-age population was 5,000; unfortunately, the county's 46 schools average attendance was only 1,000 white and 240 black children. Of the 46 schoolhouses, one was brick and the remainder were log or frame structures. Four schools were for African-American children. The 42 teachers consisted of 38 white and 4 black. The county's educational structure slowly improved from 1870 to 1900. With the beginning of the industrial economy the towns became more important as commercial centers with new job opportunities that attracted the best of Newberry's youth. The less successful tenant families and others found work in the cotton mills, which gave them steady employment, housing, and education. Education improved as one-room schools were consolidated into area schools. However, Dr. W.L. Gray reported in 1926 that South Carolina had 38,000 white and 181,000 black illiterate persons. Newberry County's population was 20,879 in 1860; 34,586 in 1910; and 40,000, in 1926.

This volume continues the practice of reviewing the county's municipal structure, sites, and activities first; the major business district second; social, cultural, and industrial facets third, and then shifting to smaller communities in the rural areas last. The city's merchants produced a normal level of commercial postcards that were sold by retailers such as the Mayes Book Store, Pelham's Drug Store, and several 5 and 10¢ stores that stocked them as small profit items. The postcard images found in this survey came from private collectors; private and public archives; and the albums of those individuals with Newberry roots. On occasion some of these postcard images were taken by the traveling factory salespersons who were trained in the art of photographing postcard-type views and many had excellent images; however, when the initial 8-by-10-inch master photographs were located, these often had sharper details and were therefore used in the book. The scale of the pictures on the cover and in the book have been altered to relate to page layout and length of caption. Additionally, "titles" that appear on the front of some postcards begin each image's accompanying caption; where a postcard has no title or where a title may be incomplete (for instance, lacking a date), the author has created one and inserted it between brackets.

What is a postcard image? The answer relates to the intended or extended use of the subjects on the photographic negative. The image could be made full scale for postcards, enlarged for framing, or reduced for montage use. Probably the most interesting postcard images relate to the extended uses of the negatives. Photographers wanted to make as many pennies from a negative as possible. One example was the 1907 fire where pictures were used in newspapers, reused as postcards, and later placed in numerous books. Another prototype is the group portrait taken for the sponsors' use in annuals and later placed on postcards for participants' correspondence. The Newberry College baseball team postcard is an example of that type. Needless to say, reprints are made years later and mailed for various reasons. Most of the views in this volume fit into the latter extended categories.

The selection criteria for images in this volume were as follows: has that subject been seen before on South Carolina postcards; did it have a historical or cultural value for South Carolina history teachers and students in 2001; and would someone want to mail the image elsewhere? Rural merchants had few requests for postcards so few were produced. Members of historical societies located rural and urban images in local private albums and those were copied at public meetings. Every effort was made to obtain pictures from each community.

The object of the previous books in this *Postcard History Series* has been to produce a body of images that reflect the lifestyles and culture of the 1890s to the 1930s of one or more counties. I hope that the two-fold experience of edification and enjoyment has been found in this volume, as well.

—Howard Woody

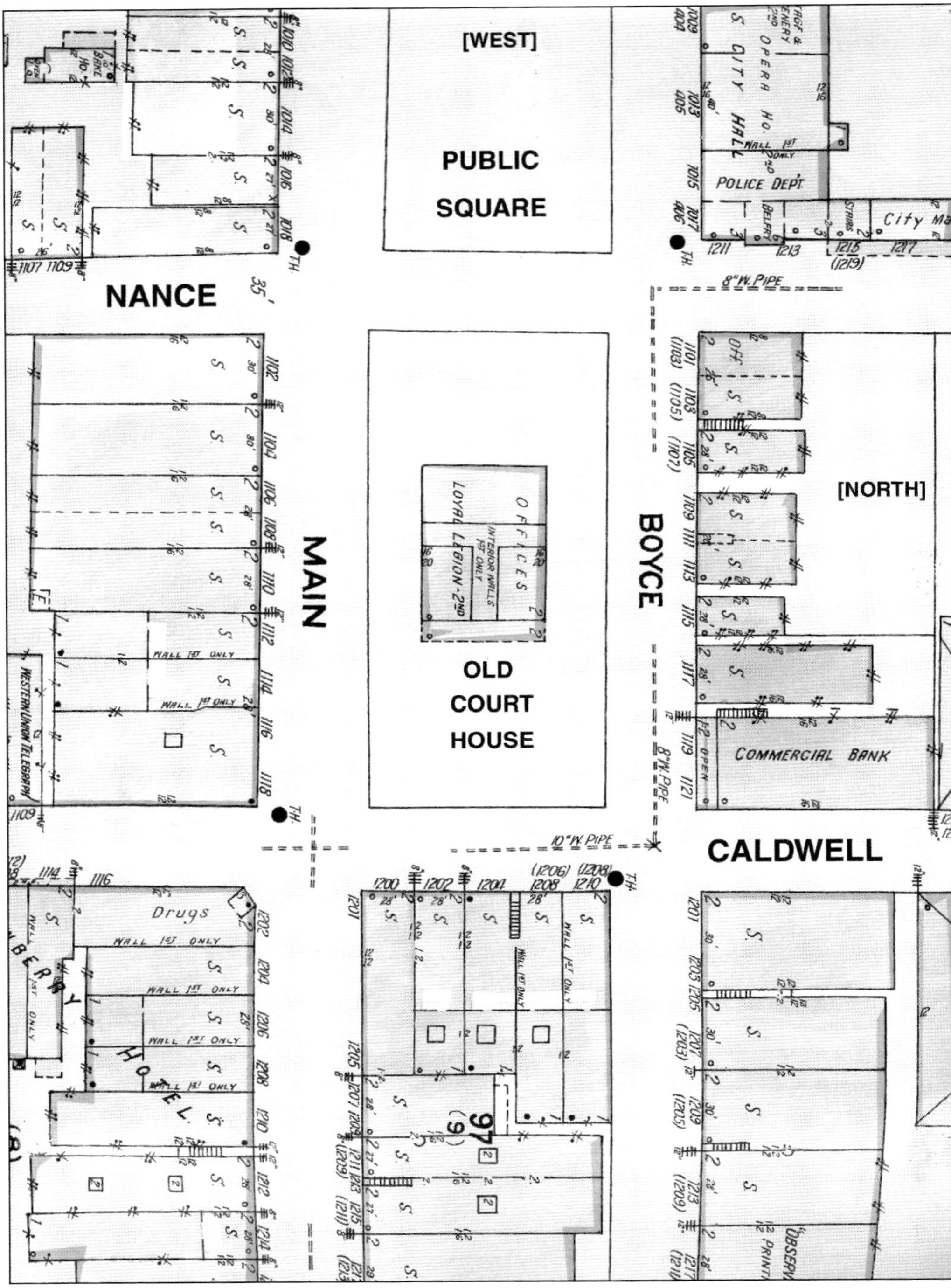

[Business District Map, 1923.] The central business district as drawn on the 1923 Sanborn Fire Insurance Map has been reproduced and adjusted so that the placement of the retail stores can be more easily understood. The 1911 street names and numbering system are used to prevent confusion.

One

Views of Newberry

The courthouse village of Newberry District evolved from an isolated site into an economic center with the establishment of the 1851 and the 1890 railroad freight and passenger services. The county facilities began with a small log structure on L. Coate's two-acre lot in 1789 that was replaced by a wood building in 1801. Being too small for public functions and without a fireproof vault to protect public records, a third one was designed by Robert Mills and built by Grafton and Beck for $10,000 in 1823. This edifice became unsafe, so a fourth one was built in 1853. Merchants quickly erected inexpensive frame stores, beginning with just a few at the courthouse and expanding to 53 stores in 1879 and then 75 in 1889. These stores surrounded the Courthouse and Public Square. Like other towns, fires continually destroyed this business center and adjacent homes. In 1886, half of the business section was destroyed; in 1877, 20 stores and many homes were lost; in 1879, 10 stores were consumed and 2 others razed; in 1883, the frame Mollohon row was gutted; and in 1907, 5 entire blocks went up in flames. Brick buildings replaced the frame ones and each time the areas were rebuilt and expanded. New cotton mills and other industries came, and the city grew from a population of 2,500 in 1879 to 7,278 by 1930.

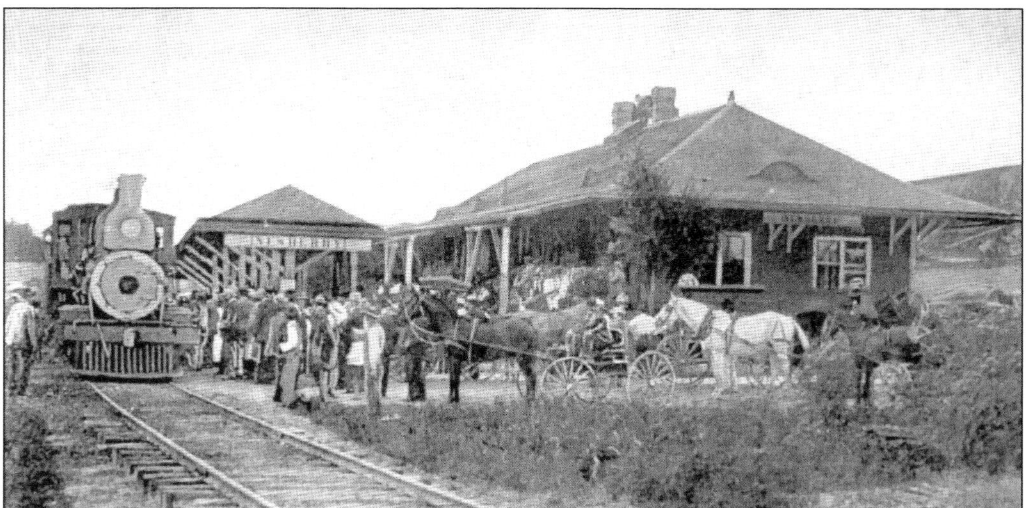

Union Station, Newberry [c. 1907]. Newberry began its development into a commercial center when the Greenville and Columbia Railroad reached Newberry in March 1851 and expanded further when the Columbia, Newberry, and Laurens (CN&L) Railroad established its depot in 1890. The Union Station was at 1105–1109 West Main Street with its freight depot at 844 West Main Street. The CN&L depot was on Friend Street while their freight depot was on O'Neal Street. Passenger service was discontinued in 1952.

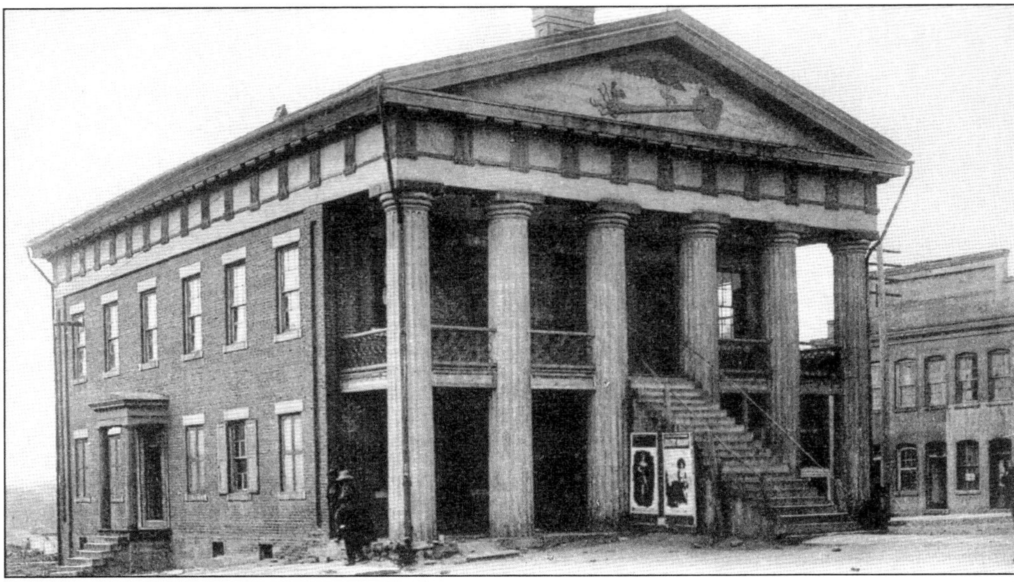

COURTHOUSE, NEWBERRY [C. 1906]. The fourth courthouse, completed in 1853 at 1203 Caldwell Street, was designed by architect J. Graves and constructed in stucco-covered brick by J. Damrod at a cost of $9,100. O. Wells repaired the building in 1876 and added a bas-relief on a front pediment of a fallen palmetto tree symbolizing a prostrate South Carolina and an American eagle with scales of justice representing the federal government.

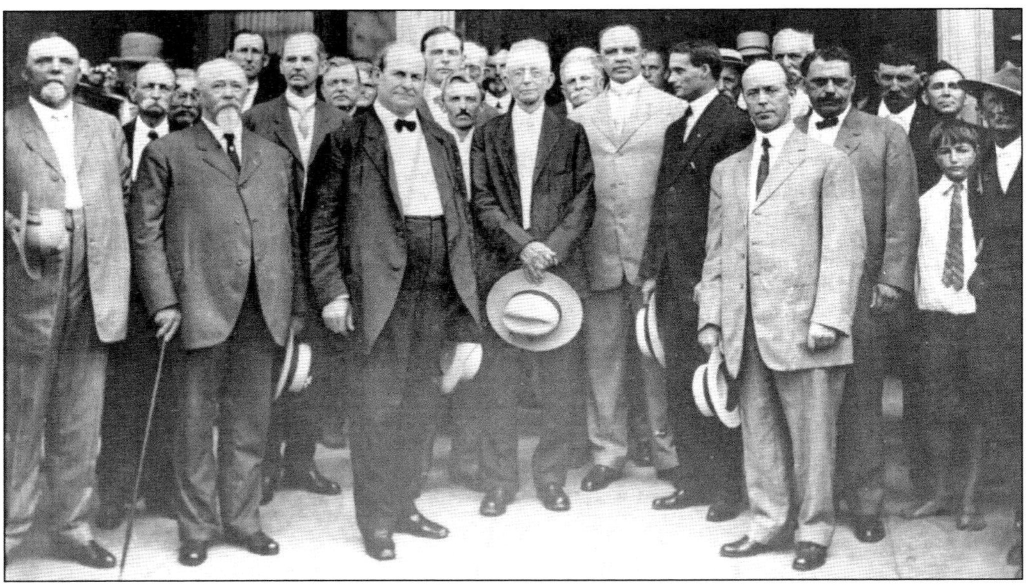

[WILLIAM JENNINGS BRYAN, NEWBERRY, 1911.] W.J. Bryan (1860–1925), the Democratic Party's nominee for President in 1896 and 1900, visited Newberry as a guest speaker for the Chautauqua festival. This picture, printed in *The Observer*, shows him standing (third from left) with the reception committee composed of H.L. Parr, G.S. Mower, Dr. McIntosh, J.H. Harms (president, Newberry College), B.L. Mathews, J. Kinard, J. Mayes, and C. Summer in front of the Crotwell Hotel. He gave a speech entitled "Prince of Peace" at the Opera House.

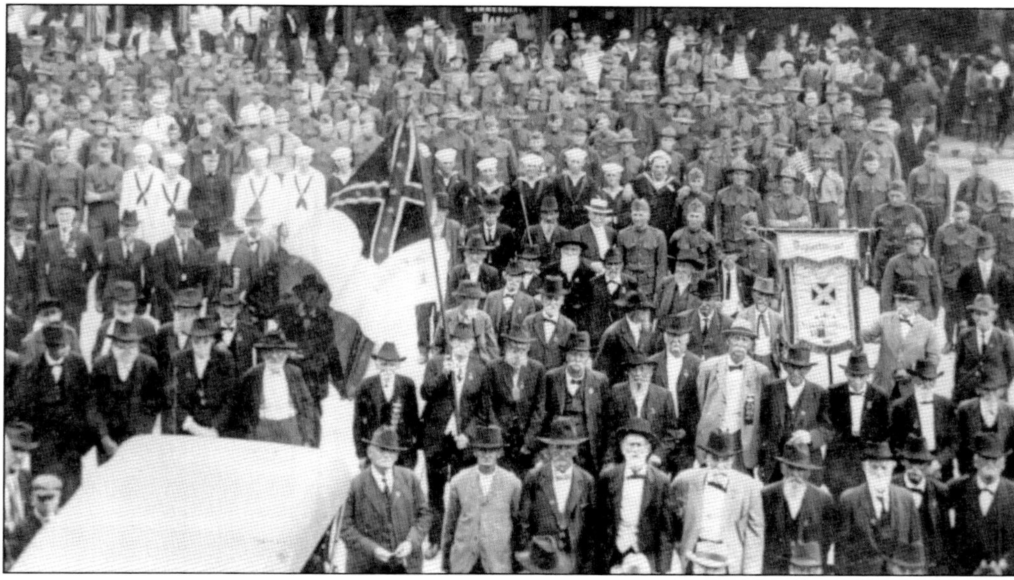

[The Memorial Day Celebration, *c.* 1919.] Newberry's American Legion organized a celebration that began in front of the Old Courthouse. Remaining veterans of the Civil War, the Spanish-American War, and World War I battles were invited to assemble for a Memorial Day program that honored the sacrifices of those who died and those who returned from the conflicts.

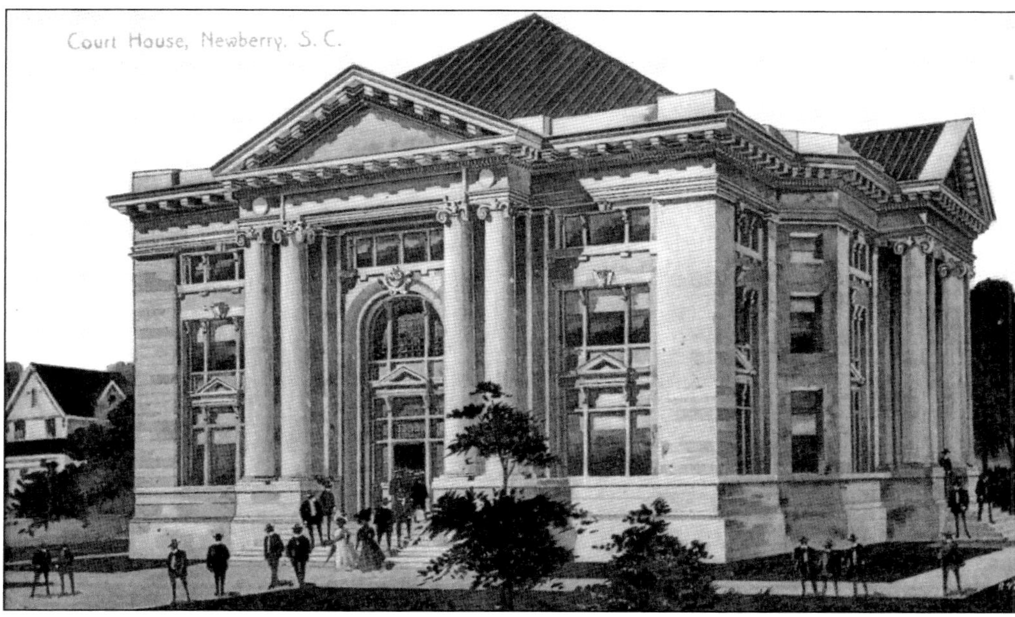

Courthouse, Newberry [*c.* 1908]. In 1906 a new, larger courthouse was deemed necessary so a commission, chaired by G.S. Mower, selected F.P. Milburn of Charlotte to design a Neoclassical-style building costing $50,000. G.W. Waring of Columbia built it using red brick and terra cotta. This fifth courthouse at 1224 College Street was completed in 1908. The architectural drawing above was used on 1908 postcards and was printed in the *Herald*.

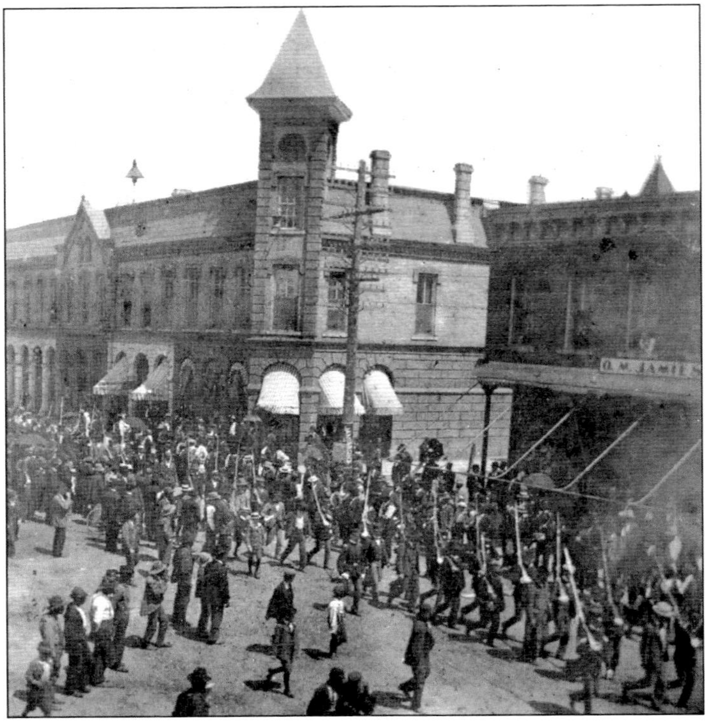

[Spanish-American Recruits Marching, 1898.] Capt. W.S. Langford, a graduate of the Citadel, organized the Newberry Guards in 1897. Members of this unit volunteered for service in the Spanish-American War. On the day of departure, the stores closed and the town came out to send off the recruits. The 96-man company formed at the armory and marched to the depot to depart for Columbia on May 10, 1898. Their officers included 1st Lt. R.H. Wearn, 2nd Sgt. J.G. Daniel, and 3rd Sgt. T O. Stewart Jr.

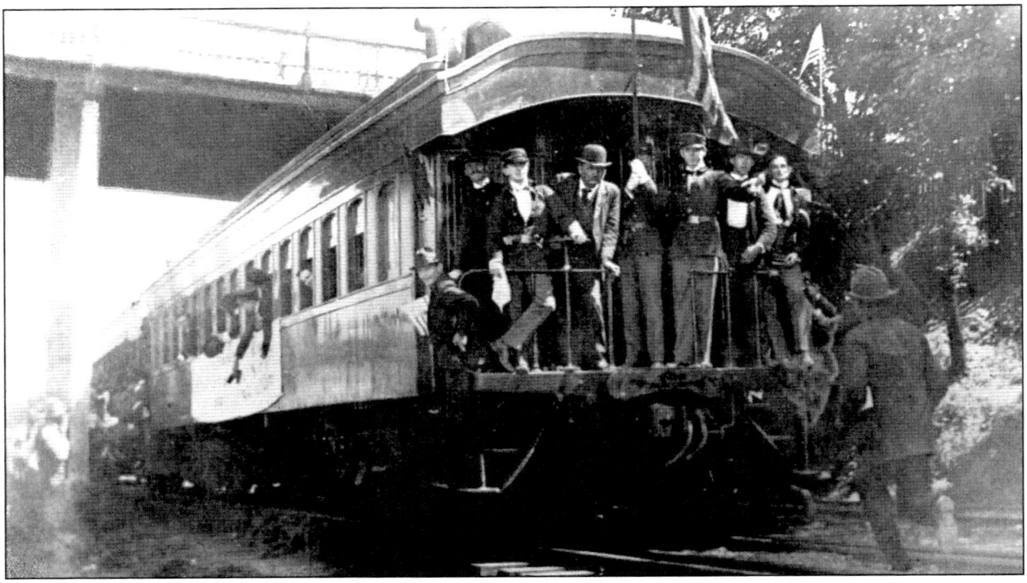

[Recruits Leaving Newberry Station, 1898.] The Southern train arrived and hooked up the Newberry Guards' two coaches. The recruits were accompanied to Columbia by Mayor H.H. Evans, Sen. G.S. Mower, Sheriff M.M. Buford, and others. They arrived in Columbia with bands playing and cheering spectators lining the streets as they marched from the depot to the post office on Main Street. From there they rode the street car to Hyatt Park and then marched to Camp Ellerbe. Forty percent of the Spanish-American recruits were rejected.

CONFEDERATE MONUMENT, NEWBERRY [c. 1907]. The Survivors Association of the 3rd South Carolina Volunteers Regiment (SCVR) secured $1,300 for the monument and a contract was let to Leavell and Speers in February 1880 to make and install a monument. A base of Newberry granite supported an Italian marble shaft that included the names of the 471 deceased Newberry District soldiers; it was surmounted by 13 cannonballs. An assembly of 8,000 observed the unveiling on June 30,1880, in the Public Square. Gen. Y.J. Pope, adjutant of the 3rd SCVR and president of the Survivors Association, presided over the ceremony and Gen. John D. Kennedy of Camden, commander of the brigade that included the 3rd SCVR, delivered the oration.

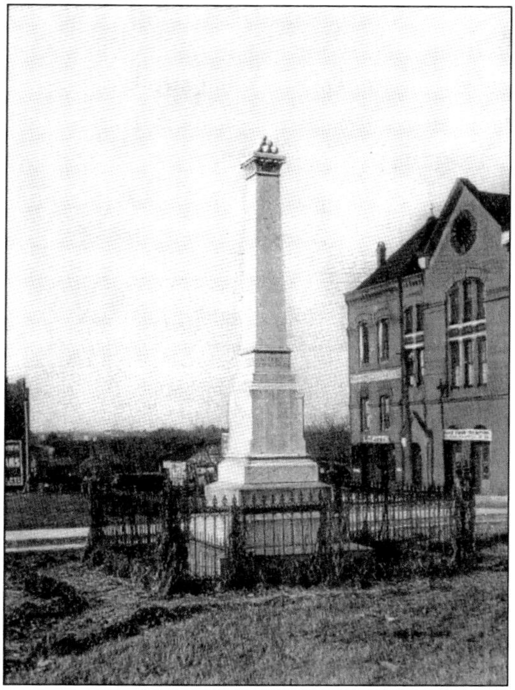

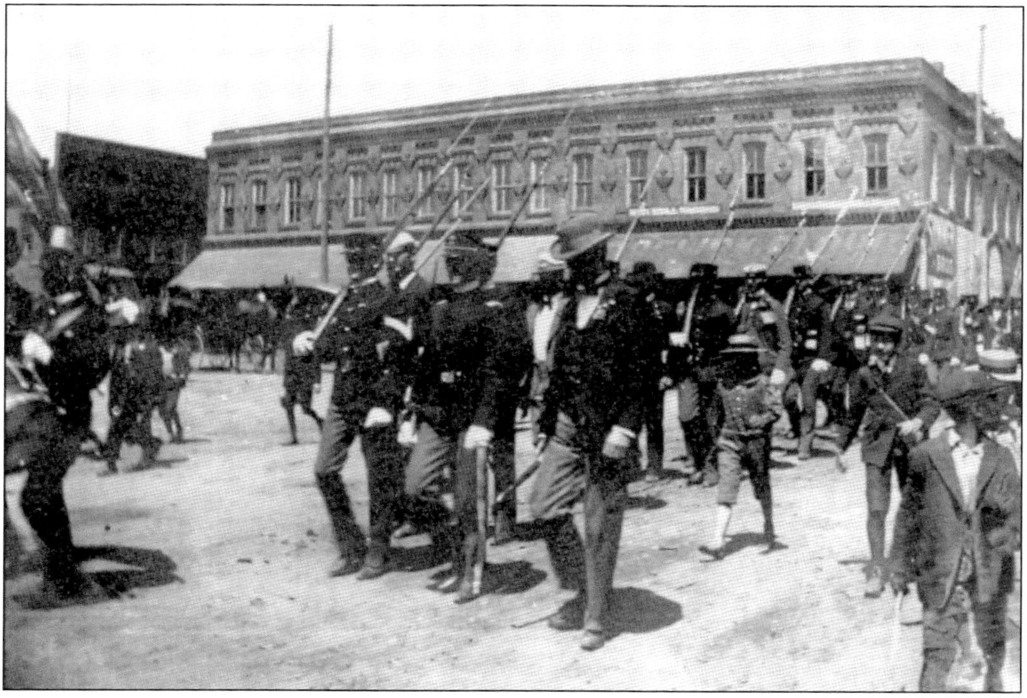

[VETERANS ON PARADE, c. 1919.] Newberry used the Confederate Memorial Day of May 10 to honor the veterans and current military men with a parade down Main Street. This picture taken after World War I shows soldiers wearing uniforms of that era and some veterans of earlier conflicts.

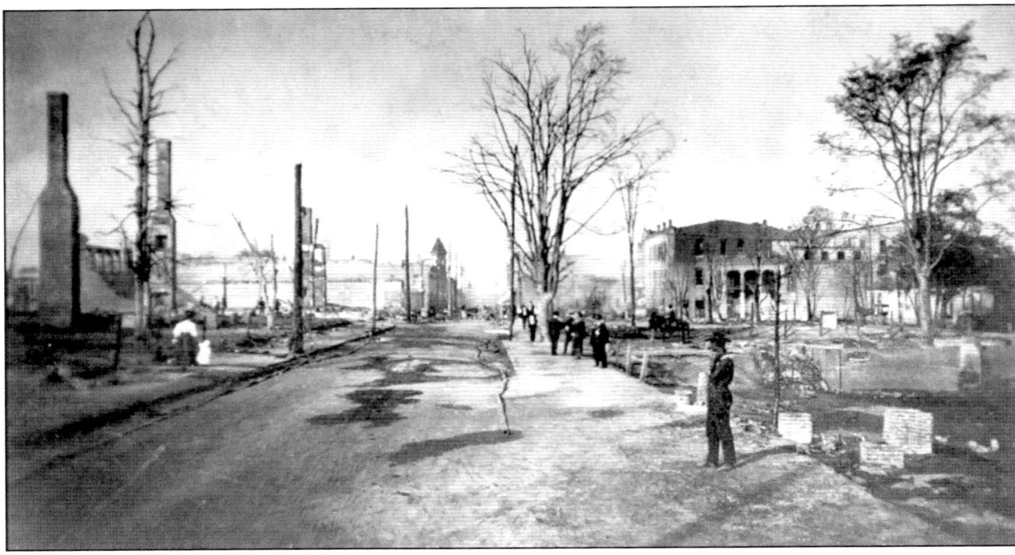

[THE BURNT DISTRICT, 1907.] The Great Fire of 1907 began on College Street and spread eastward with strong winds up Friend and Main Streets. It burned five square blocks, destroying 10 stores, 22 residences, 2 churches, and livery stables at a loss of $125,000. The fire department ran out of water and contained the fire by using dynamite to destroy houses in the path of the blaze. This westward view was taken from Main and Thompson Streets. The several-story building on the right is the back side of the Frederick Hotel. The chimneys on the left belonged to the Silas Johnstone residence.

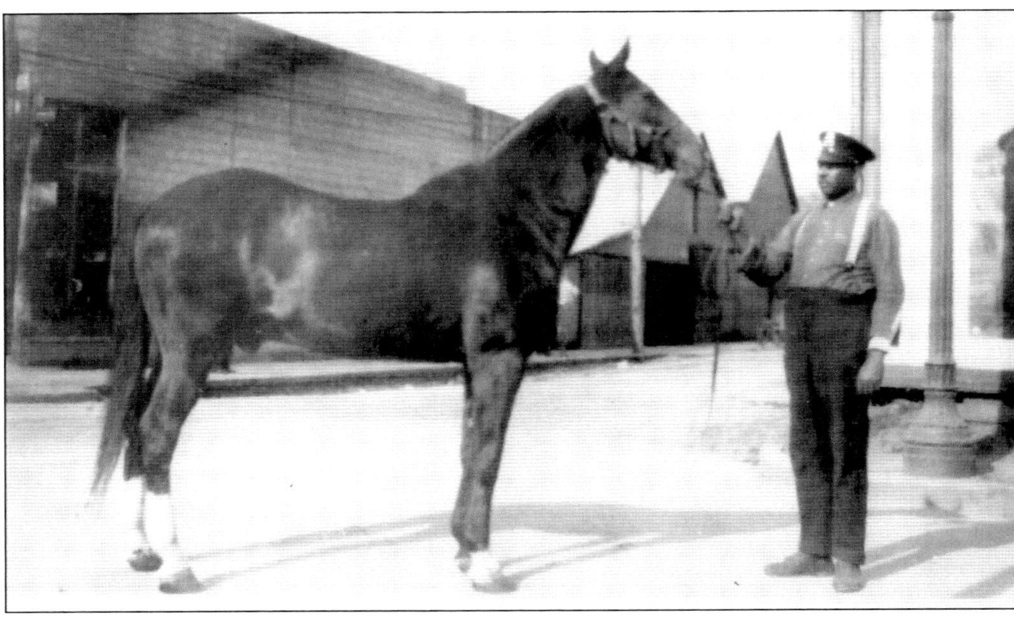

['JOE' THE FIRE DEPARTMENT'S HORSE, *c.* 1911.] Joe, bought by the fire department *c.* 1904, was trained by M. Lesesne. In 1911 at Rock Hill Joe broke the all-time state record for the 200-yard race. He competed in and won more fire tournaments than any other horse in the state. When Joe died in 1930, he was honored with a public ceremony while the town's fire bell rang 35 times, once for each year of his life. He was buried beside the fire department building.

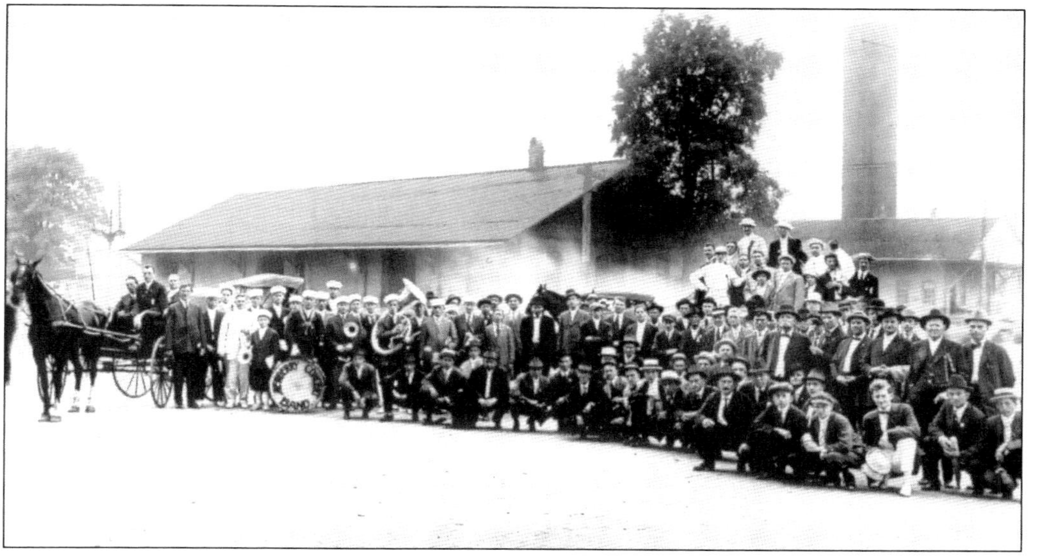

[Joe's Greenwood Victory, c. 1912.] The Fire Departments' Tournament at Greenwood was the venue for Joe to win another first place for Newberry and add to his long list of victories. The Newberry Concert Band and supporters were at the Greenwood depot, the site of this scene, to cheer their team.

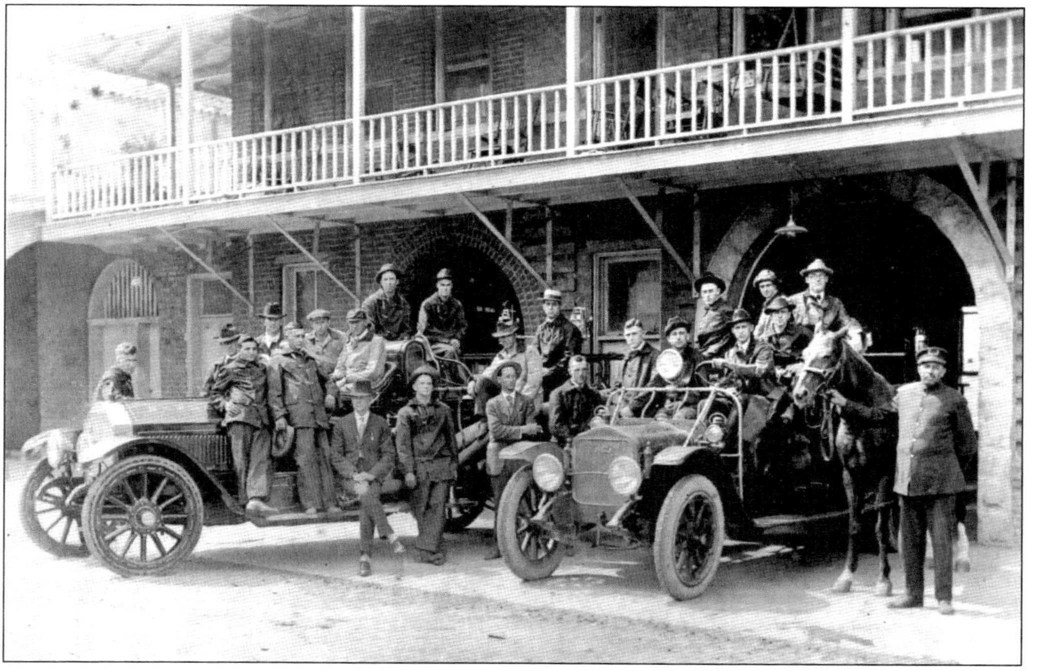

[Fire Department, c. 1920.] In 1883 the "Excelsior" fire company was established, and they purchased a La France fire engine, two heavy two-wheel reels, and 1,000 feet of hose. Later the company became the Newberry Fire Department and was located at 1227 Nance Street. H.B. Wells was the fire department chief from 1905 to 1940. The building shown above was remodeled and enlarged by adding a large back section and still stands in 2001.

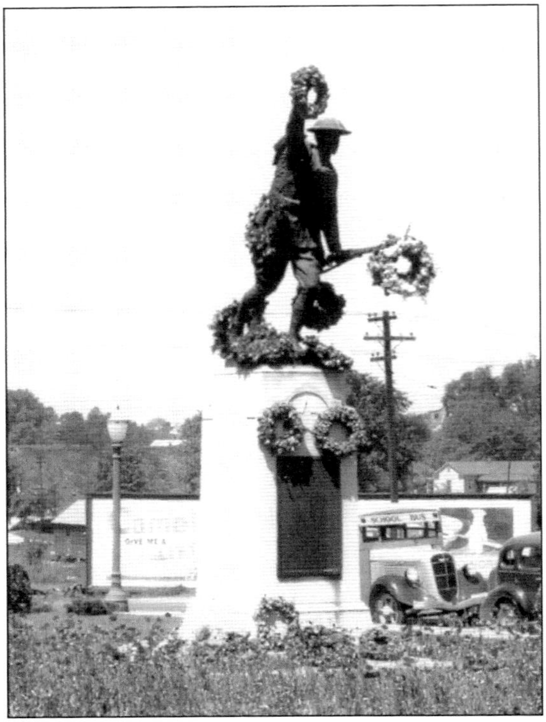

[American Dough Boy WWI Monument, 1928.] Ten years after World War I had ended a committee including Z.F. Wright and eight others was appointed to establish a memorial honoring those who died in that conflict. The popular American Dough Boy WWI Monument, which was also erected at the Olympia Mills Village in 1930 with copies used at numerous sites elsewhere at a cost of about $3,000, was chosen for a lower Public Square site. The unveiling program was held on Sunday, November 11, 1928, before an audience of 3,000–5,000 spectators. Newberry County Post 24 of the American Legion organized the program. South Carolina had 62,294 men in this war with 41 killed, while Newberry County suffered 3 deaths.

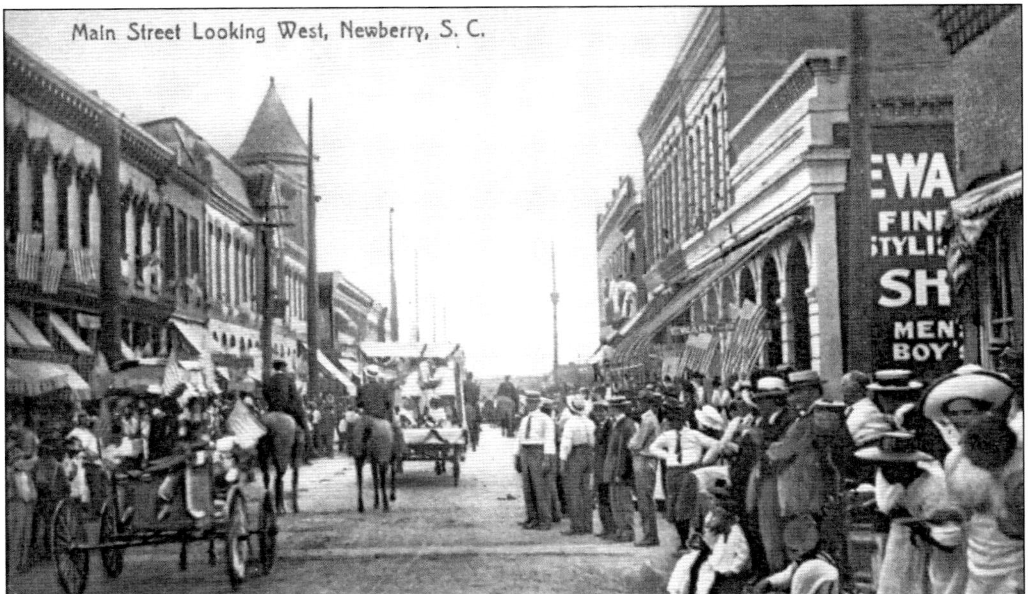

Main Street Looking West, Newberry [c. 1908]. This postcard view highlights a summer parade with horse-drawn floats moving west on Main Street. The American flags placed on both sides of the street suggests that it might be a Fourth of July celebration. On the left side of this 1200 block of Main Street are retail shops on the ground level of the Newberry Hotel. The right side shows the corner of College Street with a sign for Ewart-Perry men's store.

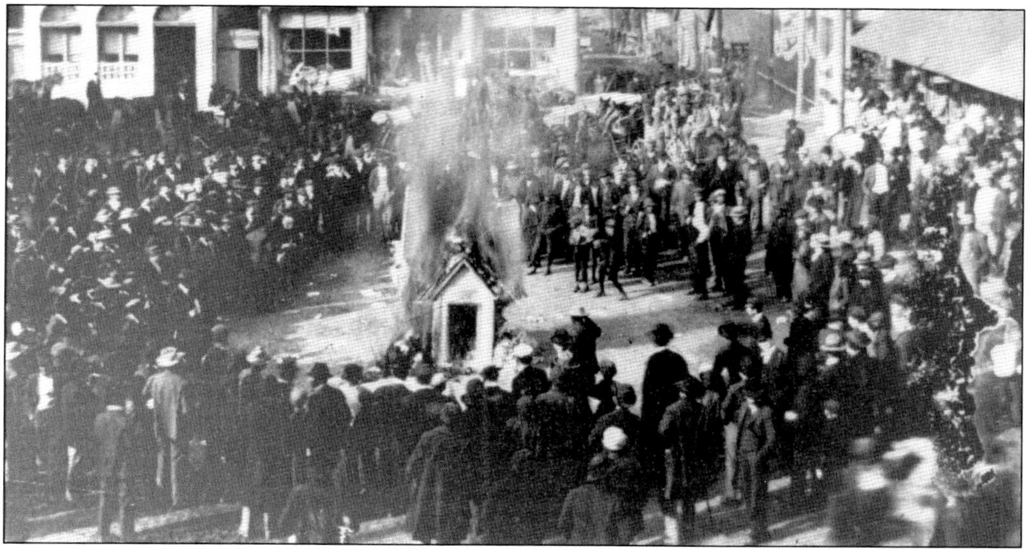

[FIREMANS' TOURNAMENT, 1902.] A large crowd assembled in front of the Old Courthouse and watched the burning of a small building in the plaza area as the Newberry Fire Department's team demonstrated their techniques of fire-fighting. Fire departments from across the state met in Newberry in 1902 for their annual tournament.

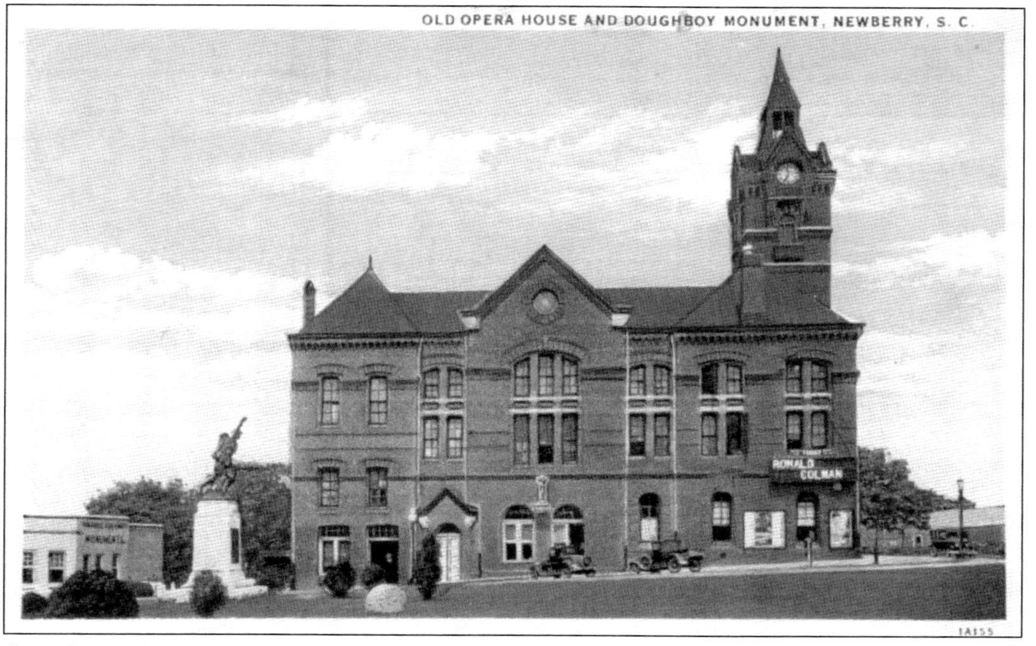

OLD OPERA HOUSE AND DOUGHBOY MONUMENT, NEWBERRY [c. 1929]. The Opera House was designed in a Gothic style by G.L. Norman and constructed by Cline at a cost of $30,000 at the corner of Nance and Boyce Streets. It was dedicated in 1882. The initial clock in the tower was replaced by a fire bell. It became the social center for the town with touring acts including Yankee Doodle Girls in 1906 and Alice in Wonderland in 1910. By 1913 moving pictures were shown there. City hall offices occupied the ground floor.

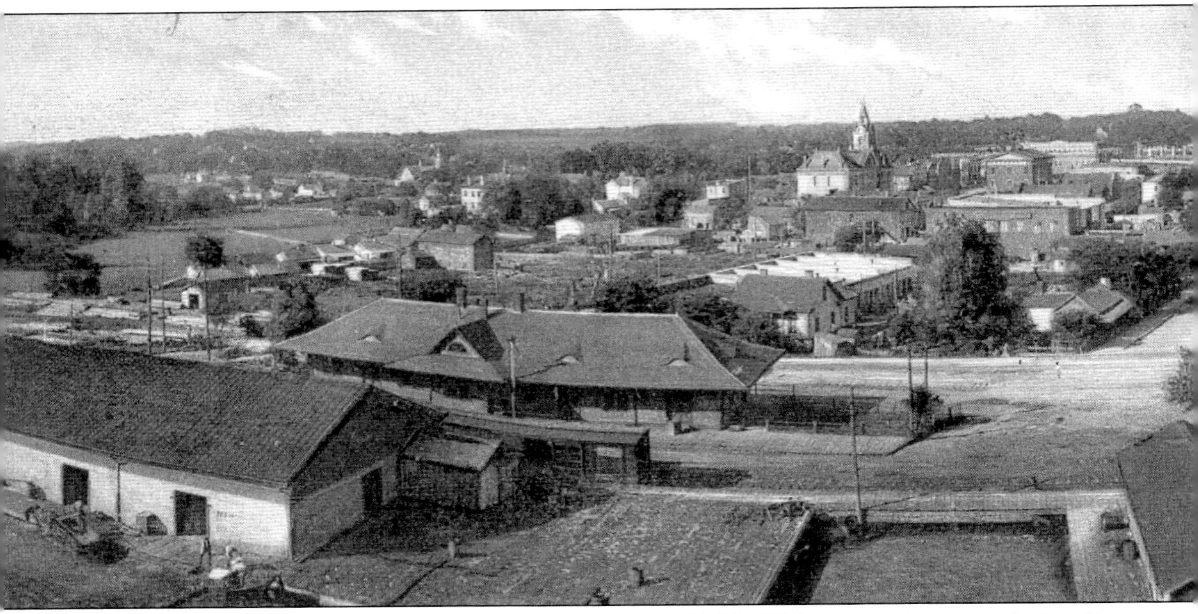

Greetings From Newberry, Birds Eye View [c. 1907]. This panoramic postcard view from the roof of the Newberry Cotton Mill on the west side of town looks east with the railroad depots and warehouses in the lower foreground and the Opera House, courthouse, and business section in the distant center of the scene. Newberry's economic lifelines were the two railroads. One was the Greenville and Columbia Railroad, which connected this town to Prosperity, Pomaria, and Columbia to the east and Chappells and the Piedmont to the west. The second was the Columbia, Newberry

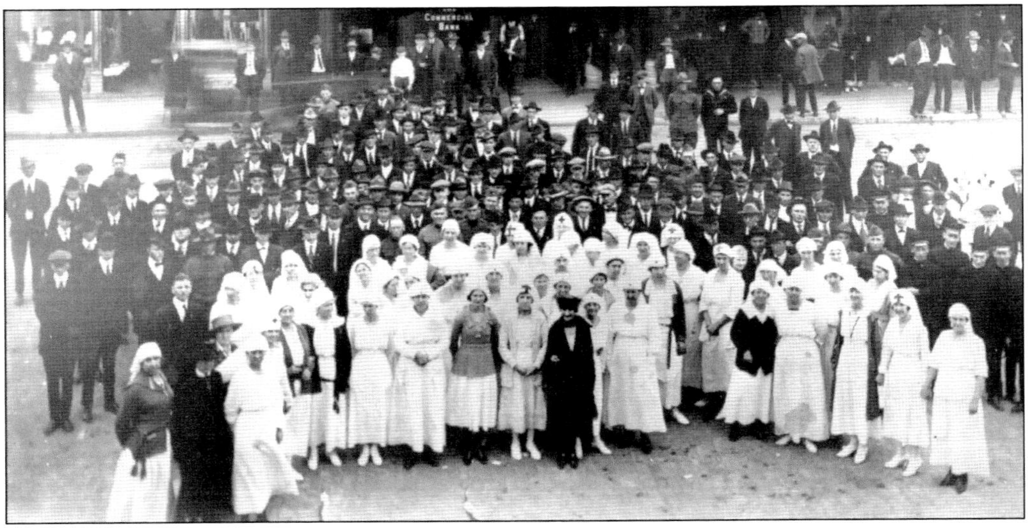

[Newberry's Armistice Day, 1918.] Newberry celebrated the end of World War I on November 11, 1918. The banks and stores closed at 11 a.m., followed by a parade down Main Street that included the military company of Newberry College, veterans of both the Civil and the Spanish-American Wars, and local bands while the church and fire bells rang. These military men along with members of the Red Cross Auxiliary, which greeted the troop trains and served snacks when they passed through Newberry, enjoyed a festive occasion.

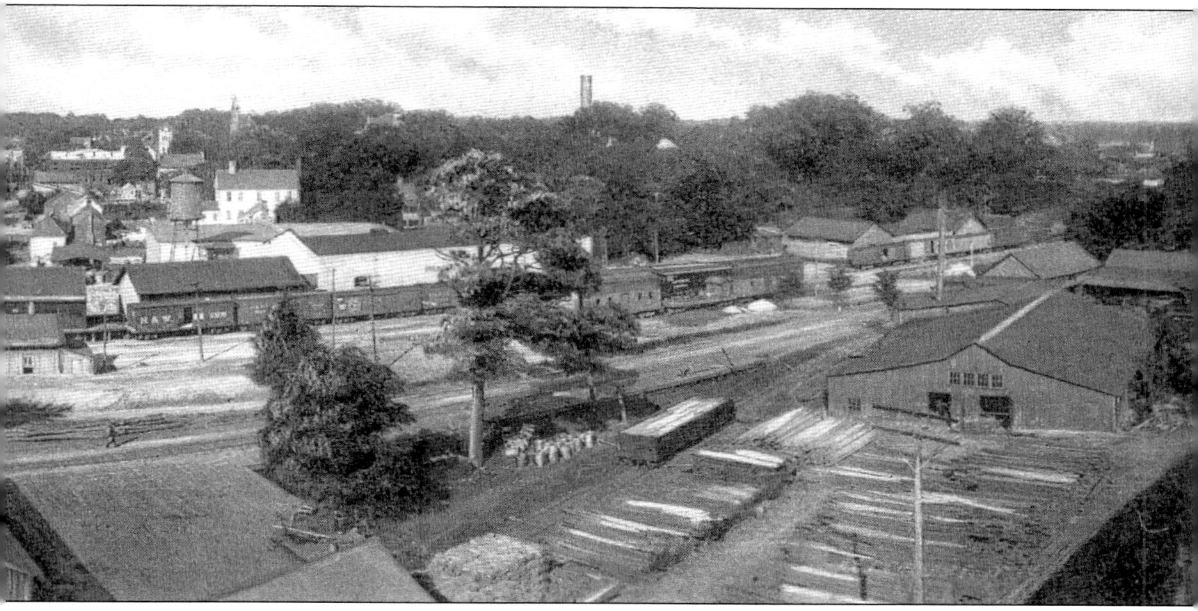

and Laurens Railroad, which linked this county hub westward to Kinards and Clinton and eastward to Little Mountain and beyond. A record volume of 24,406 bales of cotton were shipped from the Newberry depot in 1871. Newberry's economic significance expanded further when the three local cotton mills' machinery was shipped to the mill site by way of this depot while their finished fabrics were shipped to state, regional, and national destinations by the rail systems.

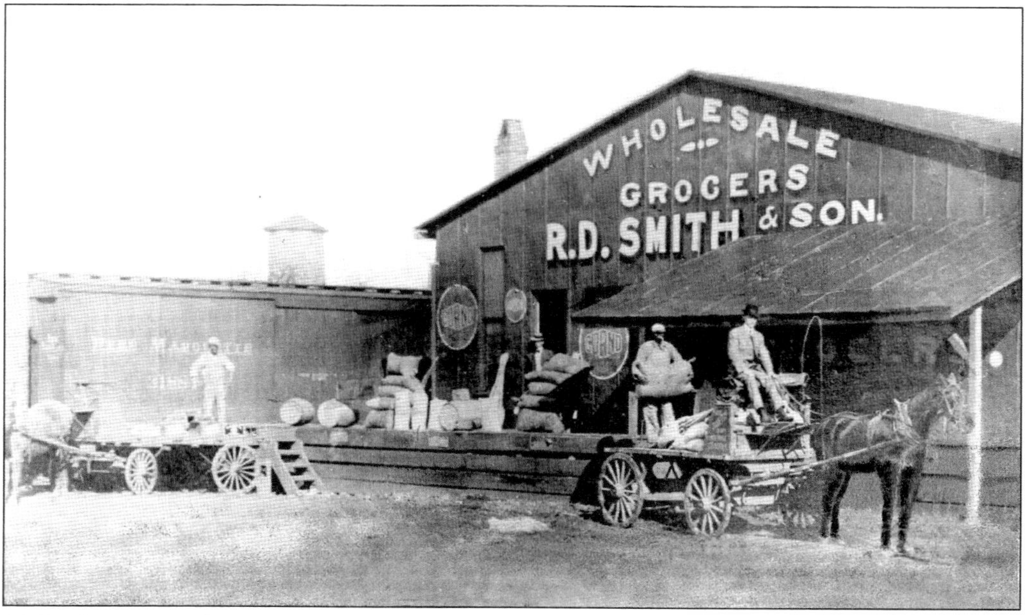

[R.D. Smith and Son Wholesale Grocers, 1915.] This business was established before 1901 at a site between the two sets of railroad tracks. The office was located at 844 Main Street. They distributed flour, grains, corn, feed, hay, and other farm supplies.

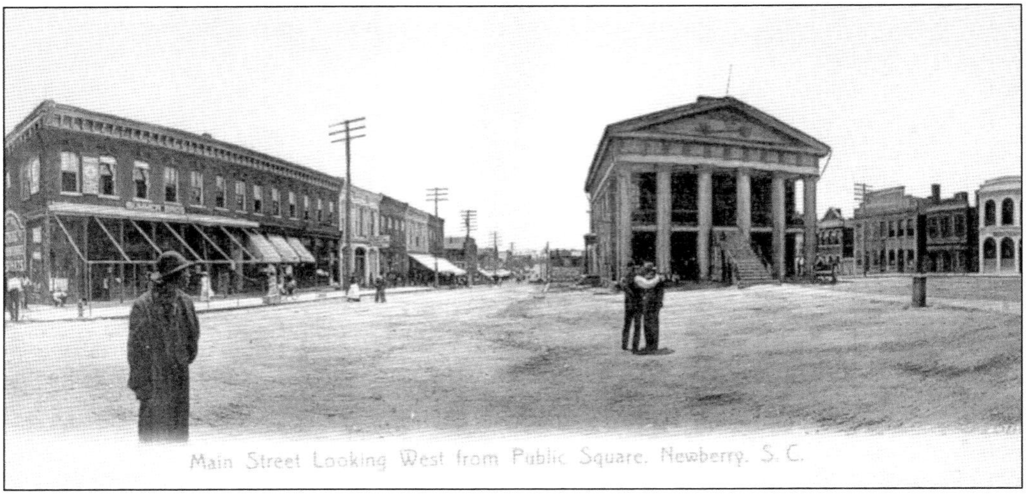

Main Street Looking West from Public Square, Newberry [*c.* 1900]. This view of the city square facing west shows the front of the courthouse in the center right. Sanborn Fire Insurance maps and newspaper ads suggest the locations of various shops. Many shops move or shut down so positions change. The south side of the square begins on the left with the east end of the J.J. Lane block on the corner of Main and Caldwell Streets. The Summer Brothers Company's clothing store is on the far left corner of that block at 1118; with their dry goods store at 1116; a grocery store at 1114; a 5 and 10¢ store at 1112; West-Martin Company [furniture] at 1110; a hardware store at 1108; Mimnaugh's Dry Goods at 1106 and—1104 and 1102 that are out of sight—make up this block.

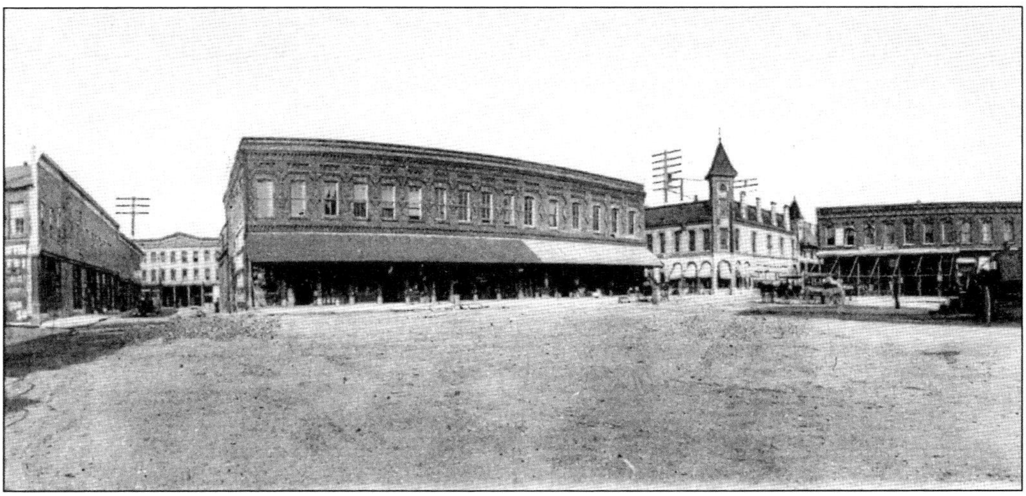

Mollohon Block, Newberry [*c.* 1900]. Mollohon Block, in the center between Boyce Street, left, and Main Street, right, is on the east side of the Public Square and faces the front of the courthouse. The initial row of old frame buildings in the Mollohon group, the 1200 block of Caldwell Street, were destroyed in the fire of July 1883 after escaping the fires of 1866 and 1877 and was rebuilt in brick. By 1900 the retail units were, from left to right, Johnson's Hardware Store at 1208; Mayes Books & Stationery at 1206; The Commercial Bank at 1204; a dry goods store at 1202; and Summer Brothers Grocery at 1200. On the left side, the 1200 block of Boyce Street, is the McCaughrin block, which in 1921 housed G.B. Summer and Sons at 1201–1203 and C.T. Summer at 1207. The right side is the Newberry Hotel and the east end of the J.J. Lane block on Main Street.

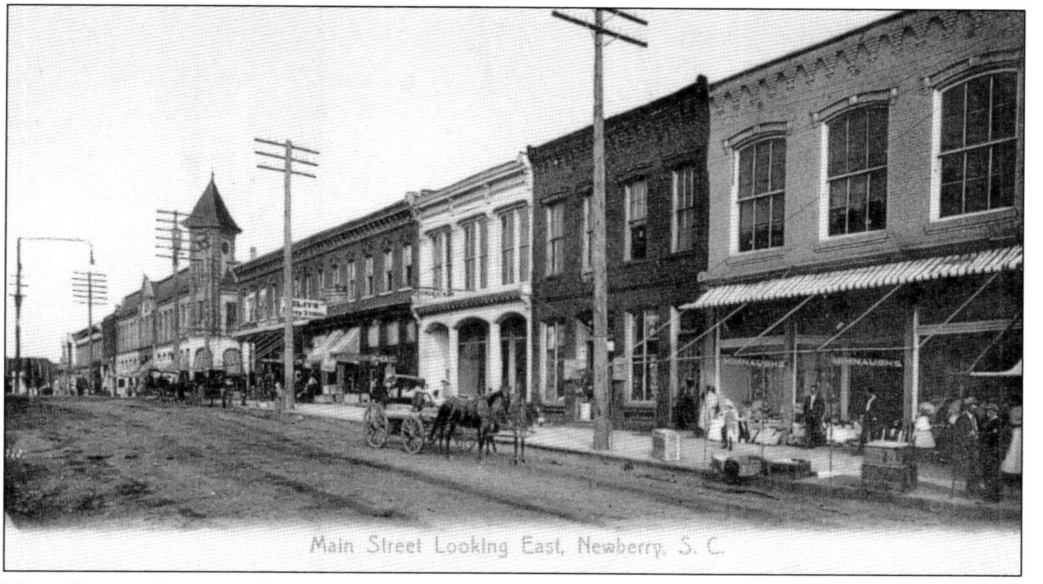

MAIN STREET LOOKING EAST, NEWBERRY [C. 1911]. This postcard view of the south side of Main Street looking east begins on the right with Minnaugh's Dry Goods store, established *c.*1889, at 1104; Busy Bee Café at 1106; Trakies Confectionery at 1108; West-Martin Company (furniture) at 1110; Anderson 10¢ Store (a January 1910 *The Observer* ad listed 5,000 new postcards) at 1112; Summer Brothers' Dry Goods on the first floor and the Elite Photo Studio on the second floor of 1114; and the Summer Brothers' clothing store at 1116 at the end of the Lane Block and Caldwell Street. The Newberry Hotel begins the 1200 block of Main Street.

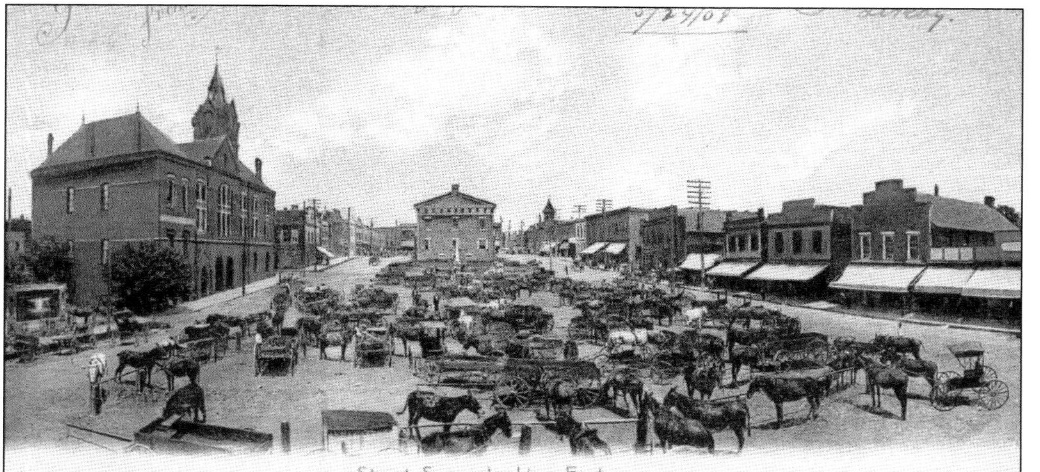

STREET SCENE LOOKING EAST, NEWBERRY [C. 1907]. This Saturday view from the west end of the Public Square was taken from McKibben Street looking east and shows the farmers' wagons loaded with their harvest that is being sold directly to the public. On the left side is the back of the Opera House that contained the police station and city hall while in the distant center is the back of the Old Courthouse and the Confederate Monument. On the right is the row of buildings making up the 1000 block of lower Main Street. Merchants in this block stocked grocery, drugs, general merchandise, clothing, and dry goods, and they offered restaurants.

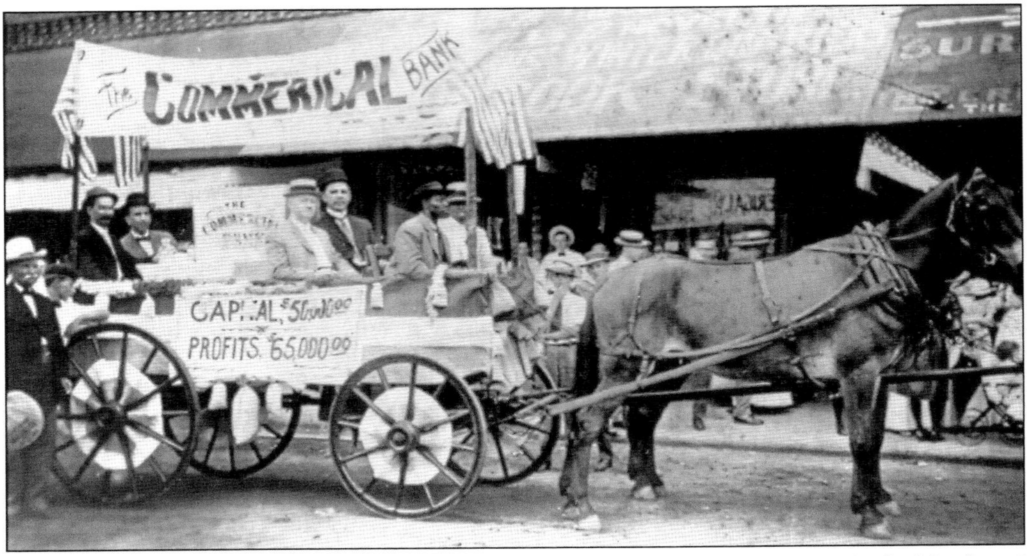

[**Commercial Bank Float, c. 1911.**] This Commercial Bank float was a participant in the Merchants' Parade in the 1911 Chautauqua Festival. The float is shown in front of their bank at 1204 Caldwell Street in the Mollohon Block. Seated in the second row is J.M. Kinard, president, and J.W. McFall, vice president.

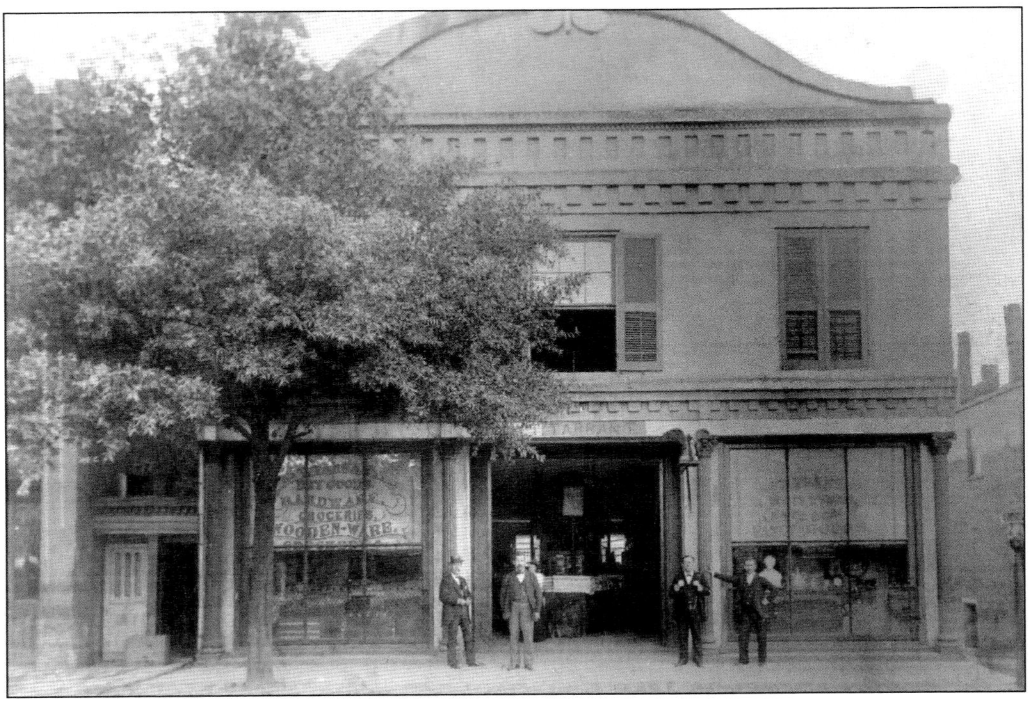

[**Tarrant General Mercantile Store, c. 1900.**] This general store was located on the corner of Boyce and Caldwell Streets in 1892. It sold dry goods, hardware, clothing, groceries, and fancy goods. Later, this 1119 to 1121 Boyce Street site was the location of the Summer and Hipp Company. In 1923 it became the site of The Commercial Bank.

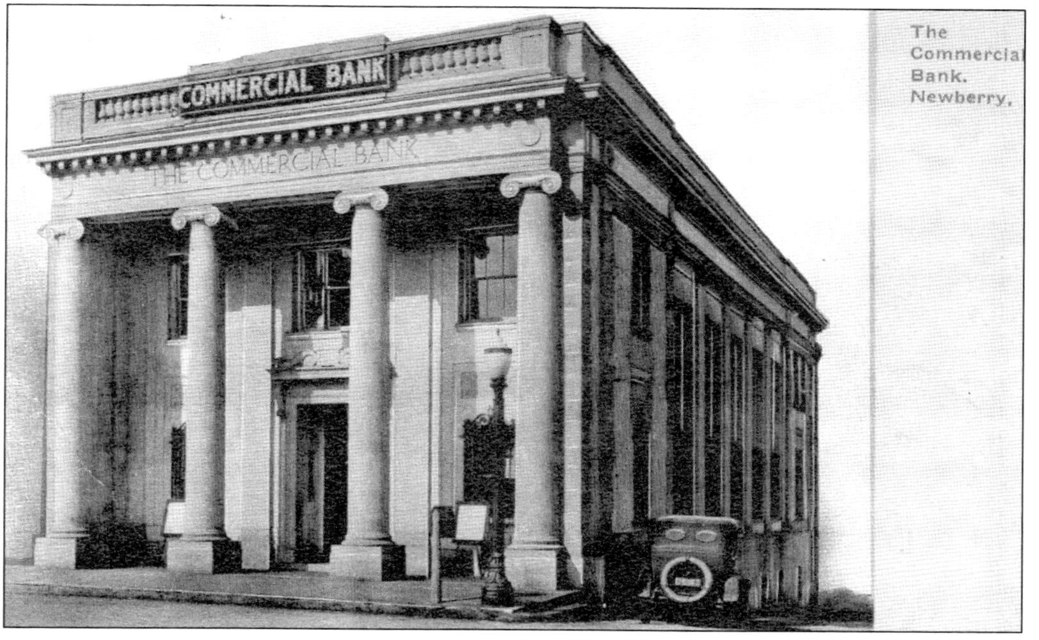

THE COMMERCIAL BANK, NEWBERRY [*c.* 1923]. This bank was founded in 1896 with resources of $50,000 and its officers were J.M. Kinard (1862–1933), president, and J.W. McFall, vice president. Its first quarters were at 1204 Caldwell Street in the Mollohon Block. In 1919 the bank purchased the G.B. Summer and Son's building at the corner of Boyce and Caldwell Streets and built a handsome structure there in 1923. The bank merged with the South Carolina National Bank in 1931 and remained open during the Great Depression. In 2001 the building houses the Wachovia Bank.

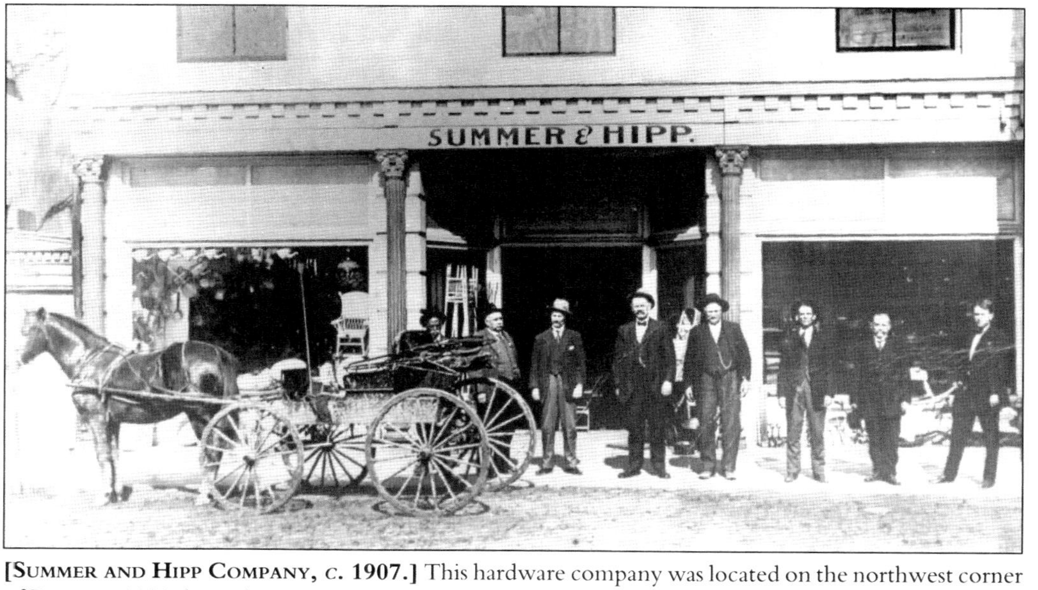

[SUMMER AND HIPP COMPANY, *c.* 1907.] This hardware company was located on the northwest corner of Boyce at 1119 through 1121 and Caldwell Streets after 1906. The Summer and Hipp Company sold stoves and aluminum cookware in 1913. The Commercial Bank bought this site from G.B. Summer and Son in January 1919, and it became the site for the 1923 Commercial Bank building.

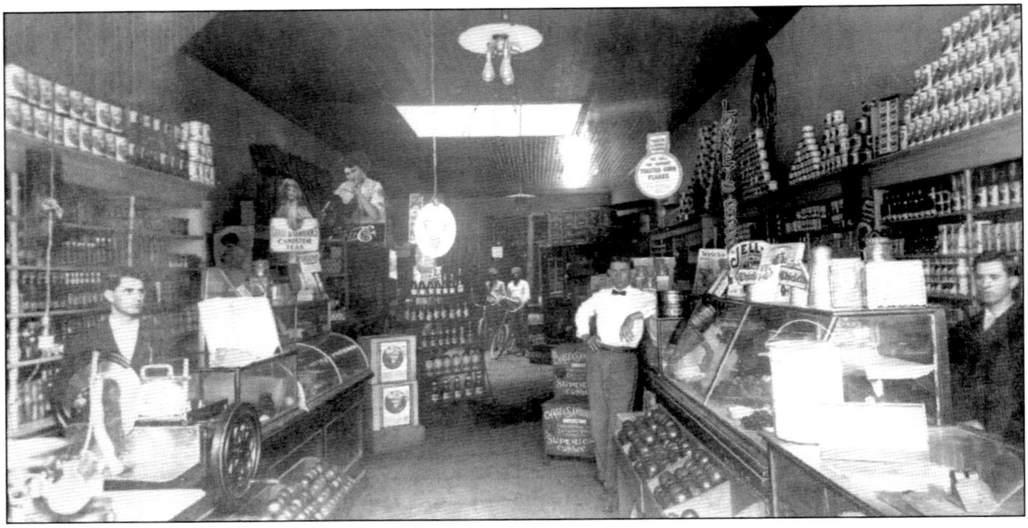

[Interior of E.M. Lane Grocery Store, c. 1910.] This interior view shows Lane in the center with clerks Andrew and Edgar Cromer behind the counters. A series of *The Observer* newspaper ads in February 1910 indicated they received weekly Wednesday and Saturday shipments of fresh Norfolk, Virginia oysters. Lane stocked Norway mackerel and other fancy groceries. In 1913 he began offering S. & H. Green trading stamps. Lane's announced that they had a sanitary meat market with refrigerators and no flies in the store in 1915.

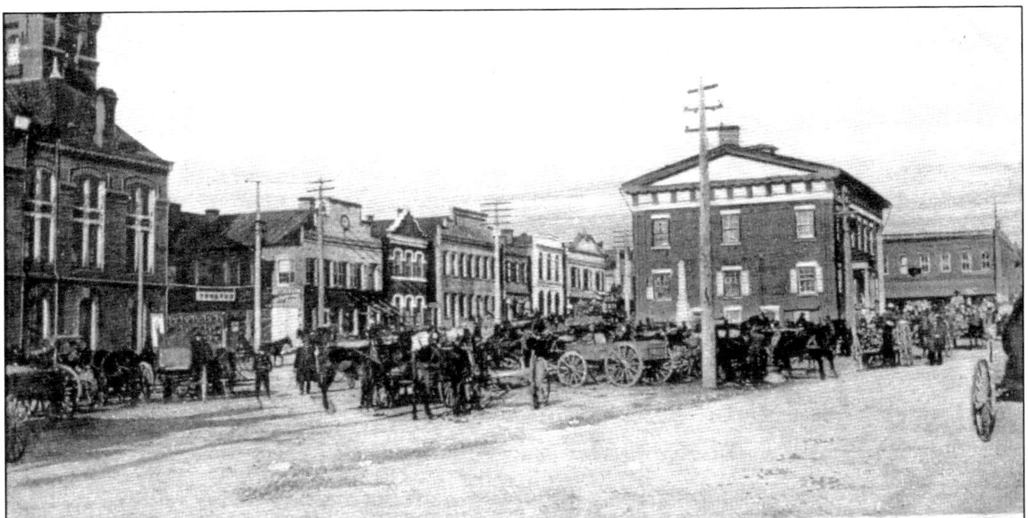

The Square on Market Day, Newberry [c. 1907]. This view photographed from the lower section of the Public Square shows the southeastern corner of the Opera House, Nance Street, and an unobstructed view of the 1100 block of Boyce Street. This block begins with Nat Gist Cotton Office at 1103; groceries shops at 1105 and 1107; offices at 1109, 1111, and 1115; the National Bank of Newberry building at 1117; and Tarrant General Mercantile Store at 1119 and 1121. In the center are farmers' wagons with produce, the Confederate Monument, the back of the Old Courthouse, and a distant view of the southern end of the Mollohon Block.

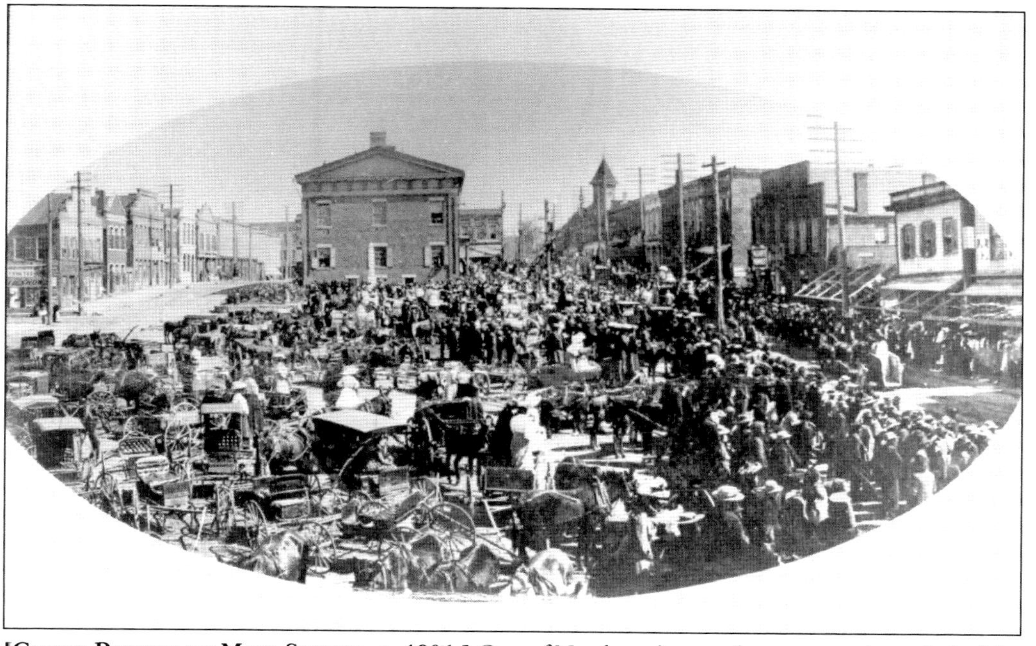

[Circus Parade on Main Street, *c.* 1906.] One of Newberry's annual events was the arrival of the circus. On October 12, 1906, the Cole Brothers United Show with its big, free street parade came to town. The large tented enterprise had numerous acts including 1,000 people and rare wild animals.

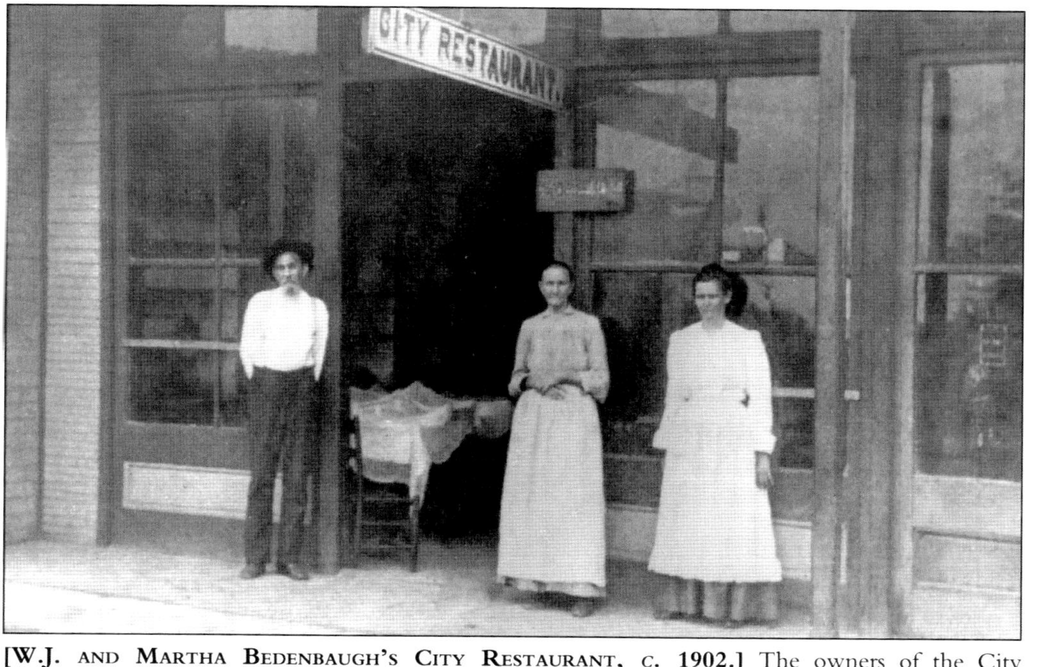

[W.J. and Martha Bedenbaugh's City Restaurant, *c.* 1902.] The owners of the City Restaurant, W.J. Bedenbaugh (1832–1906) and Martha Bedenbaught stand in front of their cafe at 932 Main Street. Mrs. Dickert (waitress) stands on the right.

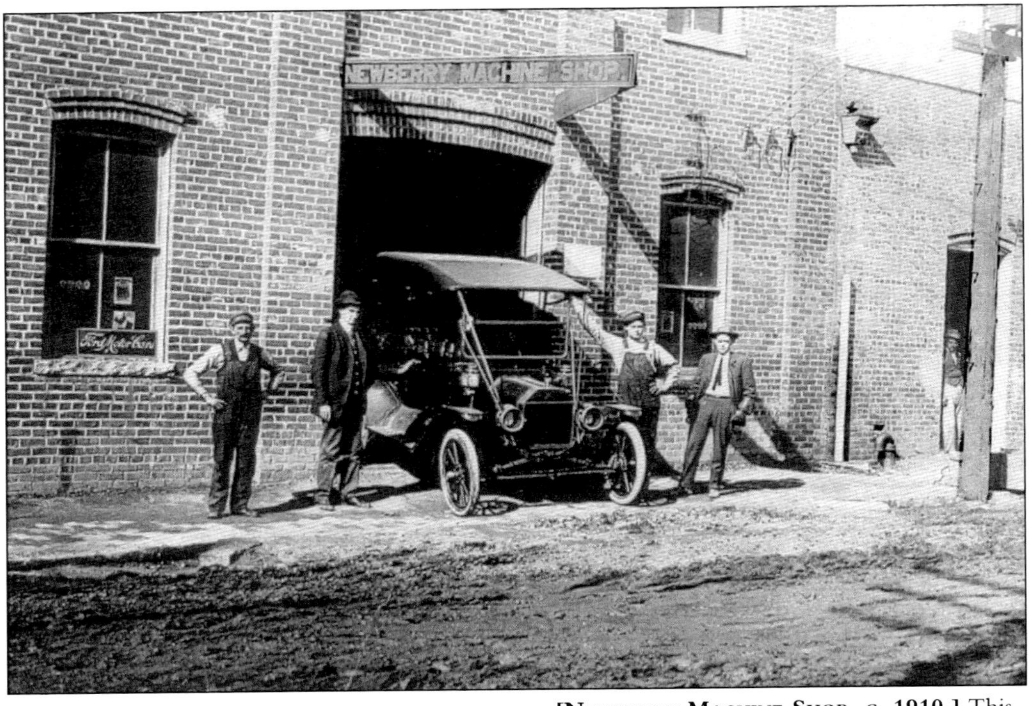

[NEWBERRY MACHINE SHOP, *c.* 1910.] This postcard scene shows the Newberry Machine Shop and garage at 335 Friend Street. It was jointly operated by Waldrop and Collins (Newberry Motor Company). A June 21, 1910 ad for the machine shop in *The Observer* indicated that Model T Fords sold for $985.

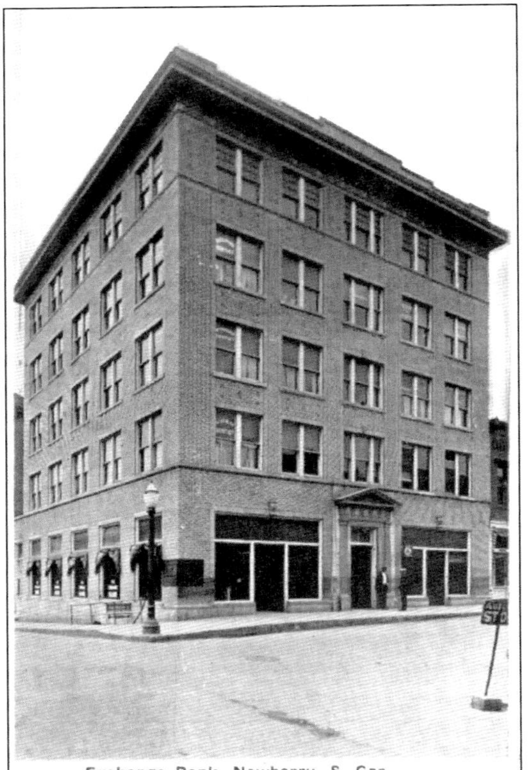
Exchange Bank, Newberry, S. Car.

EXCHANGE BANK, NEWBERRY [*c.* 1920]. The Mercantile Exchange Bank, initially located at 1210 Main Street, was founded in June 1905 with its initial officers being J.D. Davenport, president; R.C. Carlisle, vice president, and M.L. Spearman, cashier. E.R. Hipp was the second president (until his death in 1910) and was followed by H. L. Parr (1871–1931). During Parr's reign a five-story office building designed by Summer and Hemphill, architects, and costing $100,000 was built in 1918 at 1301–1305 Main Street on the corner of Main and College. It was the only skyscraper in Newberry. The bank failed in April 1931.

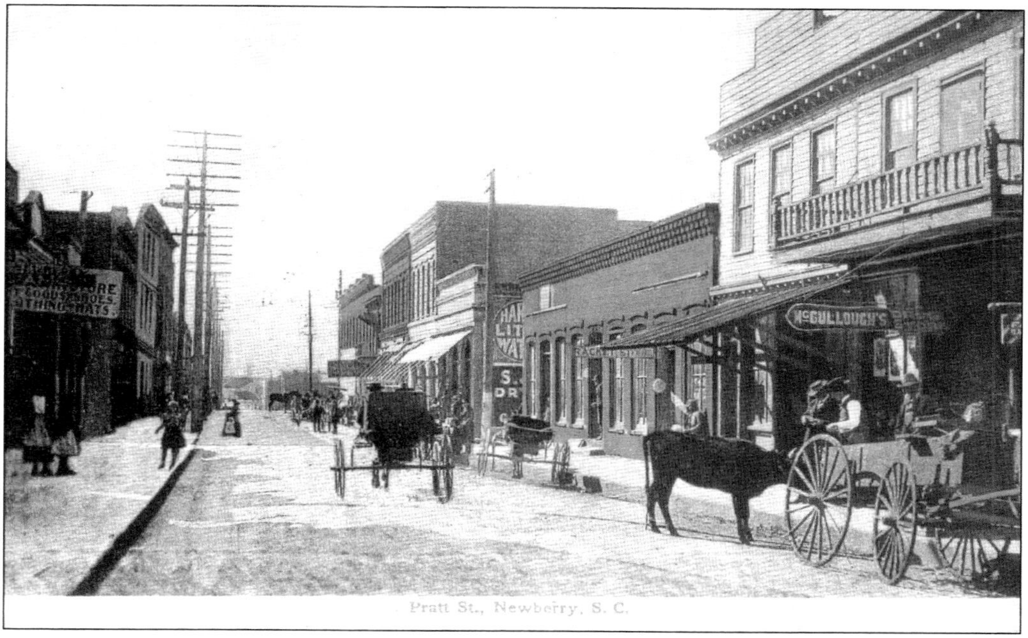

PRATT STREET, NEWBERRY [C. 1906]. This postcard view of Pratt (Main) Street looking west towards the square documents the buildings on the north side of Main Street that were destroyed in the 1907 fire. The frame building on the right was McCullough's Drug Store (a $2,500 loss) at 1307. The one-story brick unit that housed the Racket Store was at 1305, a men's store was at 1303. J.T. Dennis' grocery at 1301 was rebuilt after the fire and used until 1918 when it was razed for the construction of the Exchange Bank.

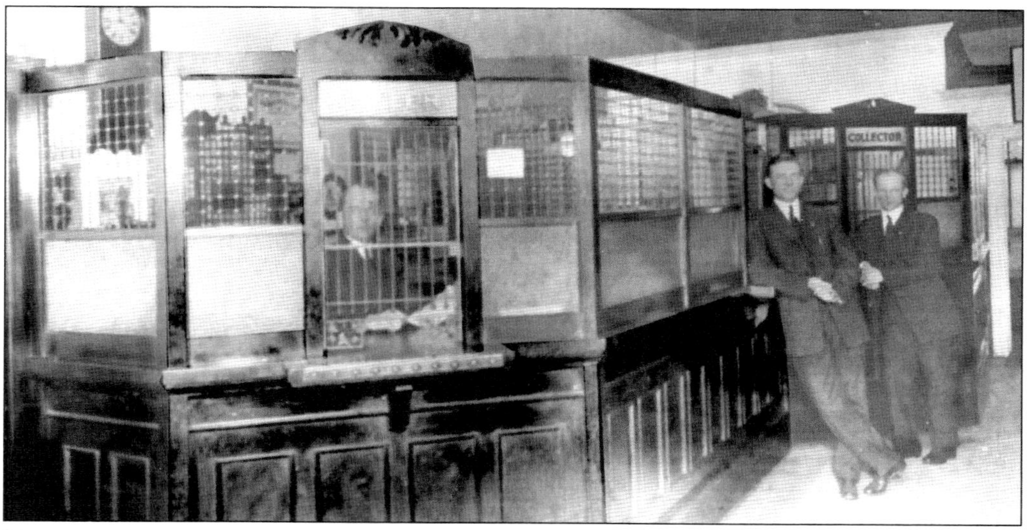

[INTERIOR, THE EXCHANGE BANK, C. 1905.] This interior view of the bank shows its initial public counter when it was located in the Newberry Hotel building's ground floor at 1210 Main Street. It is similar to other views included in ads placed in Newberry's newspapers. This view probably shows M.L. Spearman, cashier, behind the counter and the officers—J.D. Davenport, president, and R.C. Carlisle, vice-president—standing on the right.

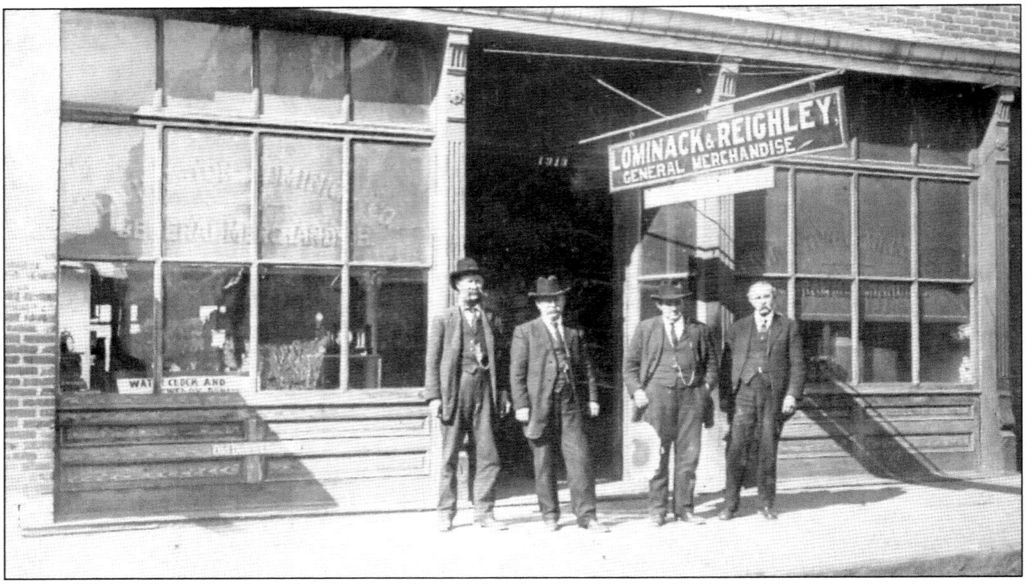

[Lominack & Reighley Store, *c.* 1910.] The Lominack & Reighley General Merchandise Store was at 1313 Main Street. The men in front of this store, from left to right, are a Mr. Asbell, watch maker; W. Reighley, owner; R.B. Lominack, owner; and a Mr. Livingston. The store's name changed to Reighley and Buford in 1923.

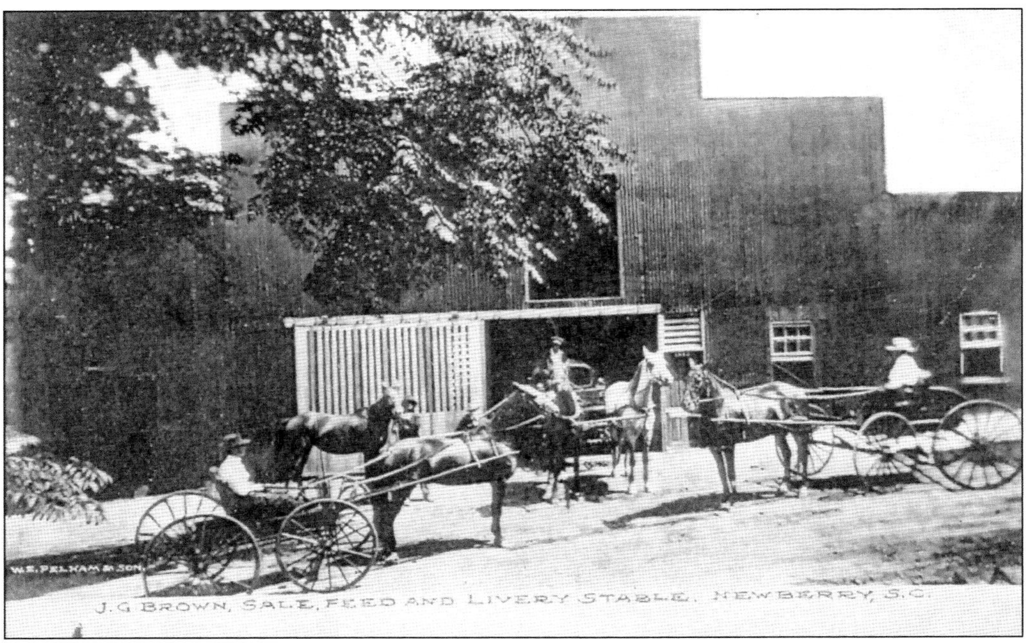

J.G. Brown, Sale, Feed & Livery Stable, Newberry [1906]. This postcard view of Brown's stable on Martin Street was taken before the 1907 great fire, which destroyed the stable at a loss of $2,500 as well as five blocks in the business area. Livery stables in 1905 were like car rental agencies in 2001. Salesmen, travelers, and residents could rent a buggy or wagon to make necessary business appointments between train stops or to visit friends living some distance away.

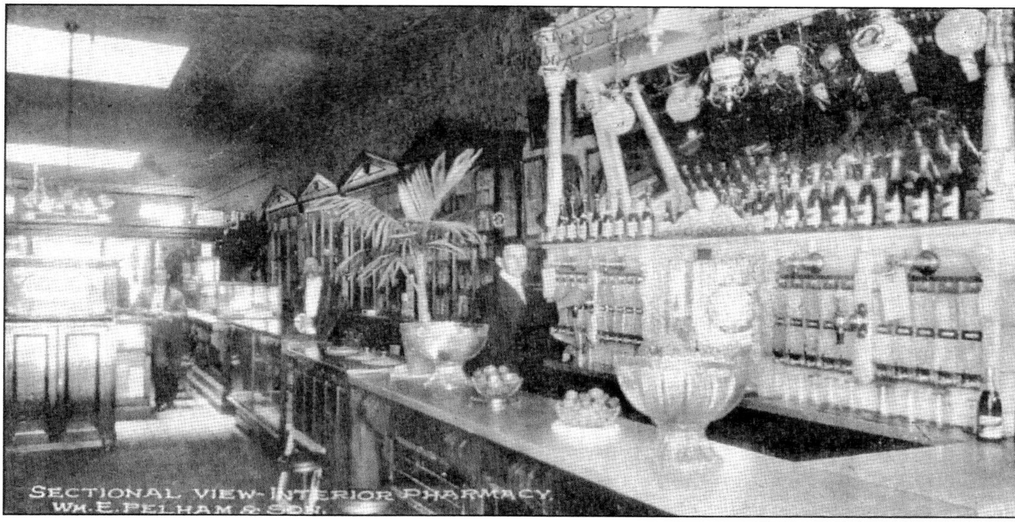

Sectional View-Interior Pharmacy [*c.* 1900]. The elegant interior of the W.E. Pelham & Son Pharmacy is shown on this postcard scene that was sold in their store and also printed in the December 1901 edition of the Charleston Exposition's monthly publication. Dr. W.E. Pelham (1854–1922) began the Pelham Drug Store in 1876. It was destroyed in the 1877 fire, rebuilt, and continued in business at 1212 Main Street until 1913 when it closed.

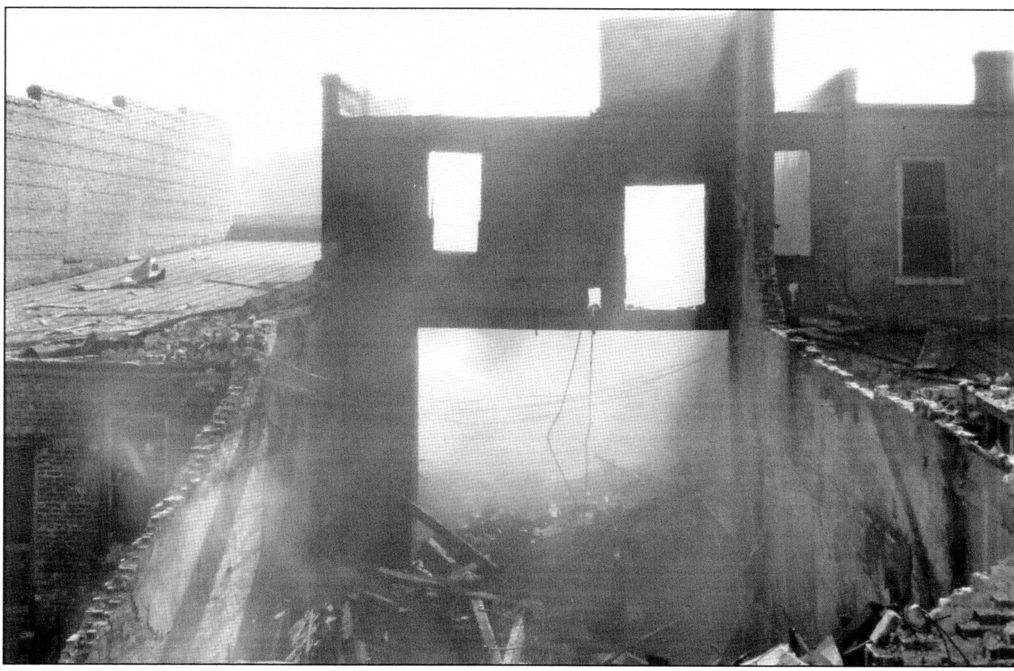

[Explosion at the Frank Lominack Hardware Store, 1934.] This tragedy killed three men and gutted the store at 1403 Main Street on November 16, 1934. A later report stated that a stray bullet fired in the basement shooting range hit packages of stored dynamite causing two-successive explosions that destroyed the building and shattered glass windows for blocks. Firemen responded quickly and saved the adjacent stores in the block.

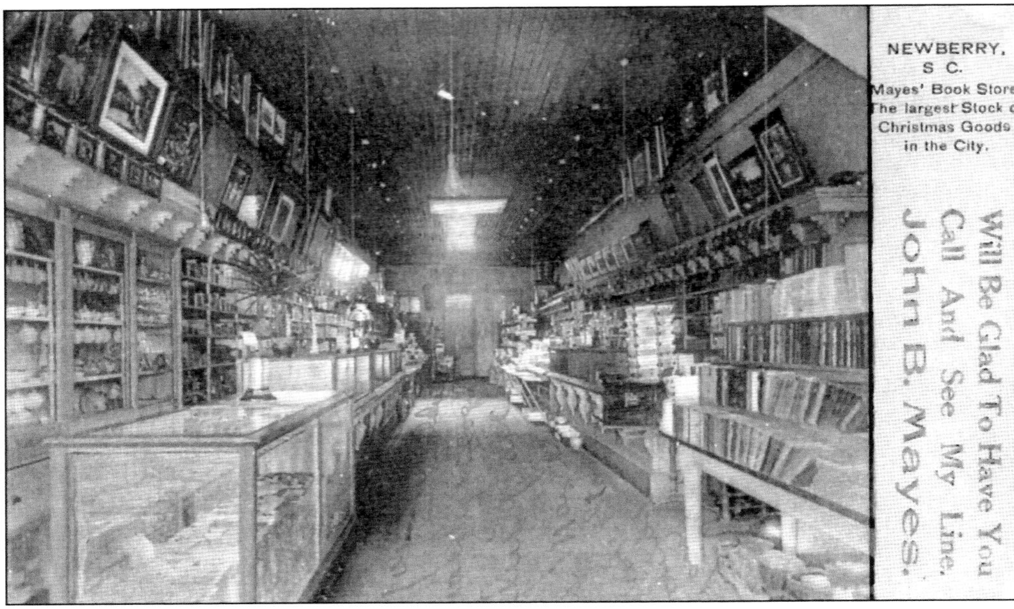

MAYES BOOK STORE, NEWBERRY [*c.* 1907]. This postcard showing the interior of the John B. Mayes Book Store, established *c.* 1900, is imprinted with an ad inviting visitors to inspect his stock of Christmas goods, books, postcards, stationery, and gift items. This store, probably at 1208 Caldwell Street, placed ads in Newberry's newspapers from 1904 to 1919, describing shipments of illustrated postcards, office supplies, and 1,000 other items.

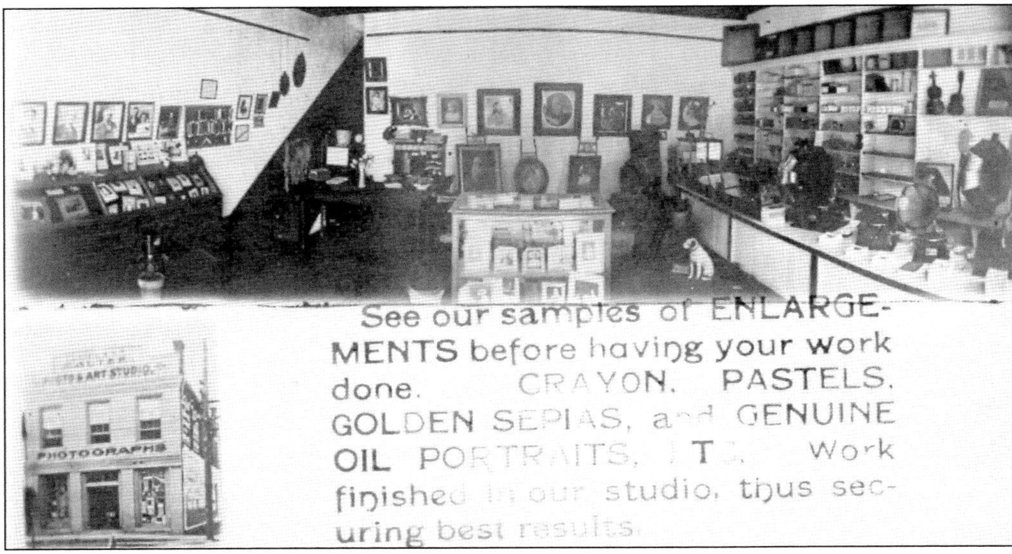

[SALTER'S ADVERTISING POSTCARD, *c.* 1911.] Jesse Zebulon Salter came to Newberry in 1882, and he and his children maintained a series of photographic shops for 50 years. Jesse called his shop the Old Reliable Photo Studio, and he operated it for 25 years. Its location at 943 Main Street was on the second floor over Leavell's Furniture store. This advertising postcard is the type LeRoy Salter used to correspond with his customers. LeRoy A. and Minnie M. Salter's studio, established *c.* 1911, was at 913 Main Street and is shown on the lower left of the card.

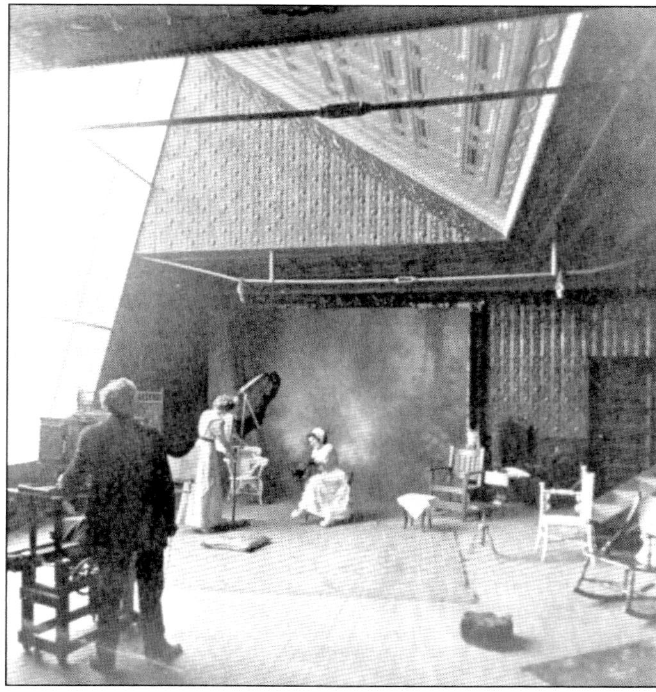

[Salter's Studio, 1912.] Reginald Otway and Temperance Elizabeth Salter, Jesse Zebulon's children, established the Elite Photo Studio on the second floor of 1114 Main Street in 1908. Their sign has been noted on early Main Street postcard scenes. This postcard view of the interior of their second studio illustrates their interest in natural lighting. The studio was built with an entire glass wall on the east side of the building. Their postcard ads show interior and exterior studio views.

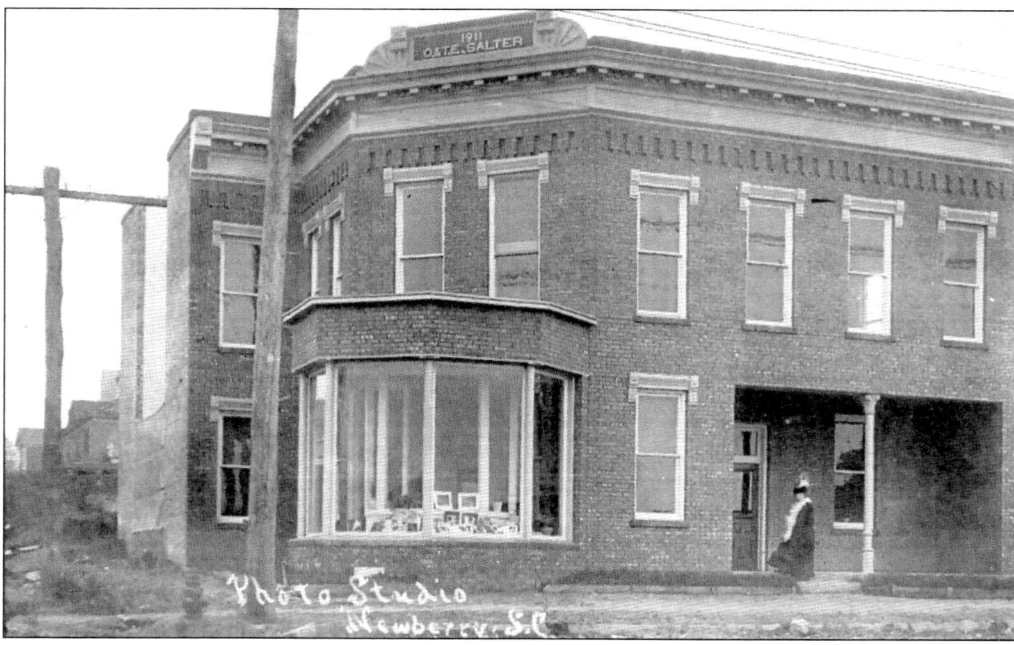

[Salter's Studio, 1911.] The first frame Elite Photo Studio at Main and Wilson was destroyed in the fire of 1907 for a loss of $2,500. The new 1911 studio was rebuilt at 1412 East Main Street and is shown on the postcard above. Salter's newspaper ads state that his portraits could be produced in oils, pastels, water color, sepia, crayon, and India ink. An ad was published in the April 10, 1923 *Observer* by R.O. Salter of California indicating this building was for sale. It no longer stands.

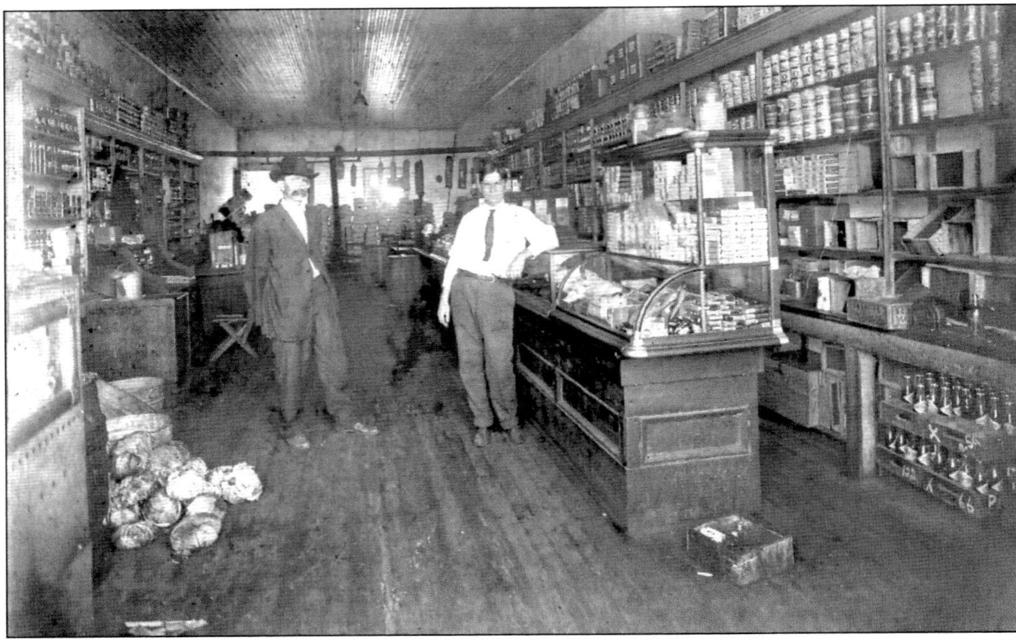

[C.T. SUMMER GROCERY STORE, 1920s.] An interior view of the Clarence T. Summer's [1880–1957] grocery store at 1207 Boyce Street is shown above. The image indicates that grocery stores of that era mainly stocked canned, bottled, and boxed food products with glass cases for the small items. In the back were large sacks of flour and hanging packages of cheese or processed meat products.

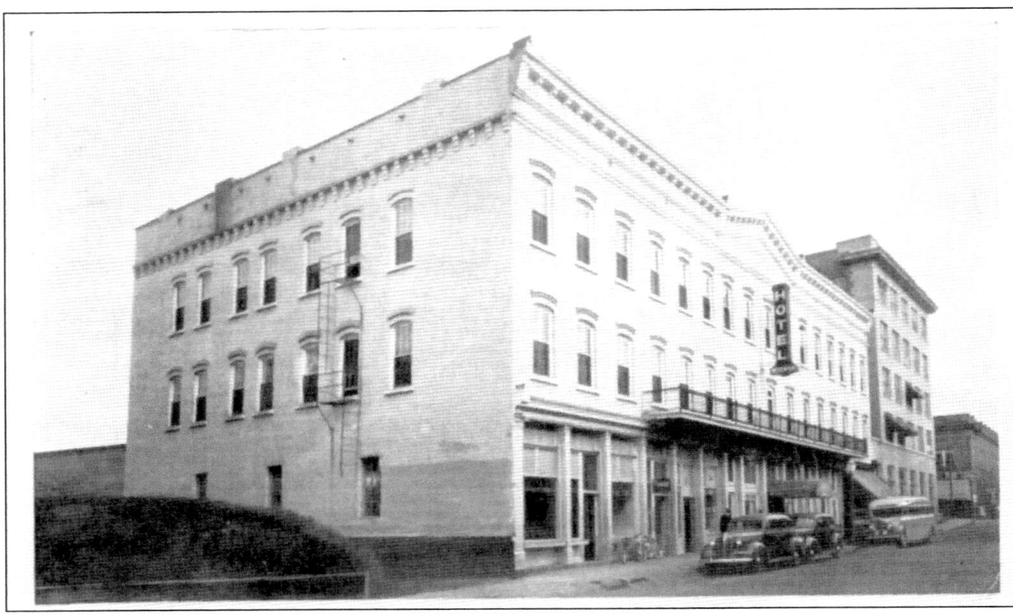

HOTEL WISEMAN, NEWBERRY [1930s]. J.A. Crotwell built this three-story hotel in 1879 on Adams (College) Street, facing Boyce Street, a block from the Courthouse Square and on the lot adjacent to the 1908 courthouse. H.L. Parr and M.L. Spearman bought the hotel in 1918 with plans to modernize it. By 1923 the hotel's name had changed to the National Hotel; it later became the Wiseman Hotel.

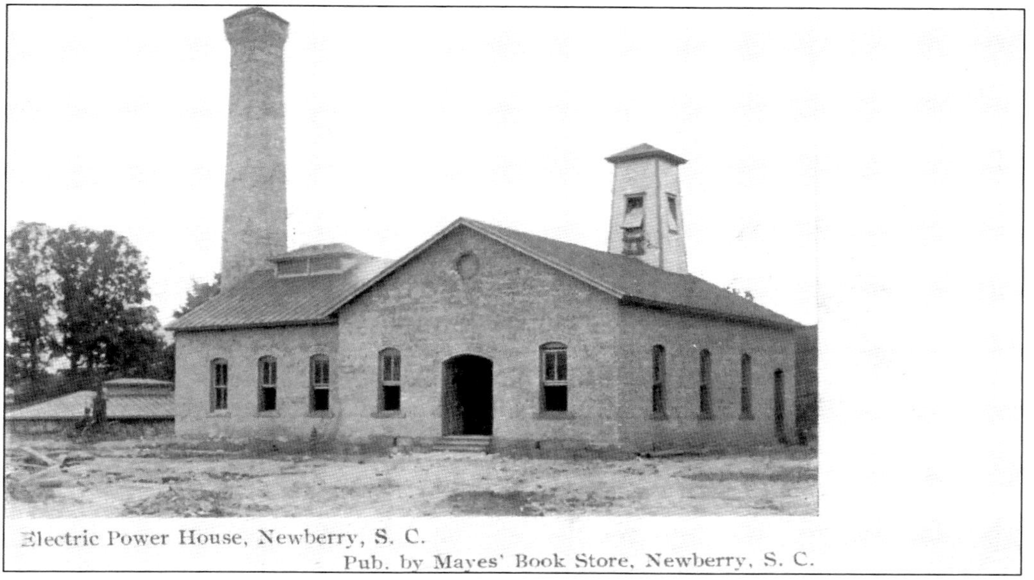

ELECTRIC POWER HOUSE, NEWBERRY [*c.* 1905]. The commission of Public Works gave an $8,209 contract for an electric power house to the General Electric Company in 1896 and went on line the next year. The sale of electricity to the public and commercial customers totaled $7,322, while the city's lights cost $5,294 in 1907. The water works plant cost $32,331 and pumped water from a 87-foot-deep well into a reservoir that held 140,000 gallons and into a stand pipe. The main line pumping engine delivered water along nine miles of pipes to 83 hydrants. The facilities were located on Power House Road.

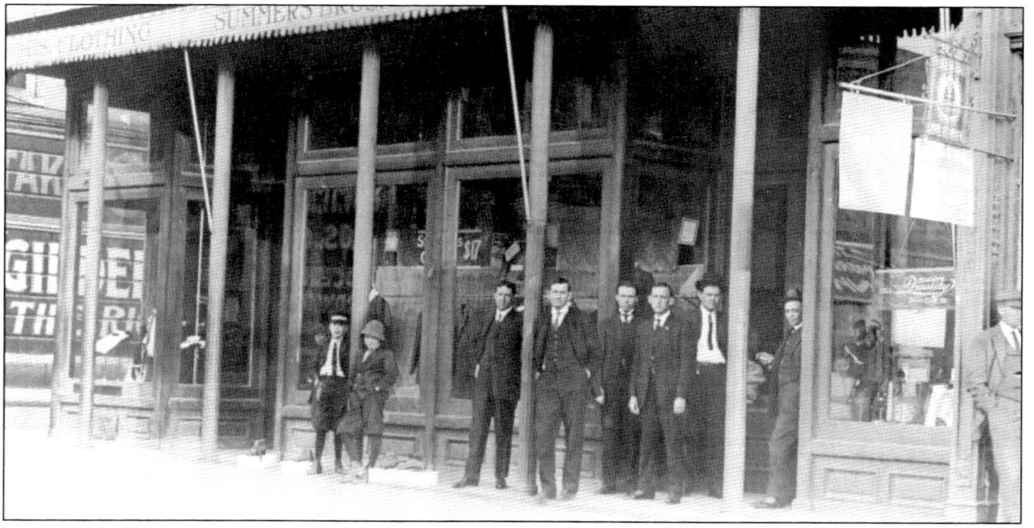

[SUMMER BROTHERS COMPANY, *c.* 1900.] The Summer Brothers general mercantile store, located on the southwest corner of Main and 1200 Caldwell Street, was established *c.* 1889 by Charles E. Summer (1859–1948), J.H. Summer (1860–1951), and G.W. Summer (1861–1944) with Charles as president. The brothers were born in the Dutch Fork area and moved to this town in the 1880s. They were leaders in various business and agricultural enterprises in Newberry. The store failed during the Depression.

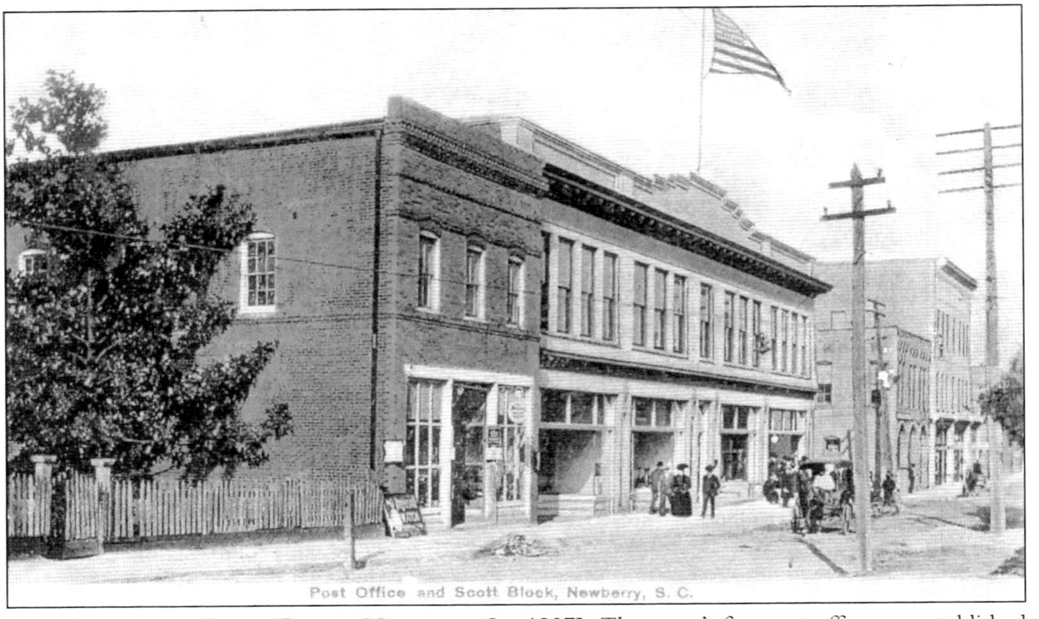

POST OFFICE AND SCOTT BLOCK, NEWBERRY [c. 1907]. The town's first post office was established in 1788. By 1877 this post office was the fourth largest one in South Carolina in mail volume. C.J. Purcell (1861–1928) was postmaster from 1902 to 1913, during which time the first home mail delivery was made. J.C. Dominick, A.J. Bower Jr., and B.H. McGraw were appointed in 1908 to be the first city carriers. The location of the Scott Block was on Friend Street opposite the Methodist Church.

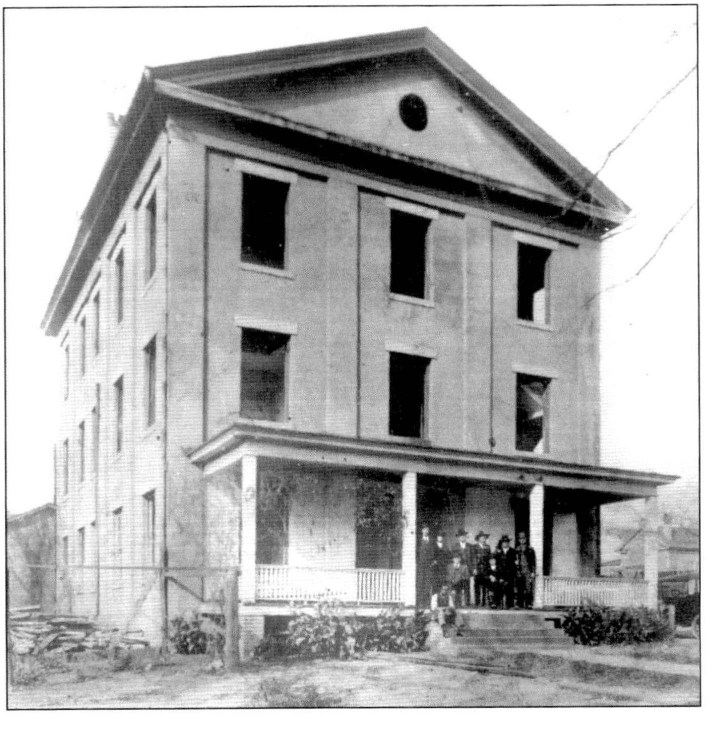

[OLD COUNTY JAIL, NEWBERRY, c. 1917.] After the fourth courthouse, designed by J. Graves, was built in 1853, the county purchased a lot on Harrington Street for a jail facility. A three-story brick jail costing $8,500, also designed by Graves, was constructed by T.W. Blease, who completed it in 1854. The jail was torn down in 1918.

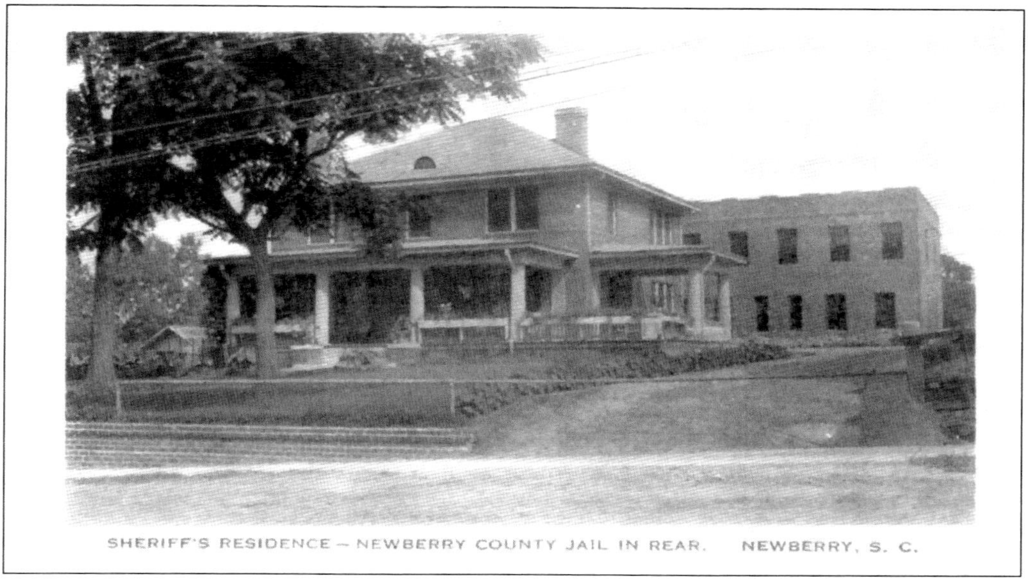

SHERIFF'S RESIDENCE-NEWBERRY COUNTY JAIL IN REAR, NEWBERRY [*c.* 1920]. Some years after the fifth courthouse was erected in 1908 a commission to create a new jail was selected with J.M. Davis as chairman. They selected architects J. Hemphill and E. Summer and the contractor was W.G. Sutherlin of Greenwood. The new jail would be placed on the Harrington Street site of the old jail. This brick jail was completed in 1919 at a cost of $68,313.93. C.G. Blease was the sheriff at that time, and the structure was considered the best jail in South Carolina. It was torn down in 1973.

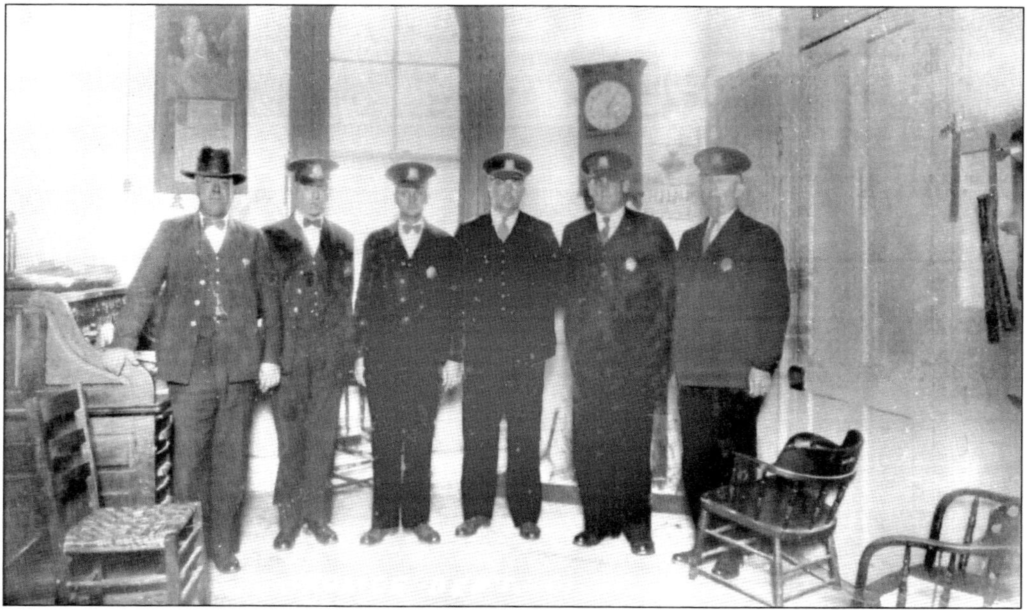

POLICE DEPARTMENT, NEWBERRY [1930s]. The police department along with city hall shared the ground floor of the Opera House. This picture of the Newberry Police Department members consisted of, from left to right, C. May (chief), T. Long, R. Bartley, C. Dowd, F. Krell, and J. Hite.

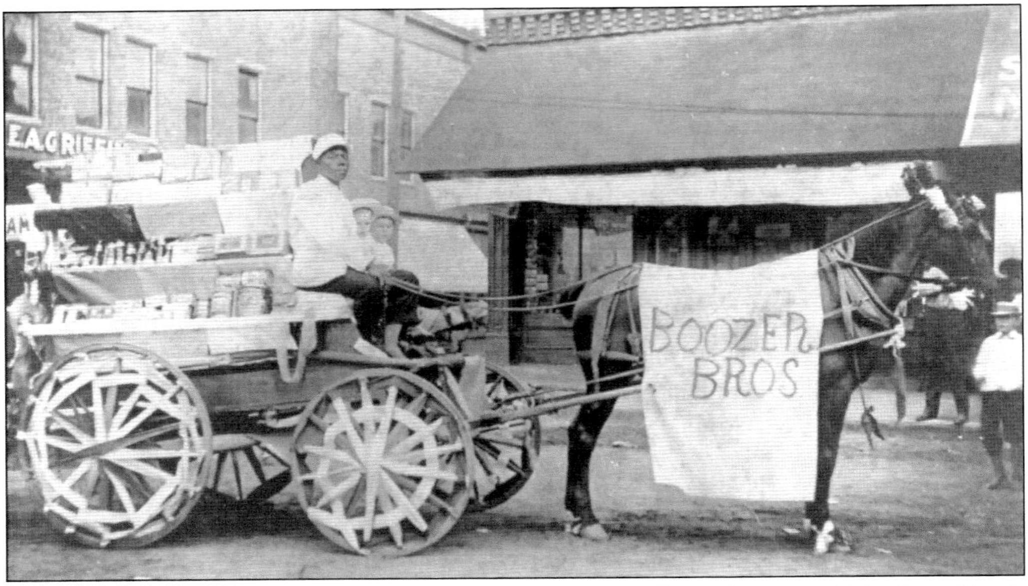

[Boozer Brothers' Wagon, 1911.] The Chautauqua Festival's Tradesmen and Merchants Parade included the wagon above, which was sponsored by the Boozer Brothers' grocery store, one of the many units signed up for this 1911 festival event. The parade traveled down Main Street and circled the business district. The festival committee arranged a wide variety of programs and events so that visitors would have a week of varied entertainment.

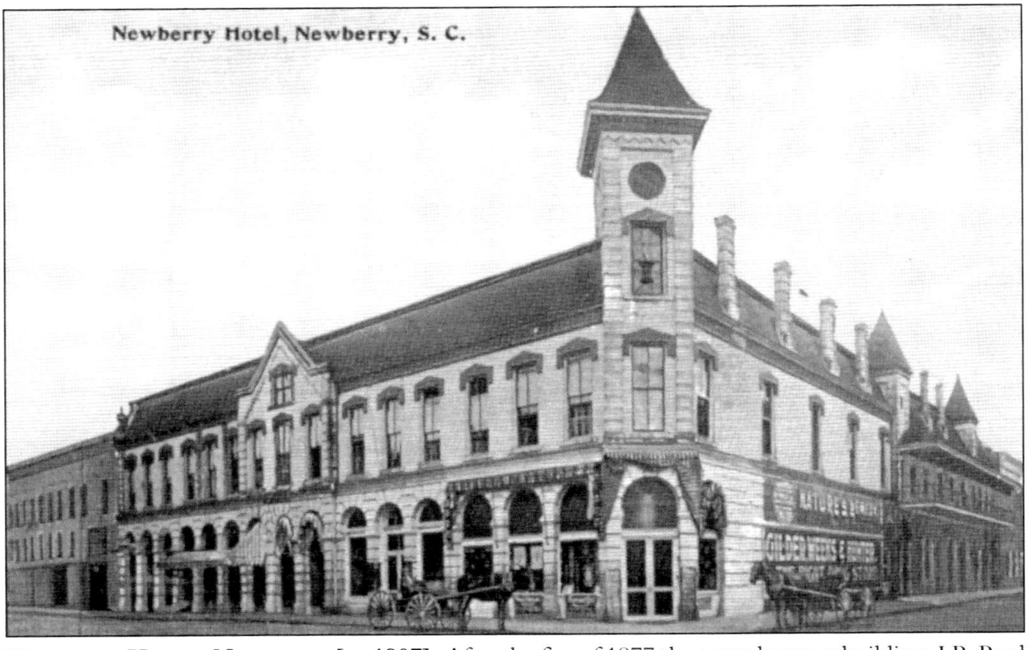

Newberry Hotel, Newberry [*c.* 1907]. After the fire of 1877 the town began rebuilding. J.P. Pool and O.L. Schumpert hired architect G.L. Norman in 1879 to design a hotel at 1112 Caldwell Street diagonally across from the front of the courthouse. Dr. Gilder, Weeks and Hunter Drugstore occupied the corner street-level retail space at that time.

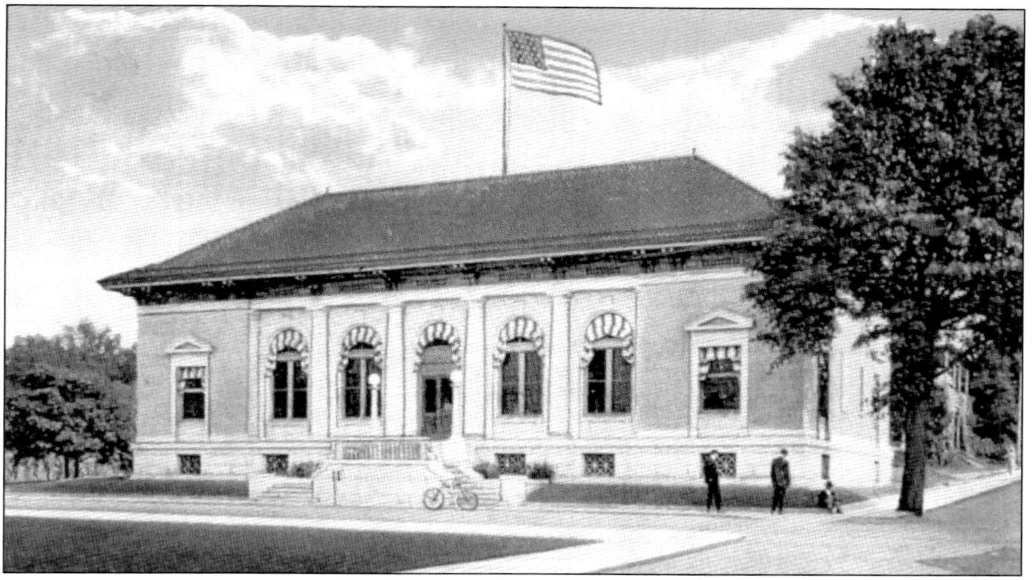

POST OFFICE, NEWBERRY [c. 1914]. The site of the new post office on the corner of Friend and College Streets was selected in 1909. J.K. Taylor was the supervising architect of this Renaissance Revival structure, which was finished on May 6, 1913 when C.J. Purcell was postmaster. Rural Free Delivery began in 1899 to Prosperity, and routes were established in 1901 to Townships 5 and 6. W.G. Peterson was the rural carrier with a salary of $500 a year.

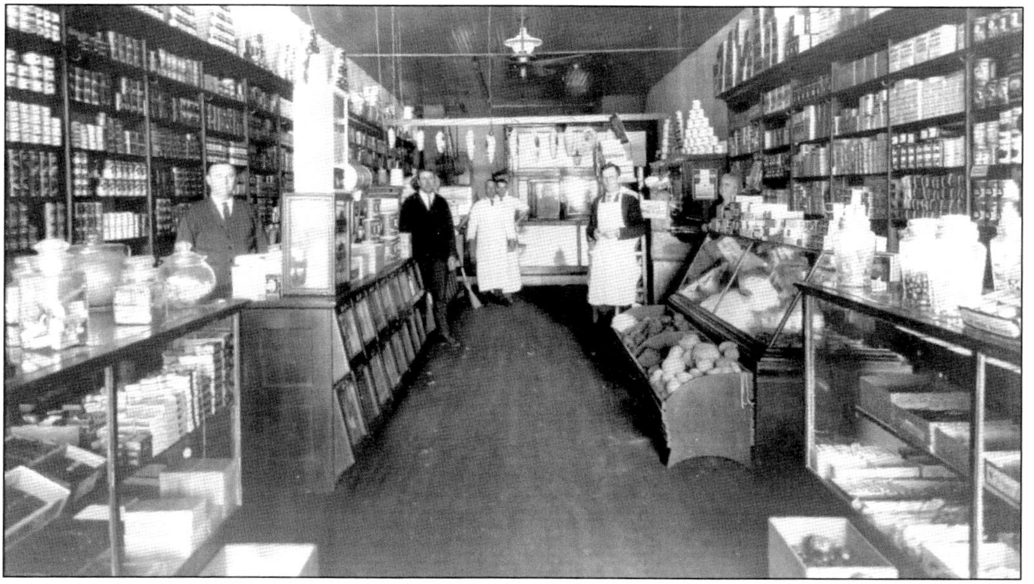

[BOOZER BROTHERS' STORE, c. 1910.] The J.R. and J.L. Boozer Brothers' grocery store was at 1311 Main Street, and the initial one-story frame building was destroyed in the 1907 fire for a $1,000 loss. The business continued and was described as being one of Newberry's leading grocery stores. An April 1910 *The Observer*'s ad listed its choice cuts of steak at 15¢ with other cuts from 10¢ to 12.5¢. The interior view above shows, from left to right, Reuben Boozer (1879–1933), Milton Hendricks, Jacob Boozer (1884–1950), Ralph Haile, and Miss Minnie Todd.

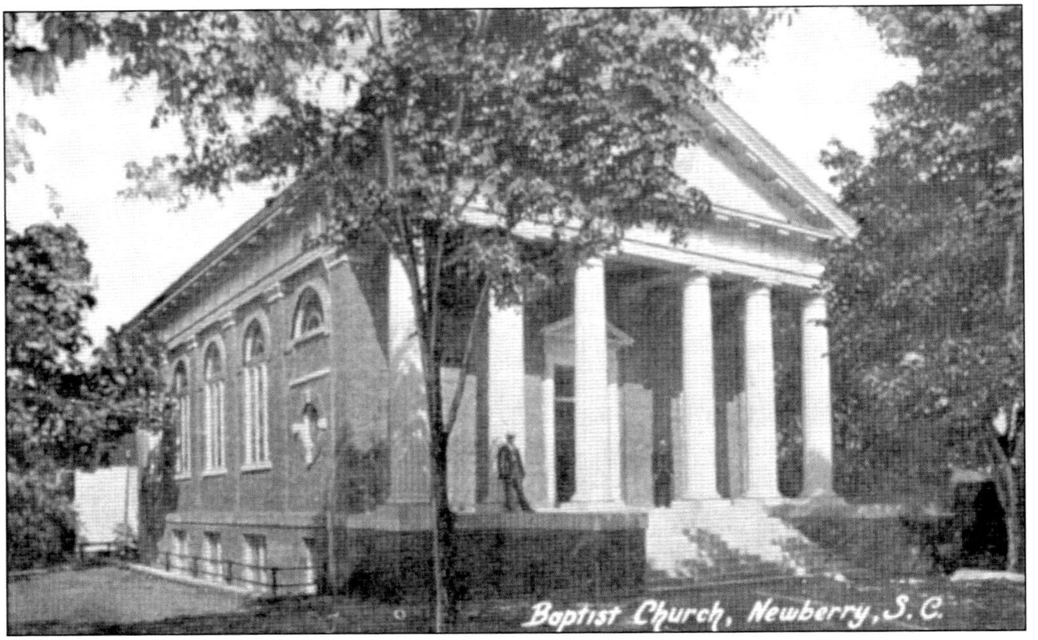

Baptist Church, Newberry [1908]. In 1905, a Newberry Baptist Church building committee, chaired by J. McIntosh, selected the Roman Revival Temple plan of Columbia architects Wilson and Edwards. The Mallard Lumber and Construction Company of Greenville built it in 1908. The original church and parsonage placement were reversed so that the new one could be built while services were being held in the old one. The 745 Caldwell Street church changed their name in 1914 to the First Baptist Church of Newberry.

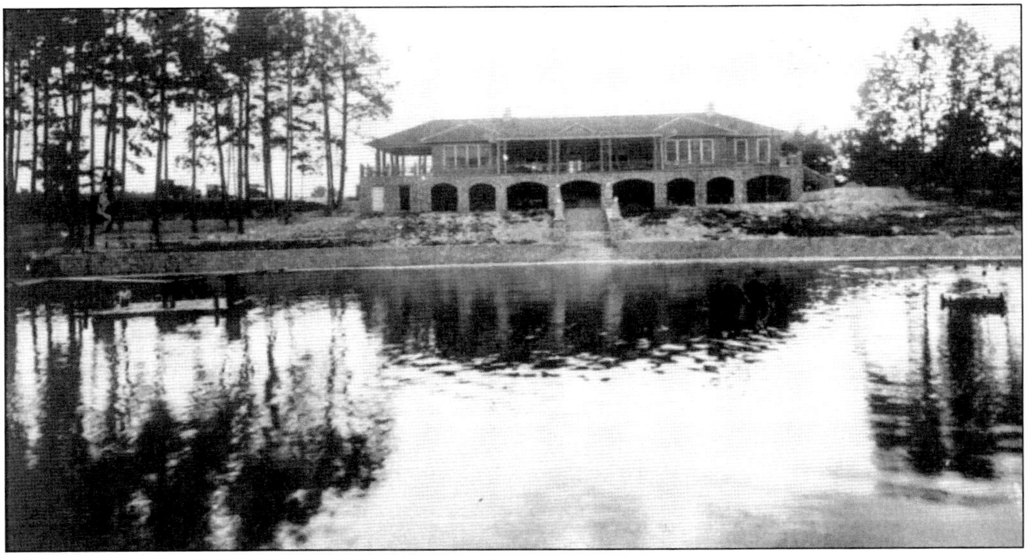

Newberry County Club, Newberry [c. 1924]. In 1922 leaders of the business community purchased a 55-acre tract of land three miles north of town. A club house, a nine-hole golf course, and a lake for boating and swimming permitted the members' families a variety of recreational activities. The original County Club House was destroyed by fire in 1939 and was quickly rebuilt.

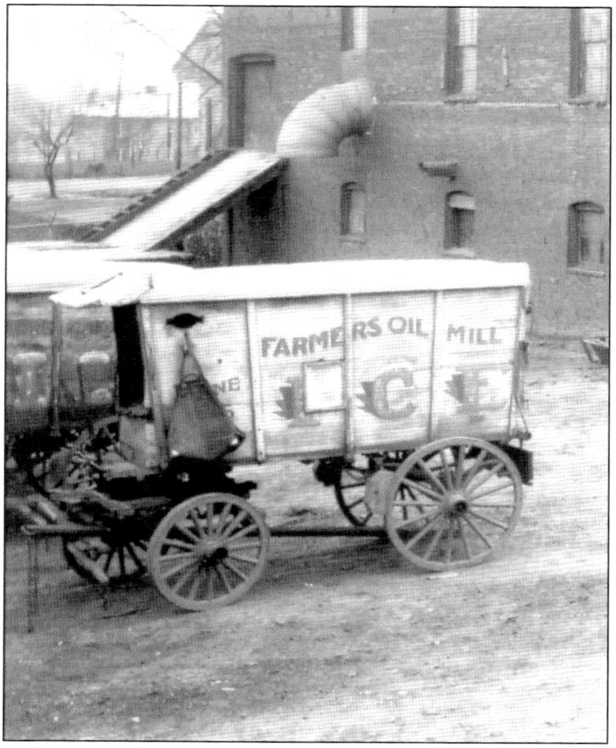

[Ice Wagon, 1908.] The Farmers Oil Mill on Drayton Street was established in May 1904 with W.K. Sligh, president, and J.H. Wicker manager. It processed oil from cotton seeds, ginned cotton, and ground flour. An ice plant was built in 1907 with ice deliveries made twice a day. Later the company also sold coal.

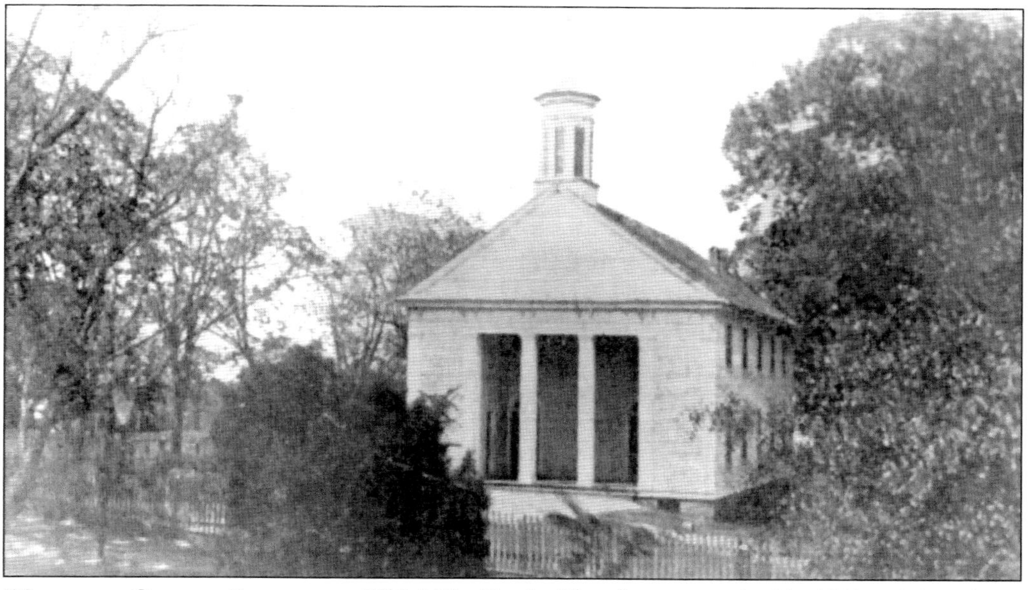

[Newberry Baptist Church, c. 1900.] The Baptist Church was organized in 1831 and their frame church built in 1832. During that era the church held services once or twice a month. The services were enriched with the addition of an organ in 1855 and a regular choir in 1888. A baptistery was built in 1889. After the dedication of the 1908 edifice, the old frame structure was taken down, moved to the Mollohon Mill village, re-assembled, and later called the Glenn Street Baptist Church.

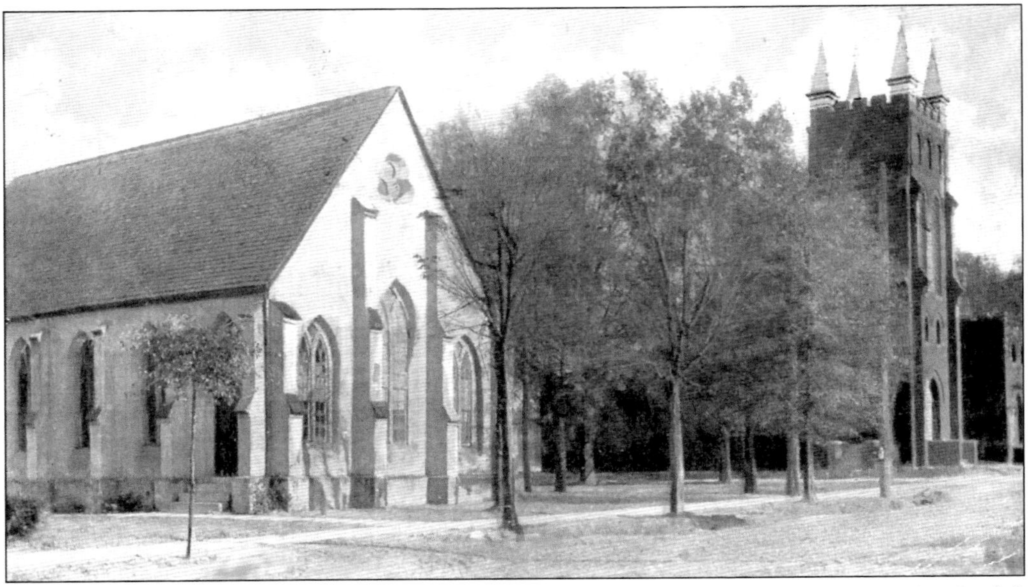

St. Luke's Episcopal Church and the A.R.P. Church, Newberry [c. 1908]. On the left side of this postcard is St. Luke's Episcopal Church, which was organized in 1846 and was the only Episcopal Church in the county. Its lot was purchased in 1854; and the Gothic sanctuary, which cost $4,000, was designed by G. Walker of Columbia and contracted by Hamilton of Charleston. It was consecrated in 1855. This church at 1609 Main Street was damaged during the Civil War, destroyed in the 1984 tornado, and rebuilt. On the right side is the A.R.P. Church at 1710 Main Street.

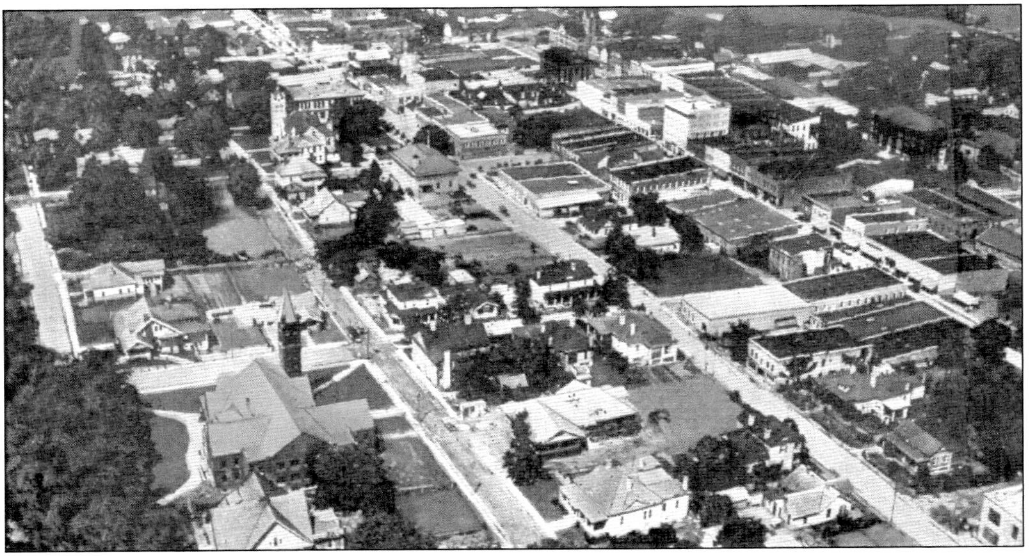

Aerial View of Newberry [c. 1926]. This view, published in a May 1926 edition of *The Observer*, shows the Lutheran Church by Johnstone Street in the lower left. An inch above its tower is the Central Methodist Church, and a half inch to the lower right is the post office on Friend Street. From this center position an inch and a half to the right is the Exchange Building on Main Street. A half-inch to the upper left is the Old Courthouse and Opera House. Finally, an inch to the right of the Exchange "Skyscraper" is the new courthouse.

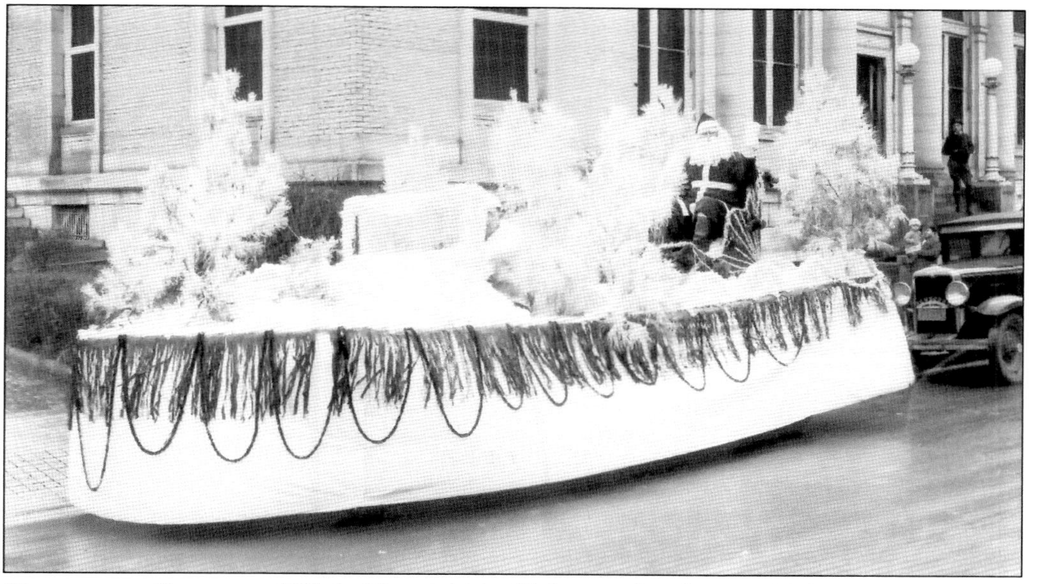

[Christmas Parade, 1935.] The initial Christmas Parades, established *c.* 1910, had two units. The first was the Newberry Concert Band, and the second one was Santa Claus seated in a wagon drawn by two horses. The parade started on upper Main Street and ended in the Public Square. Over the years tractors and then trucks replaced the horses. The 1935 float above is photographed in front of the Post Office on Friend Street. These parades continue in 2001.

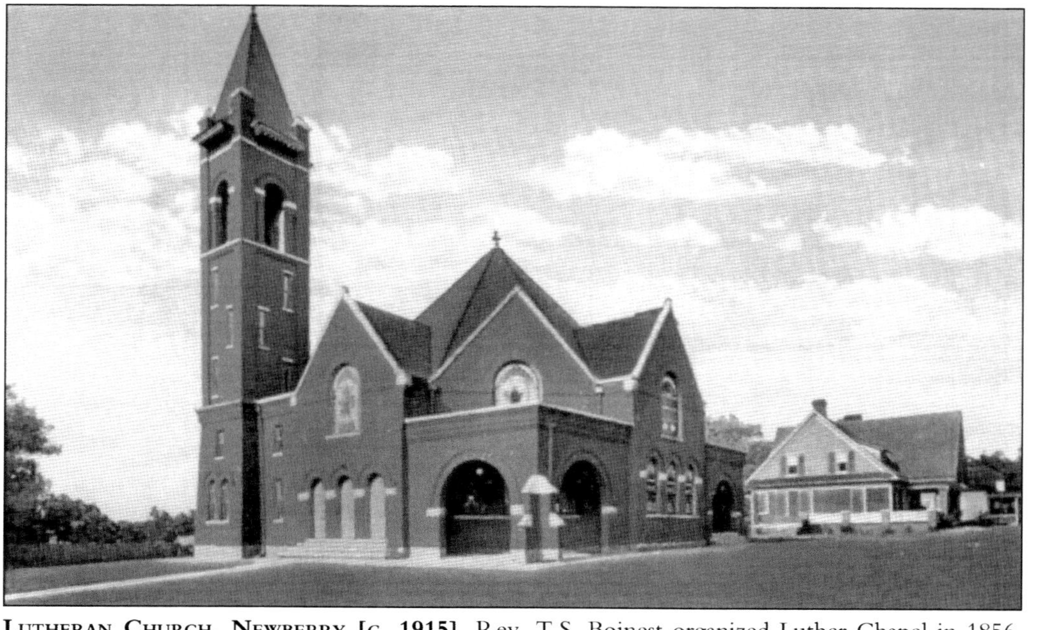

Lutheran Church, Newberry [*c.* 1915]. Rev. T.S. Boinest organized Luther Chapel in 1856. The first Gothic frame structure, designed by G. Walker of Columbia, was built just after 1856 on Caldwell Street and cost $4,000. In 1890 a site on the corner of Johnstone and Wilson Streets was bought, a new edifice built in 1897 for $14,500, and the Lutheran Church of the Redeemer became its new name.

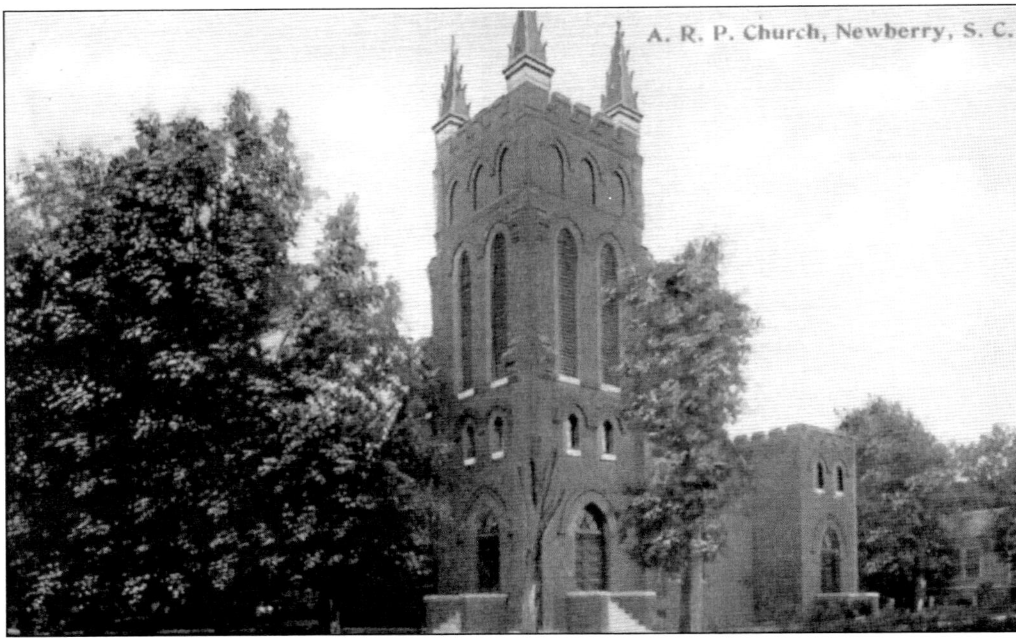

A.R.P. Church, Newberry [1908]. The Associate Reformed Presbyterian Church was organized in 1854. The original building on Thompson Street was destroyed by the fire of 1907. The edifice above was designed by F. Milburn and built by C.C. Davis for $13,000 at 1710 Main Street. The A.R.P. adherents are the fourth-oldest denomination in the county.

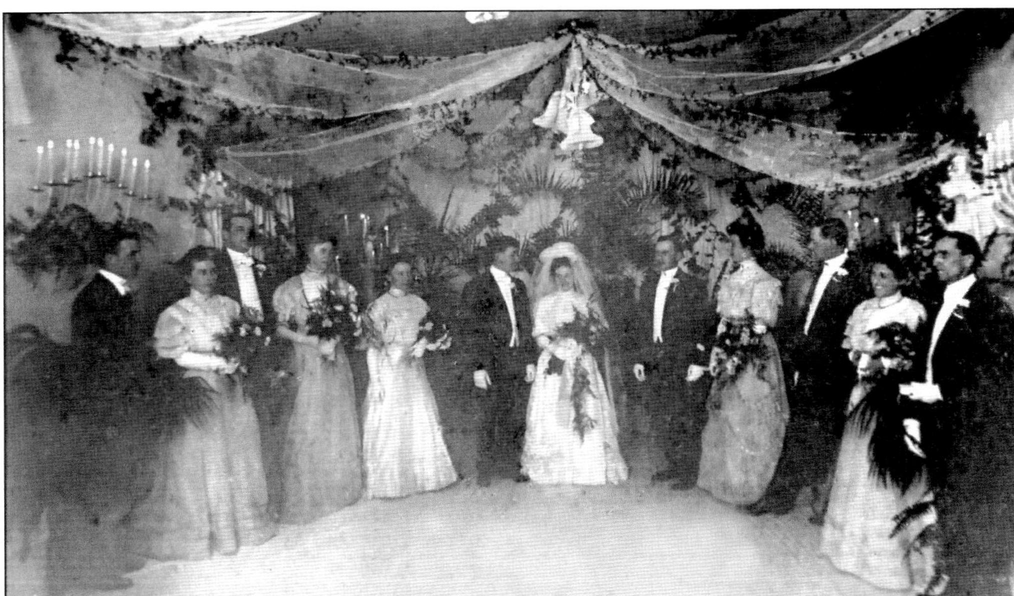

[Wedding Scene, 1907.] The Douschka Martin and Henry Sweets 1907 wedding was held in the wide entrance hall of the F.N. Martin House at 1531 Main Street. Every dark wood surface was covered with white sheets, and crepe paper streamers hung above the guests. The bride, groom, and attendants, shown above, pose for the formal wedding pictures.

[MRS. LONG, C. 1910.] Ladies at the turn of the century considered long flowing hair a feature of beauty. Some stylish young women, like Mrs. Long, never cut their hair and spent long hours grooming it. Miss Annie L. Smith's shop at 942 Main Street sold long human hair switches that were a perfect match to any variety of hair. The prices began at $2.00. She also sold "stick up's" (probably small hair pieces used to help disguise problems of thinning hair), and fancy shell hair goods.

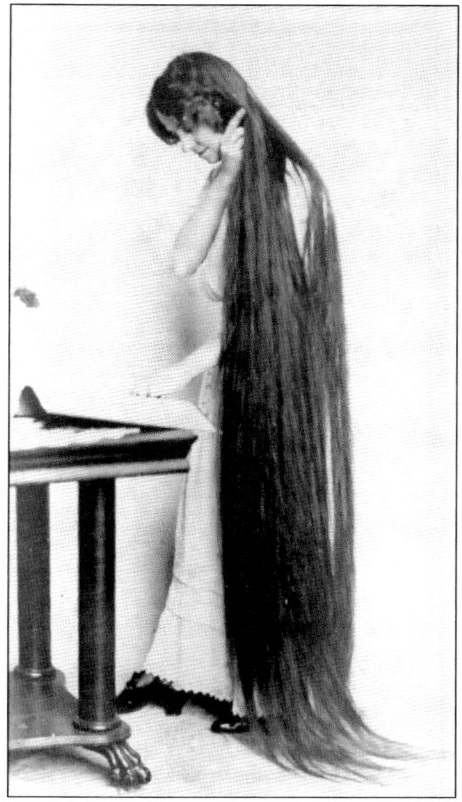

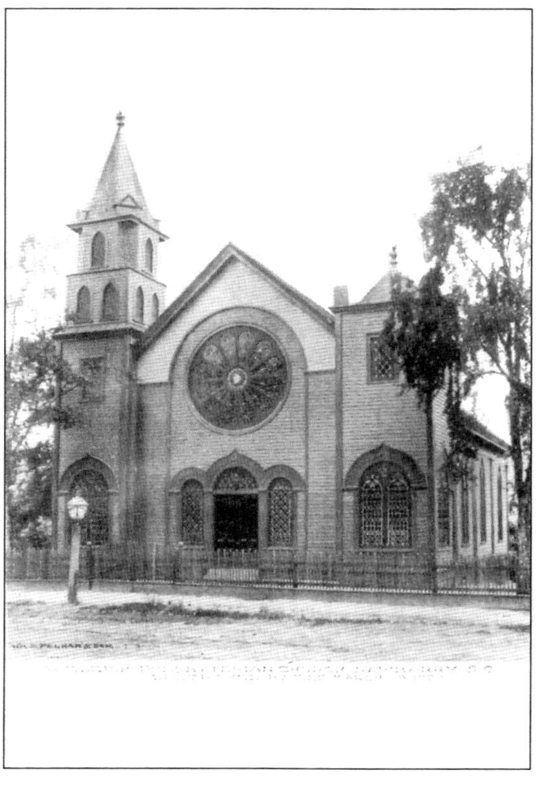

AVELEIGH PRESBYTERIAN CHURCH, NEWBERRY [C. 1906]. This church was organized in 1832 with 32 members and was located at Hunt's Crossroads [Highway 34 and 76]. In 1852 the congregation moved into town and erected a sanctuary on a lot at the corner of Calhoun and Martin Streets. In 1901 the edifice was remodeled at a cost of $3,500. This second oldest Presbyterian Church was destroyed in the Great Fire of 1907; the congregation rebuilt immediately on the same site at a cost of $6,500 and remodeled in 1930.

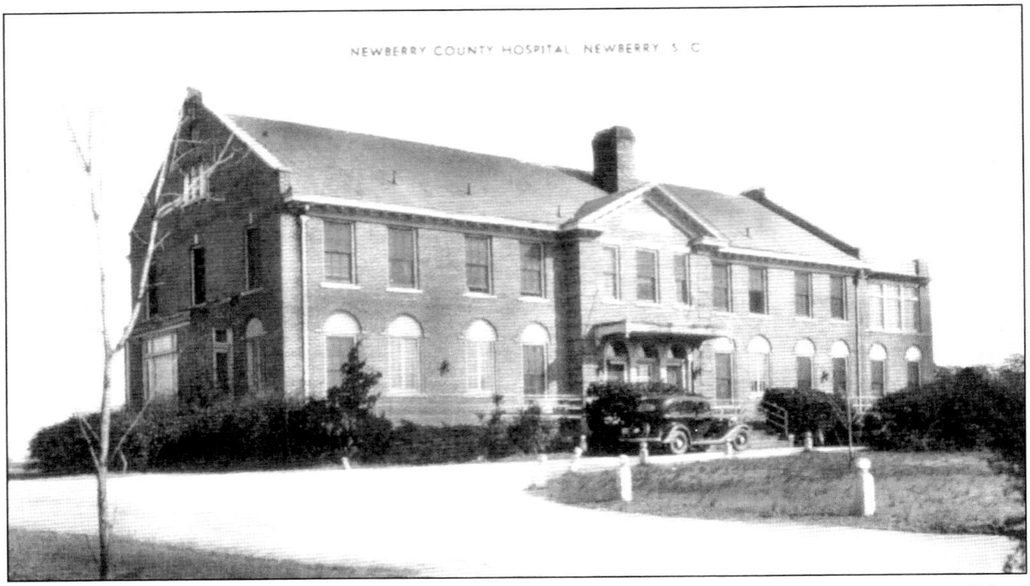

NEWBERRY COUNTY HOSPITAL, NEWBERRY [1925]. The County Health Department was established in 1920 with Dr. R.F. Finney as the first health officer. In December 1923 a Newberry County Hospital Association board of directors was selected with Dr. G.B. Cromer as chairman to plan for a new hospital. The new 25-bed hospital at 1320 Hunt and Kinard Streets opened in 1925 at a cost of $62,000, which came from voluntary contributions. Rooms were furnished by local gifts of $175 a room. Dr. H.G. Callison served as both the superintendent of Newberry Hospital and the county health officer until 1932.

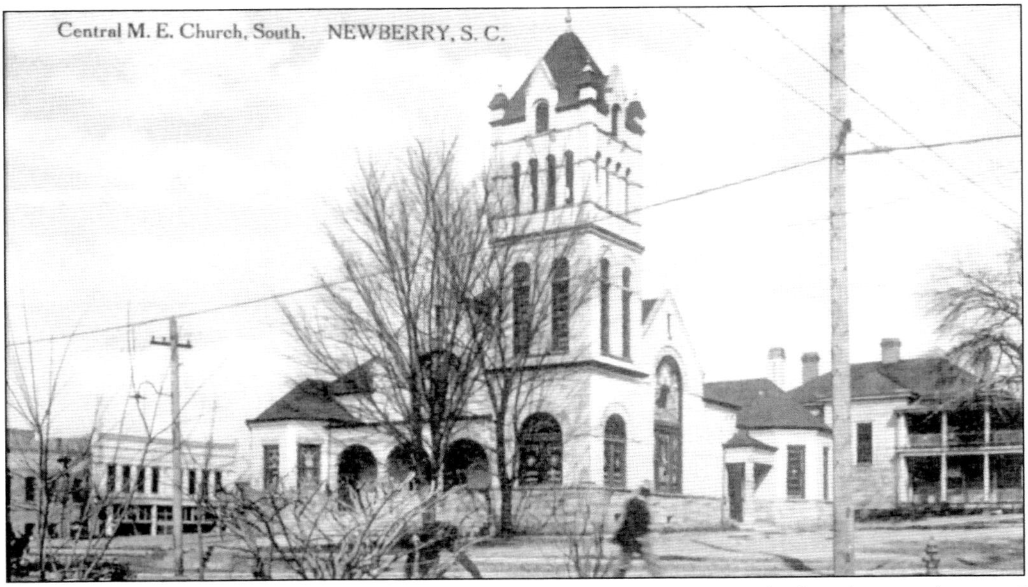

CENTRAL M.E. CHURCH, SOUTH, NEWBERRY [C. 1905]. Newberry Methodist, the town's second church, was founded in 1832 with its first structure built in 1833. A new Gothic-style sanctuary designed by R.H. Hunt of Chattanooga with a tall tower was built at 1004 Caldwell Street in 1901 at a cost of $15,000. Central Methodist Church became its name in 1901.

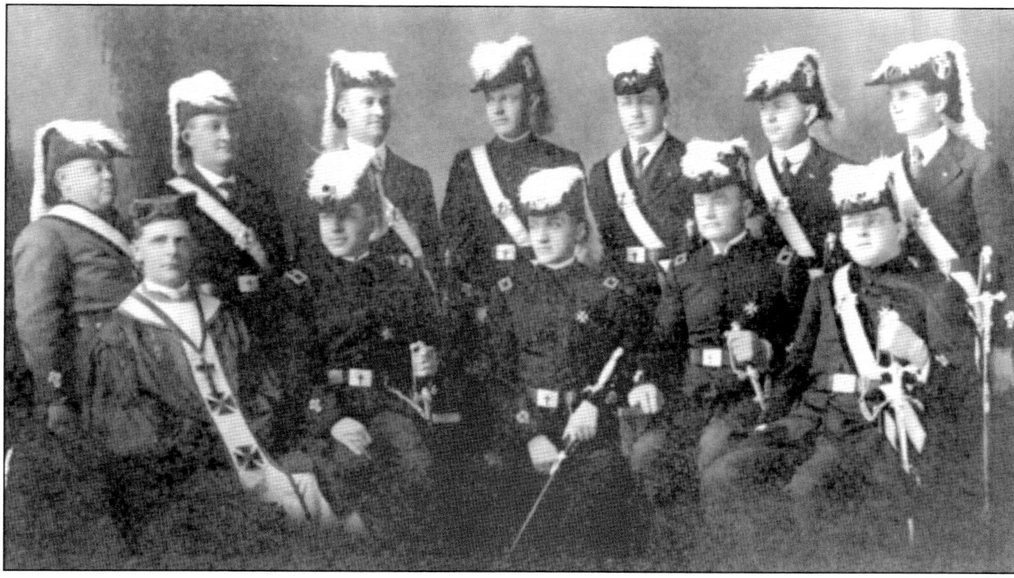

[Knights of Columbus, c. 1915.] The Knights of Columbus members in this portrait, from left to right, are (front row) J.H. Harms, H. Dominick, H. Wright, unidentified, and ? Eskridge; (back row) B. Martin, three unidentified individuals, H. Cannon, T. Johnson, and H. Wells. This international fraternal and benevolent organization of Roman Catholic men was founded in New Haven, Connecticut in 1882.

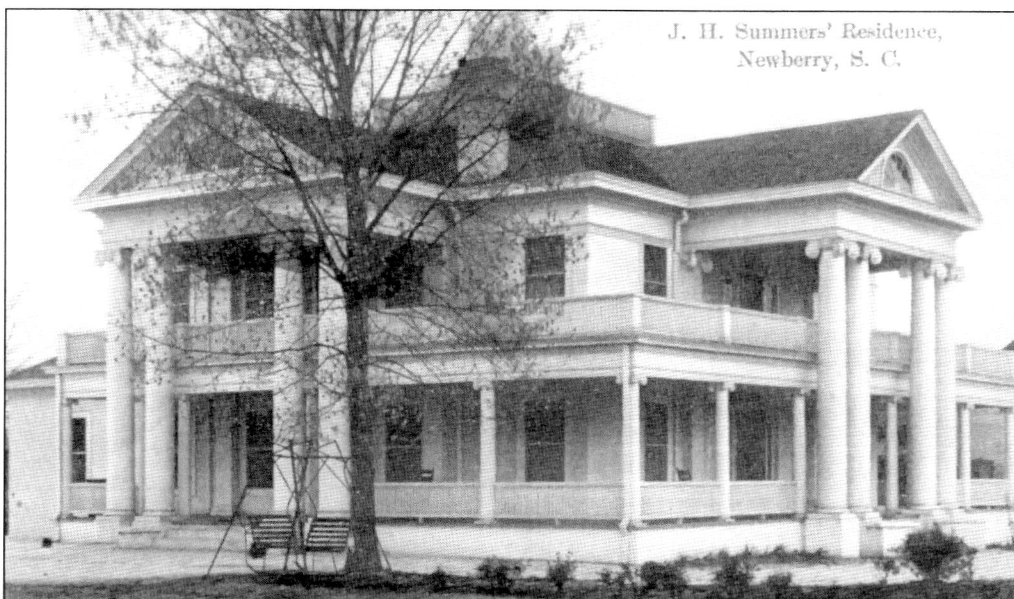

J.H. Summer's Residence, Newberry [c. 1910]. J.H. Summer (1861–1951) was born in the Dutch Fork area and moved to Newberry in the 1880s. Initially, he was a partner in the family's businesses. Summer's residence was built in the Classic Revival style. Newberry's public works supplied homes with electrical service, a one-to-five light rate being 40¢ each per month, and water service, which was $6 for the first faucet and additional faucets at $2 each. Each bathtub was $1 per month.

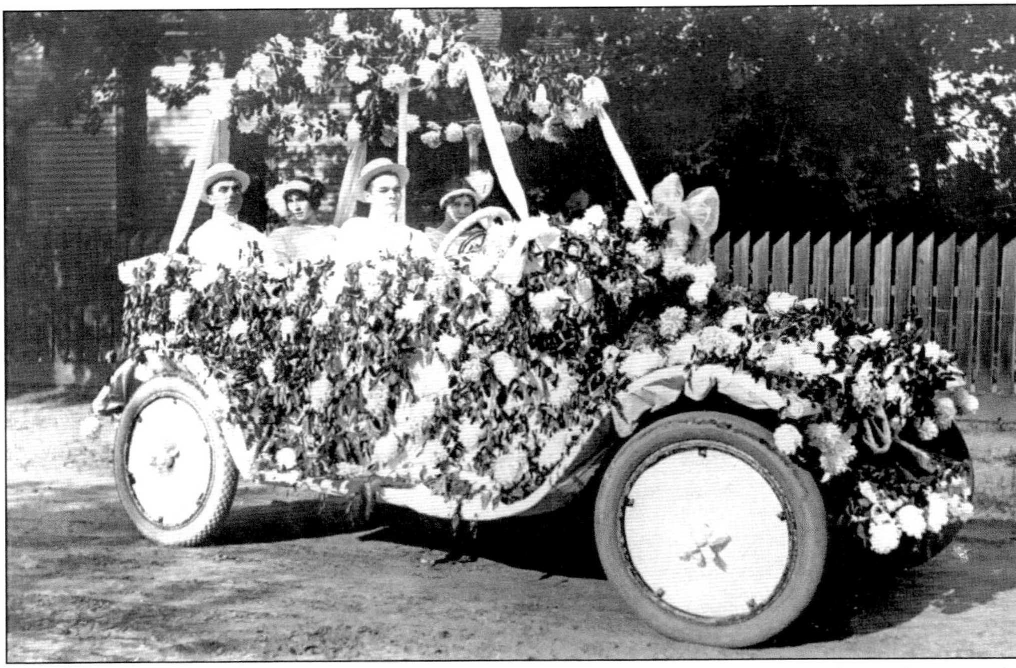

[Chautauqua Festival Parade, 1911.] The Chautauqua Automobile Parade of 1911 began at the Old Courthouse at 5 p.m. and traveled through the residential sections before returning to the Public Square. Dr. R. Houseal, his two sisters, and Zack Wright are in this automobile.

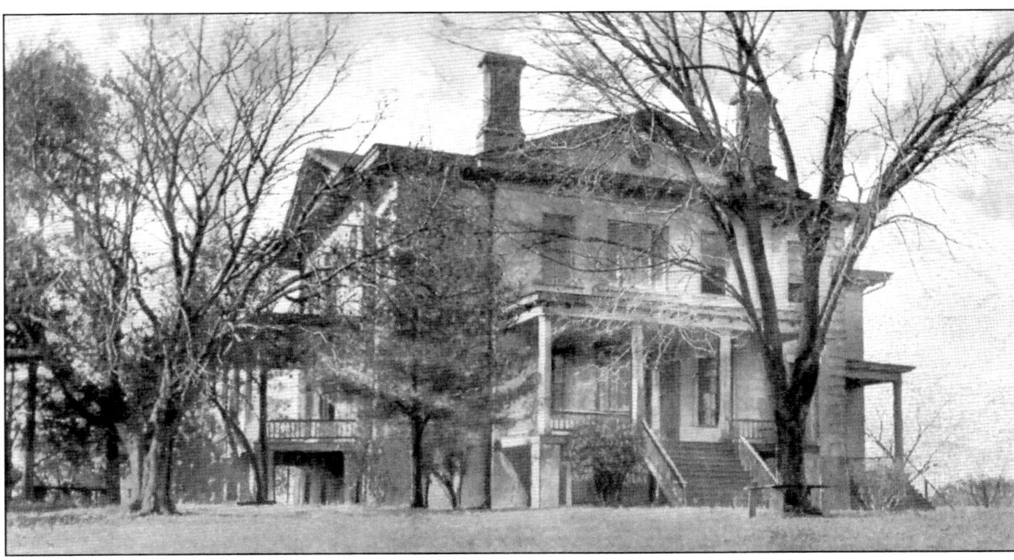

Pope School, Newberry [1909]. Judge Y.J. Pope (1841–1911) served in the Confederate army and later became a lawyer and county judge. He was elected to the following state offices: Newberry County's representative in the South Carolina legislature, attorney general, associate judge, and then chief justice of the South Carolina Supreme Court. In 1909 the city bought this residence, which was designed by G. Walker of Columbia in 1857, to be used as a school. It was altered and called the Spears Street Elementary School.

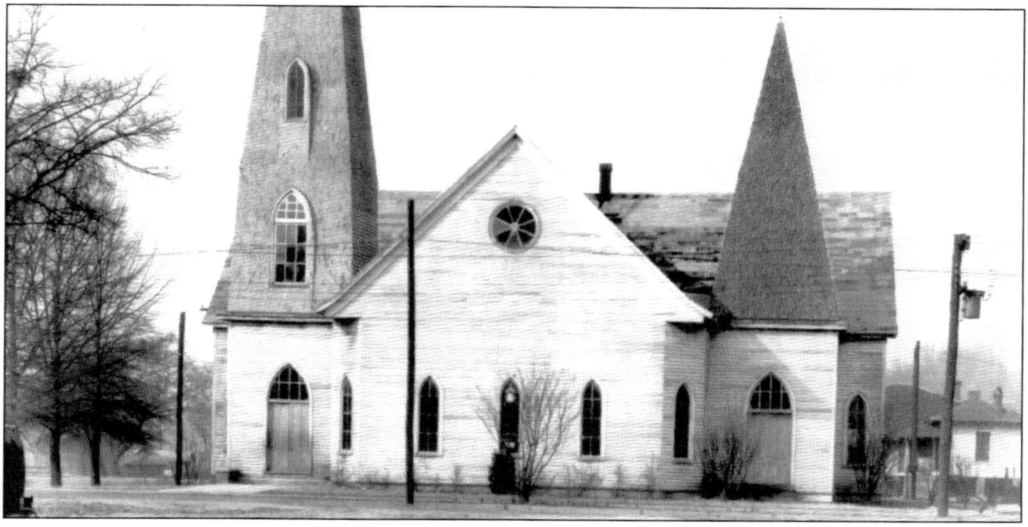

[Bethlehem Baptist Church, *c.* 1910.] Mr. G.D. Scott gave a lot on the south side of Scott's Creek to elders I. Lewis, D. Rutherford, J. Kinard, and J. Baxter, trustees of the Colored Bethlehem Baptist Church, which was chartered in 1872. The first house of worship was erected in 1873. In 1901 the church bought six lots across the creek and erected the present sanctuary at 1500 College Street. A parsonage was built on Vincent Street in 1919.

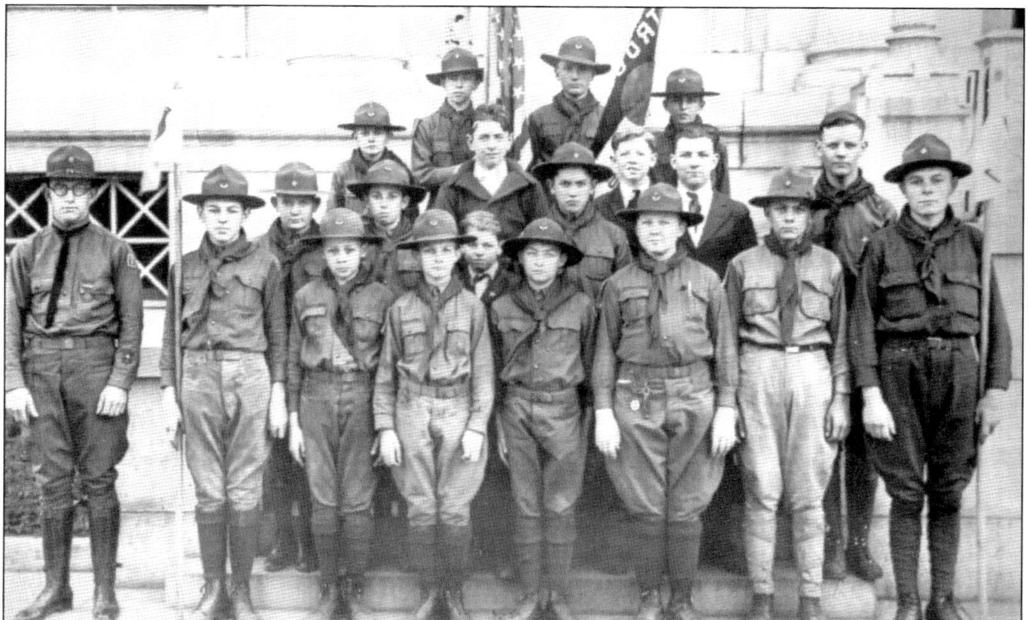

[Boy Scout Troop #1, *c.* 1918.] The first boy scout troop was organized under pastor G. Smith of the O'Neal Street Methodist Church. This troop picture includes, from left to right, (first row) J. Clarkson (scoutmaster), E. Summer, F. Martin, C. Hutchinson, S. Wise, G. Martin, A. Clarkson, and T.E. Epting; (second row) V. Taylor, M. Caldwell, J. Ward, O. Whitaker, F. Devore, and J. Nobles; (third row) A. Green, T. Rogers, and ? Turner; (fourth row) W. Bullock, J. Boyleston, and L. Anderson.

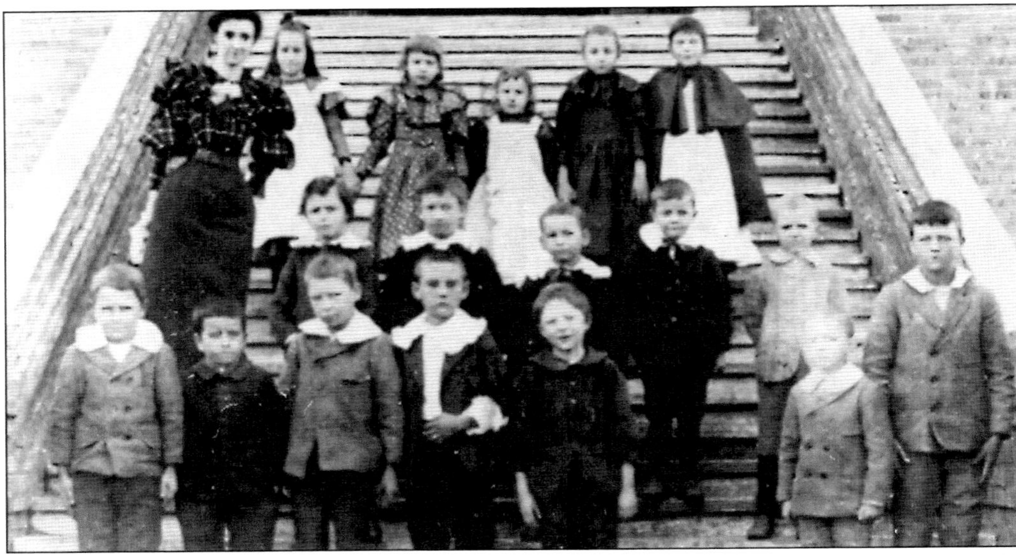

[Boundary Street School Class Picture, *c.* 1897.] The school class picture above was taken by the J.Z. Salter's photographic studio. The town's educational structure started with a male academy, established *c.* 1806, and one for girls in 1839. Newberry County had 102 schoolhouses, including 4 brick, 19 log, and 79 frame one- or two-room buildings in 1893. The students were taught by 72 white teachers and 58 black teachers.

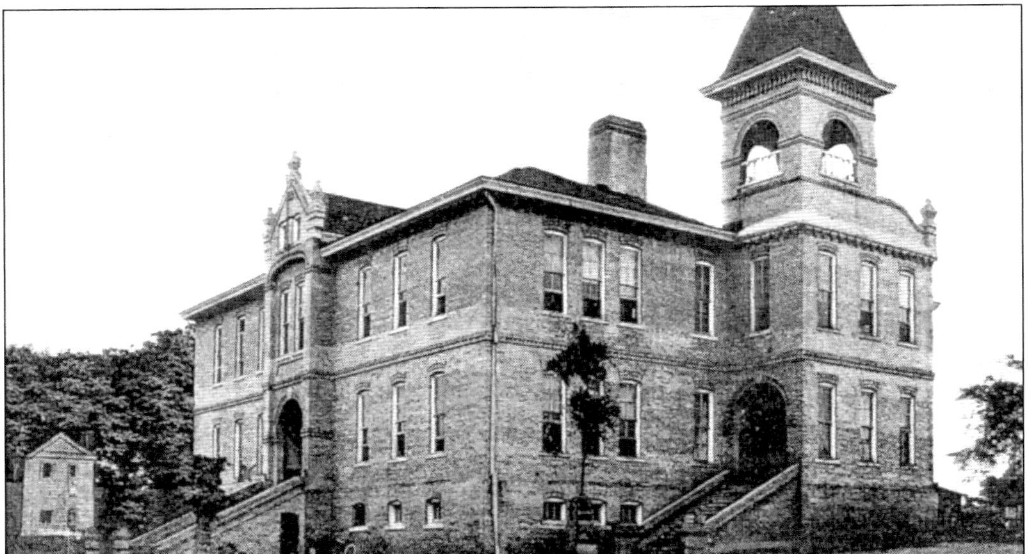

Newberry Graded School, Newberry [*c.* 1907]. This school, also called the Boundary Street School, was located at 1406 Boundary and Coates Streets. It was designed by the Atlanta firm of Bruce and Morgan and was occupied in January 1892. Newberry County had 57 school districts in 1899. The two-story brick Boundary School, above, had 11 teachers and 527 students, while each of the other districts had one white school and one black school. The average white school term was six-and-a-half months for 3,240 students while the black term was five months for 4,220 students. This structure was razed in the 1960s.

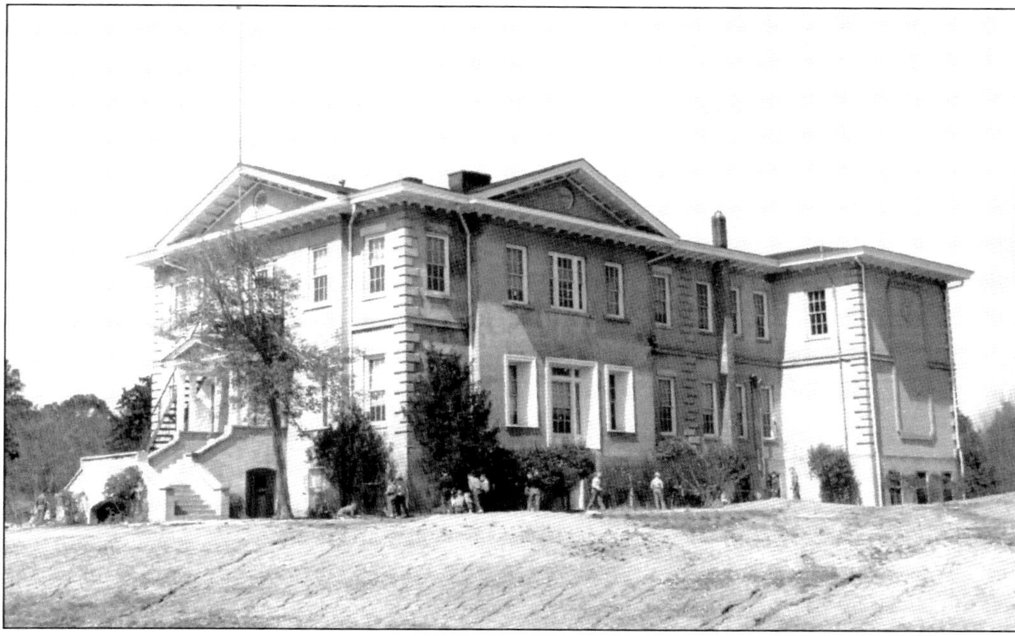

[Speer Street School, Newberry, *c.* 1915.] The Speer Street School was an altered and expanded version of the Y.J. Pope's home purchased in 1909 at 1201 Speer Street. In 1921 Mrs. S.B. Setzler was principal and was assisted by eight teachers. This building was razed in 1962.

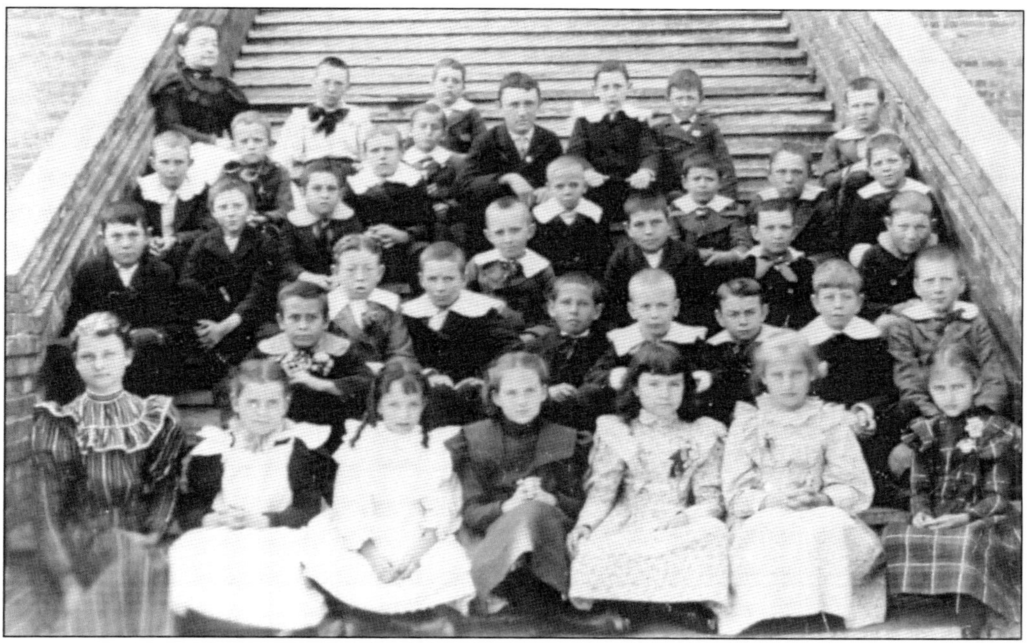

[Boundary Street School Class, *c.* 1900.] The Boundary Street School class students are shown sitting on the steps of the grammar school with teacher M. Burton. In 1900 Newberry's District #1 (town) had 2 white schools with 13 teachers and 511 students and 1 black school with 4 teachers and 328 students.

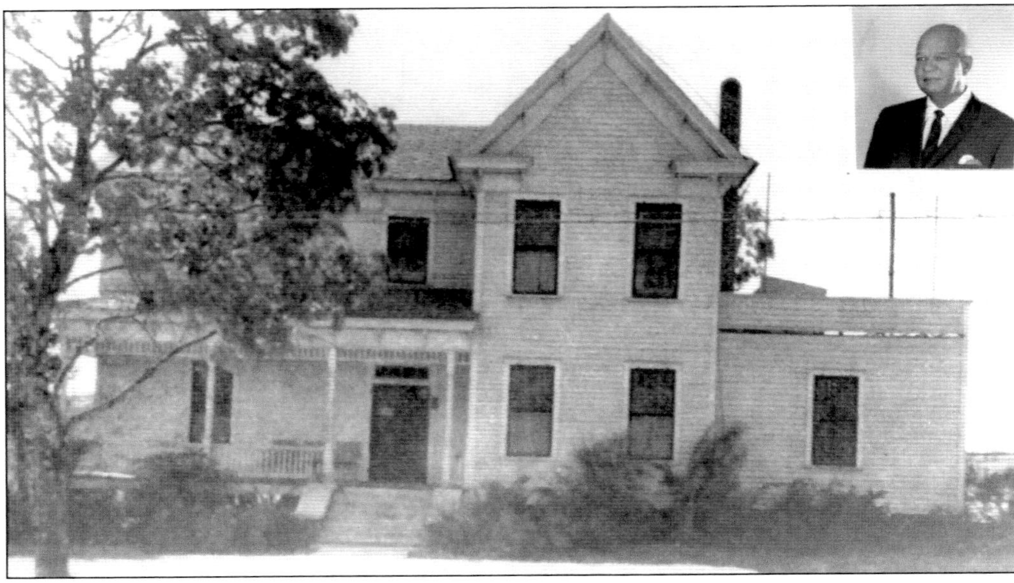

[Peoples' Hospital, 1930s.] The Peoples' Hospital at 1719 Vincent Street in the Cannon Town section of Newberry, was created for the African-American community by Dr. J.E. Grant and with the assistance of Dr. E.G. Able in the 1930s. Dr. Grant's picture is inset in the upper right corner.

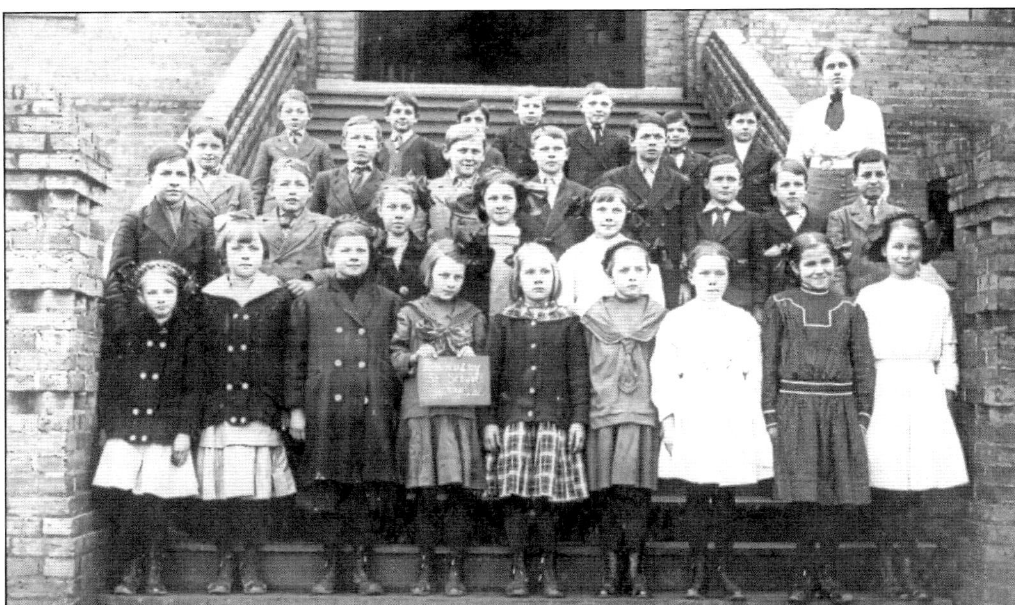

[Boundary Street School Fourth Grade Class, *c.* 1912.] Newberry County's 1912 class groupings were as follows: first grade, 424 white students and 1,552 black students; second grade, 398 w. and 918 b.; third grade, 437 w. and 776 b.; fourth grade, 450 w. and 560 b.; fifth grade, 317 w. and 383 b.; sixth grade, 291 w. and 830 b.; seventh grade, 348 w. and 164 b.; eighth grade, 125 w. and 87 b.; ninth grade, 73 w. and 73 b.; and tenth grade, 55 w. and 21 b. The totals are 2,918 white students and 5,364 black students for a grand total of 8,282 county students in 1912.

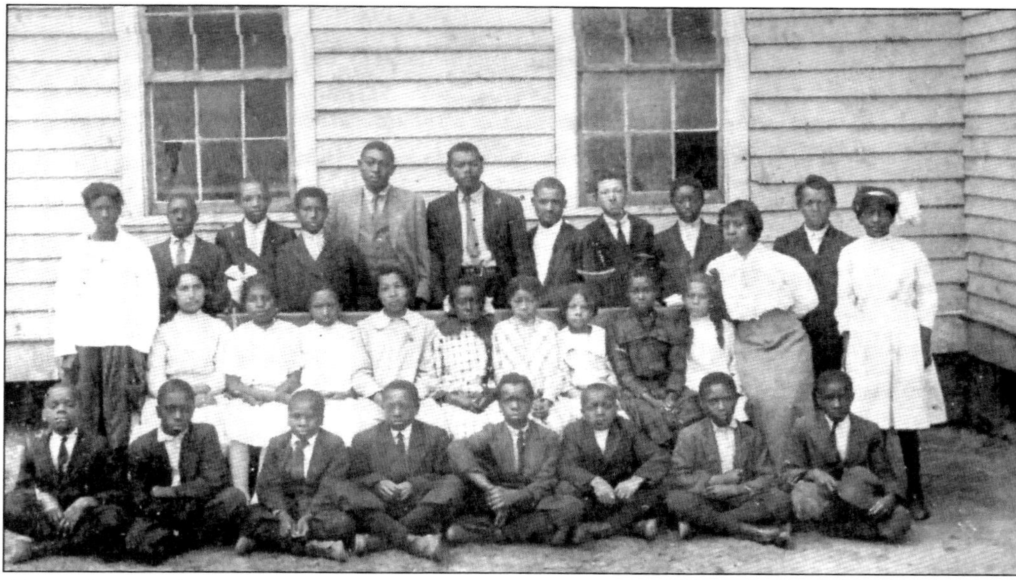

[Hoge School Students, *c.* 1920.] On October 10, 1869 J.W. White conveyed a three-quarter-acre lot in the Gravel Town section of Caldwell Street to the trustees of the Freedmen's School. This school was named in honor of S.L. Hoge, a U.S. Army captain from Ohio who became a member of the South Carolina Supreme Court, comptroller-general of South Carolina, and a member of Congress during Reconstruction. In 1890 A.P. Butler was principal of Hoge School and Misses M. Tillman and J. Kennedy were teachers. In 1921 the teaching staff included J.M. Johnson, principal, and nine teachers.

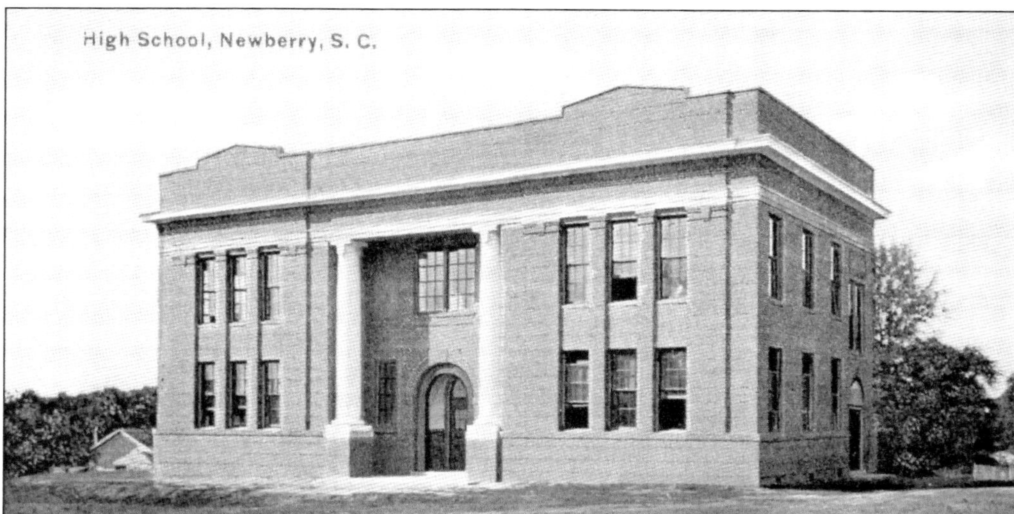

High School, Newberry [*c.* 1911]. In 1910 a new two-story brick high school, built by McCullough and Rutherford, was erected on Martin Street with five classrooms and an auditorium. In 1919 the high school student body consisted of 63 first-year students, 40 second-year students, and 11 third-year seniors for a total of 114 students. They were taught by one part-time and six full-time teachers. The building became a junior high school in 1927 when a new high school was built. It has since been razed.

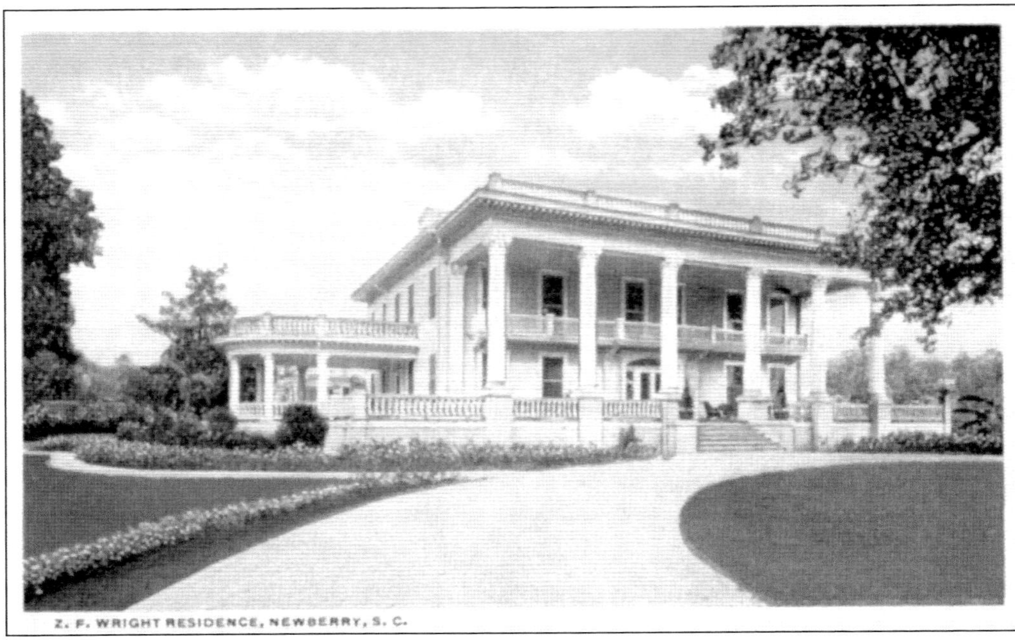

Z.F. Wright Residence, Newberry [c. 1908]. The Z.F. Wright (1869–1949) residence on Caldwell Street reflected the owner's significance in this town. After initial jobs Wright served as president of Newberry Cotton Mills from 1905 to 1946, as a director on the governing boards of all the local cotton mills, and as a board member of The Commercial Bank. He was mayor of Newberry for nine years and president of the Newberry Chamber of Commerce. Wright was active in committees that related to the city, county, educational, and social facets of his era.

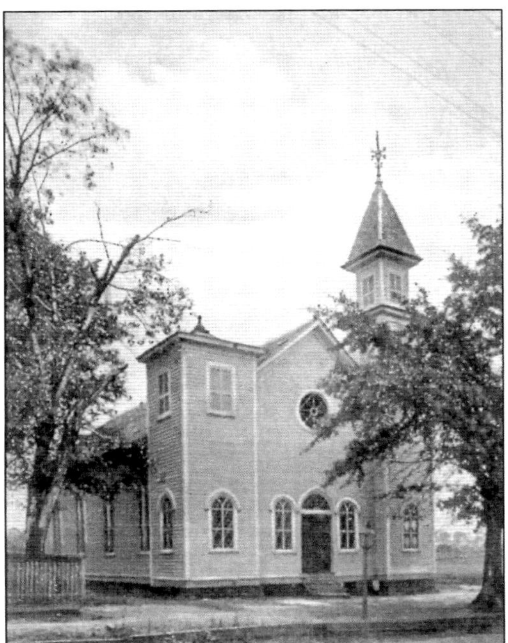

Colored M.E. Church, Newberry [c. 1907]. This frame sanctuary is now know as Miller's Chapel. The Methodist Episcopal Church South established several churches in Newberry County in 1866 under the name of Colored Methodist Episcopal Church of America. In 1869 E.K. Christian conveyed one-eighth of an acre to J. Boston and other trustees of the Colored M.E. Church. Later B. Raines gave them the adjoining quarter acre. A Freedmen's school was taught by Rev. S. Miller at 500 Caldwell Street in the Gravel Town section.

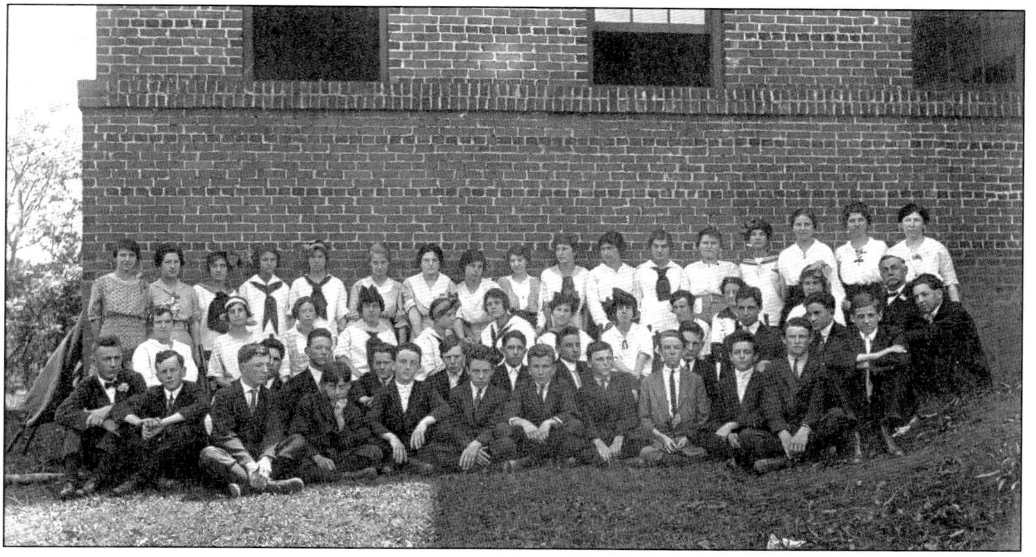

[Graduating Class, c. 1917.] This view of the *c.* 1917 graduating class was taken in front of the Martin Street High School. In 1917, Newberry County had 3,600 white students and 6,510 black students. The 1920 census reported that South Carolina had 74,000 white high school–age youth. It further detailed that 7,492 white students were enrolled in the eighth grade; 5,921 in the ninth; 4,683 in the tenth; and 3,222 in the eleventh for a total of 21,318 students. Only 28% of this age group were enrolled in classes.

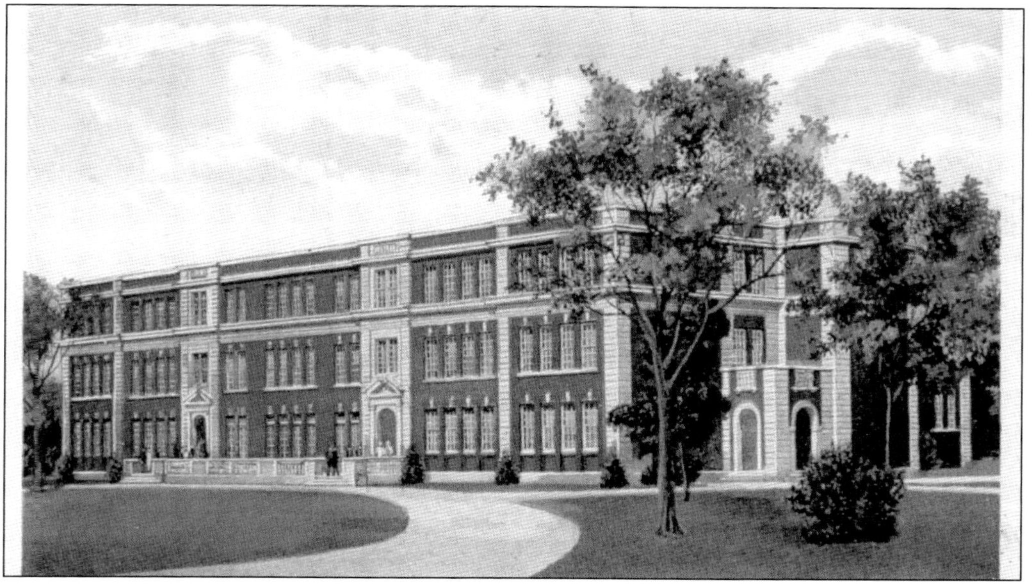

Newberry High School, Newberry [1927]. The new high school on Nance Street was constructed in 1927 by the Gallivan Building Company. Coach Hedgepath joined the high school in 1926 and coached three sports. With the consolidation of small local schools into larger area ones, the busing of school students began in the late 1920s. In 1929 the county used 31 buses to transport 1,108 white students at a cost per pupil of $20.13. The county had 4,899 white students and 4,890 African-American students in 1929.

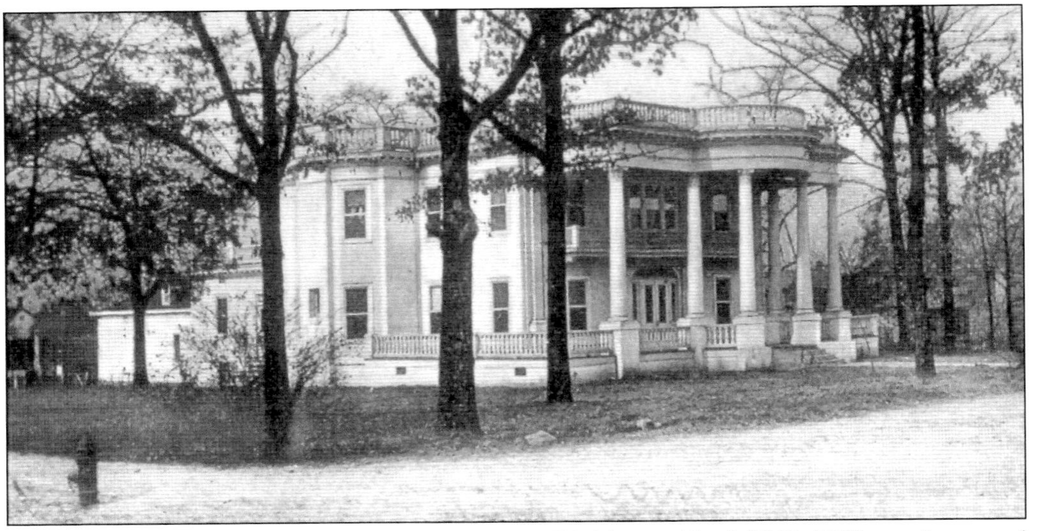

L.W. Floyd Residence, Newberry [c. 1907]. Lou Washington Floyd (1860–1928) was the general manager of the Newberry Cotton Seed Oil Mill and Fertilizer Company that was organized in 1890. He obtained the Southern Bell Telephone and Telegraph Company franchise, established *c.* 1896, when there were 21 telephones in Newberry. The annual fee began at $40. Later, he acquired the franchises of six other South Carolina cities. In 1903 he sold his entire system to Southern Bell. By 1909 Newberry County had 819 telephones and the city had 382. Floyd's Calhoun Street house was an example of neoclassical architecture.

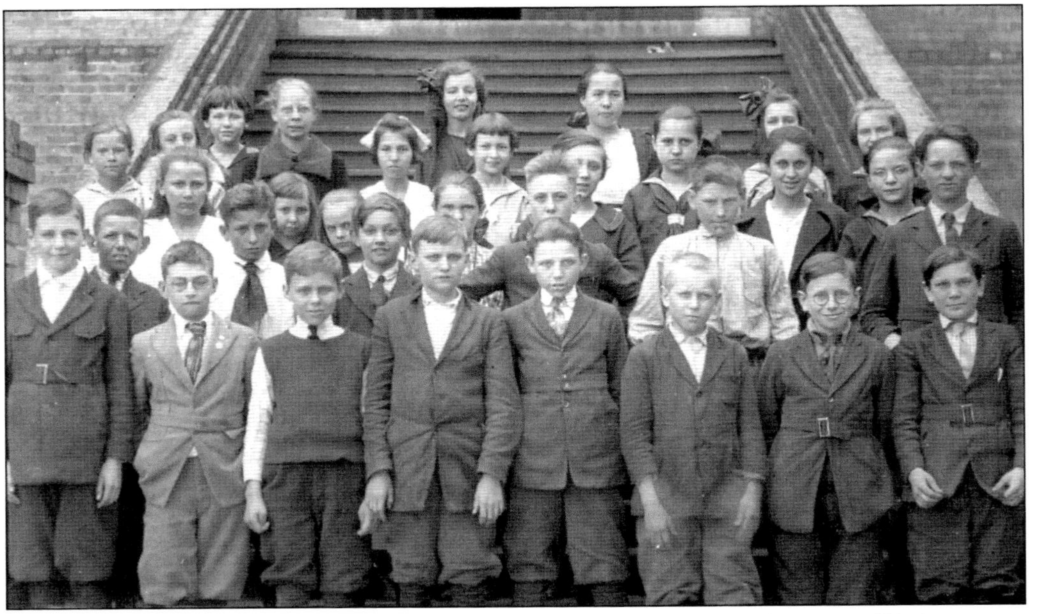

[Boundary Street School Fifth Grade Class, c. 1920.] Newberry's District #1 elementary, junior, and senior high school student distribution by grade level was as follows: first grade, 225 students; second grade, 147; third grade, 160; fourth grade, 165; fifth grade, 112; sixth grade, 95; seventh grade, 81; eighth grade, 80; ninth grade, 36; tenth grade, 23; and eleventh grade, 7, for a total of 1,131 students in 1920.

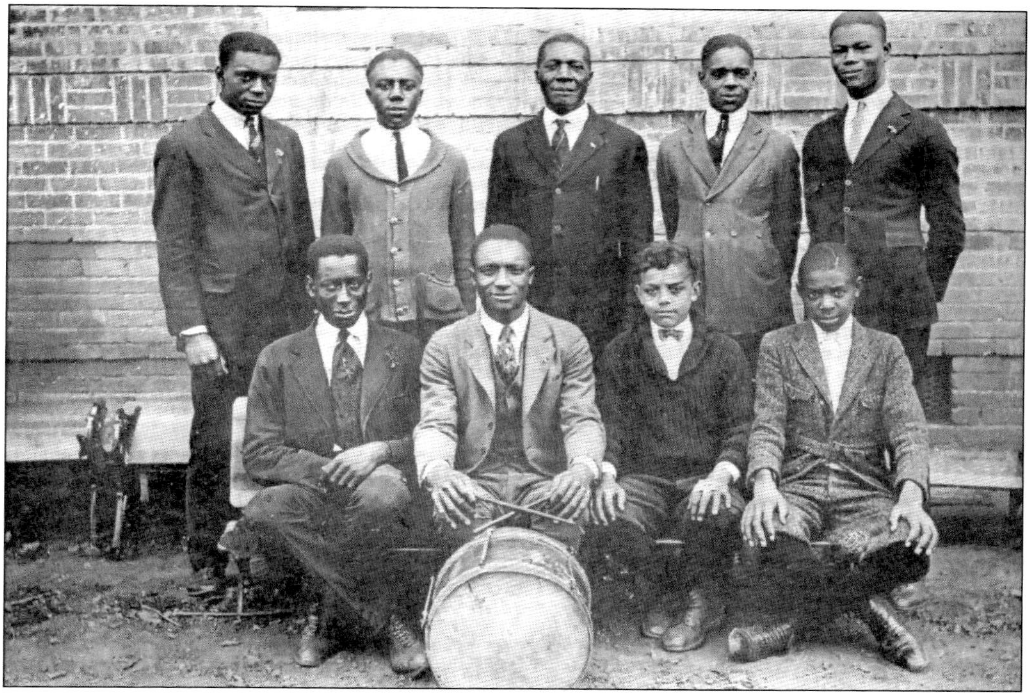

[Drayton Street High School Class, 1921.] The Rev. J.M. Johnson, the first principal of the new Drayton Street High School for African-American children, opened each day by having the students march to assembly to the beat of a drum.

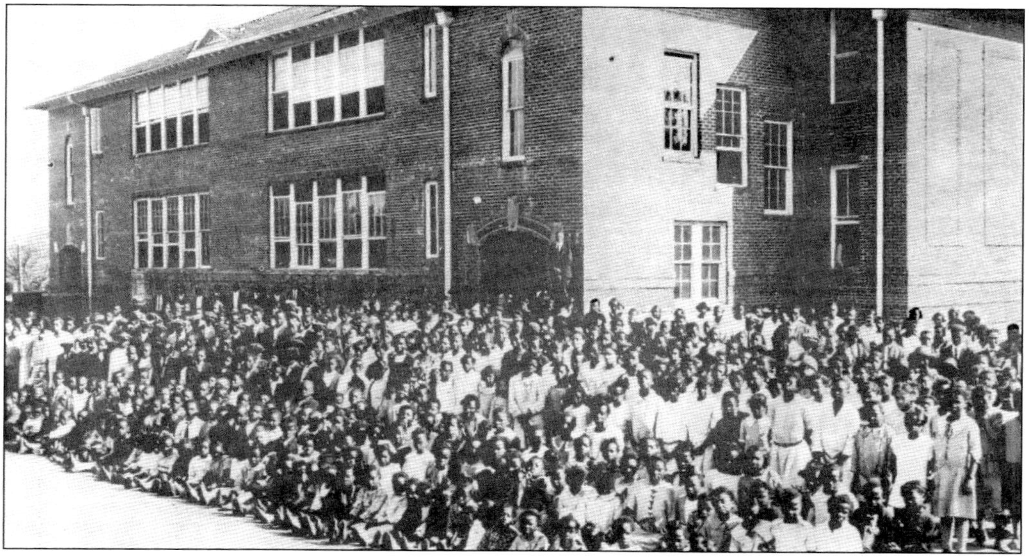

[Drayton Street High School, 1921.] This two-story brick school, costing $25,000, opened in 1921 and received students from Hoge and other small African-American schools. The Rev. J.M. Johnson was the first principal in 1921–1922. The number of students by grade were: first grade, 184 students; second grade, 72; third grade, 59; fourth grade, 65; fifth grade, 62; sixth grade, 61; seventh grade, 57; eighth grade, 46; ninth grade, 23; and tenth grade, 10, for a total of 639 students.

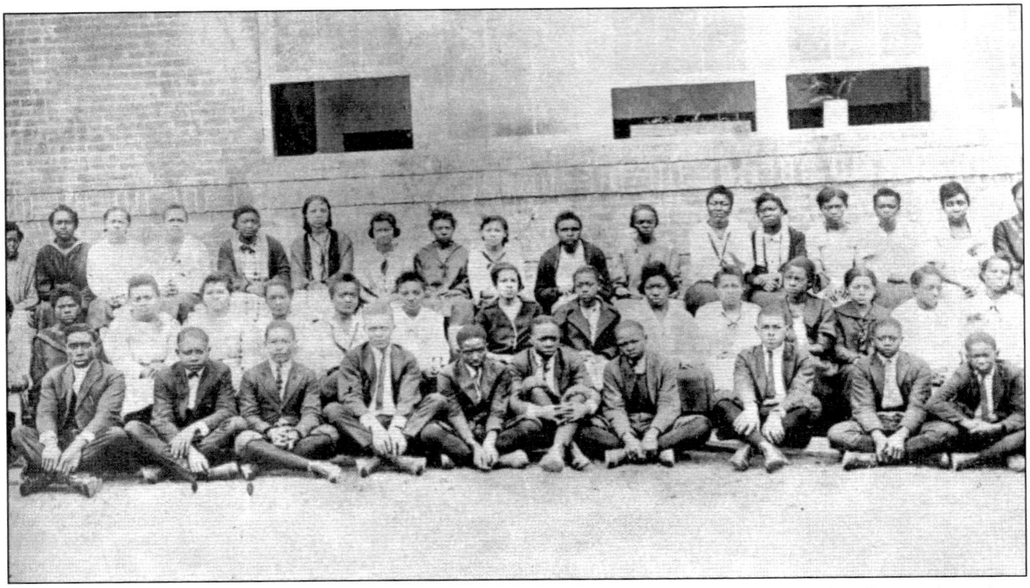

[Drayton Eighth Grade Students, 1925.] The 1920 census of South Carolina's African-American high school–age youth totaled 84,000. The black student enrollment was eighth grade, 583 students; ninth grade, 344; tenth grade, 232; and eleventh grade, 48, for a total of 1,207 students. This shows a 1.5% enrollment rate, or 98.5% of the black high school–age group not taking classes.

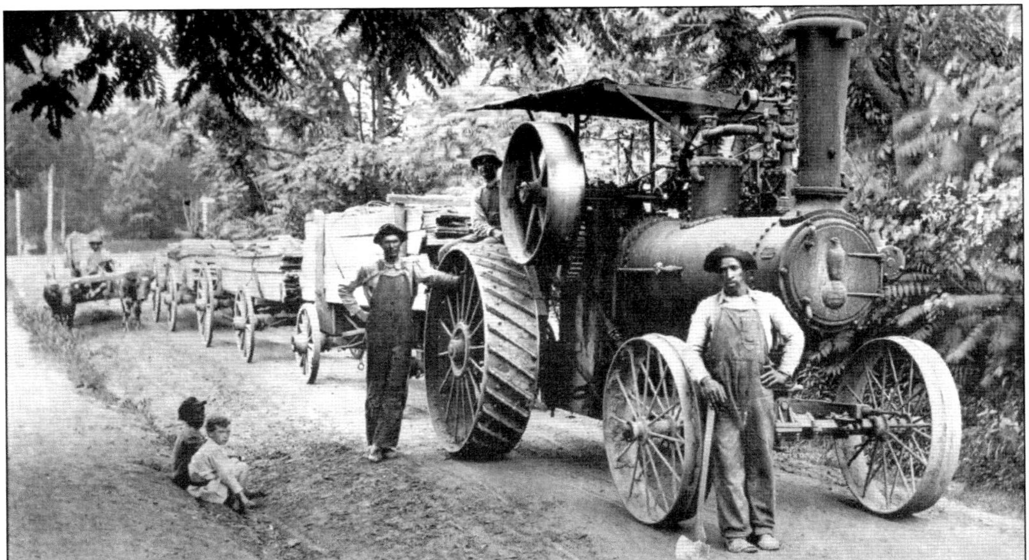

[Steam Engine on Johnson Street, 1920s.] Daily transportation of heavy construction materials began to change in the 1920s. This view of the early steam tractors hauling lumber to the Cam Davis Lumber yard documents the replacement of oxen or mule power. Since this inefficient machinery needed wood to fire the boiler and maintain the required steam levels, a second wagon pulled by oxen was used to carry the seasoned wood for the boiler. The men in this picture, from left to right, are M. Oxner, standing by the large wheel; H. Franklin, seated in the cab; J. Carter, in front; and J. Corley, driving the ox cart.

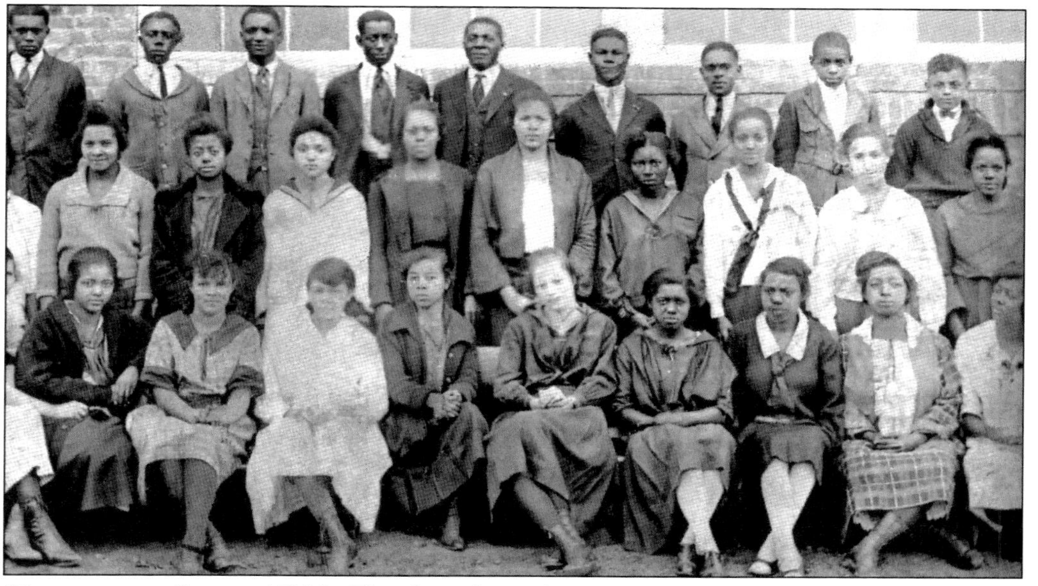

[GRADUATING CLASS, 1923.] The first class of Drayton High School is pictured above. Members, from left to right, are (first row) M.R. Bradley, A. Cunningham, H. Wheeler, H. Grimes, L. Wilson, B. Pratt, G. Maffett, two unidentified people, and R. Caldwell; (second row) H Martin, unidentified, ? Gary, unidentified, ? Jeter, unidentified, ? Haigler, ? Cora, and unidentified; (third row) two unidentified people, B. Gary, T. Teague, Rev. J.M. Johnson (principal), J. Rutherford, G. Douglas, J. Gary, and R. Williams.

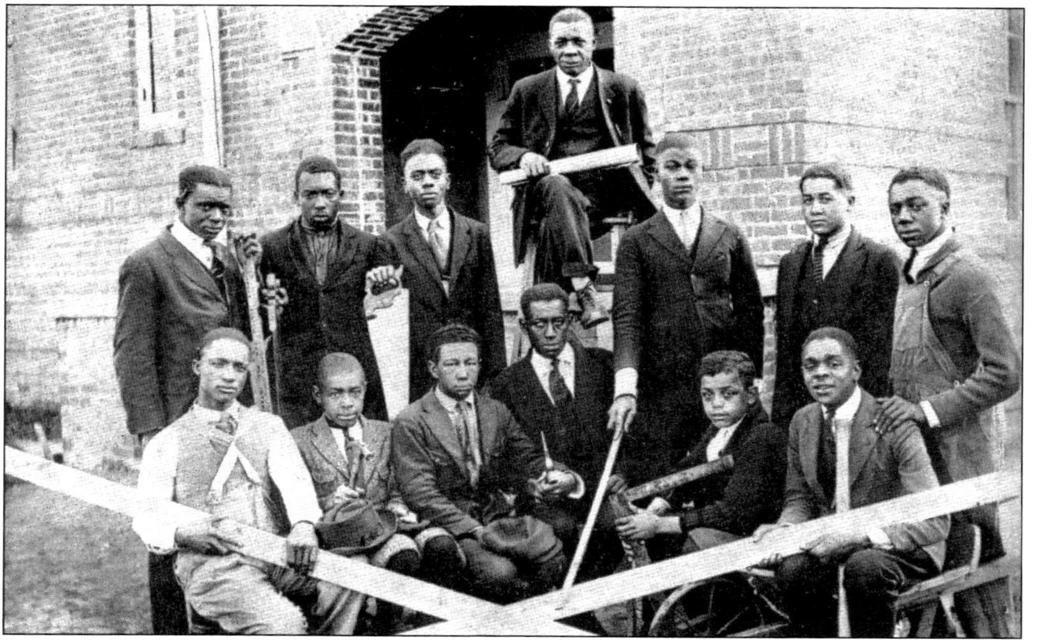

[CARPENTRY CLASS, DRAYTON HIGH SCHOOL CLASS, 1921.] Industrial arts classes were directly related to available jobs. The class goal was to train students to be efficient workers who knew the basics.

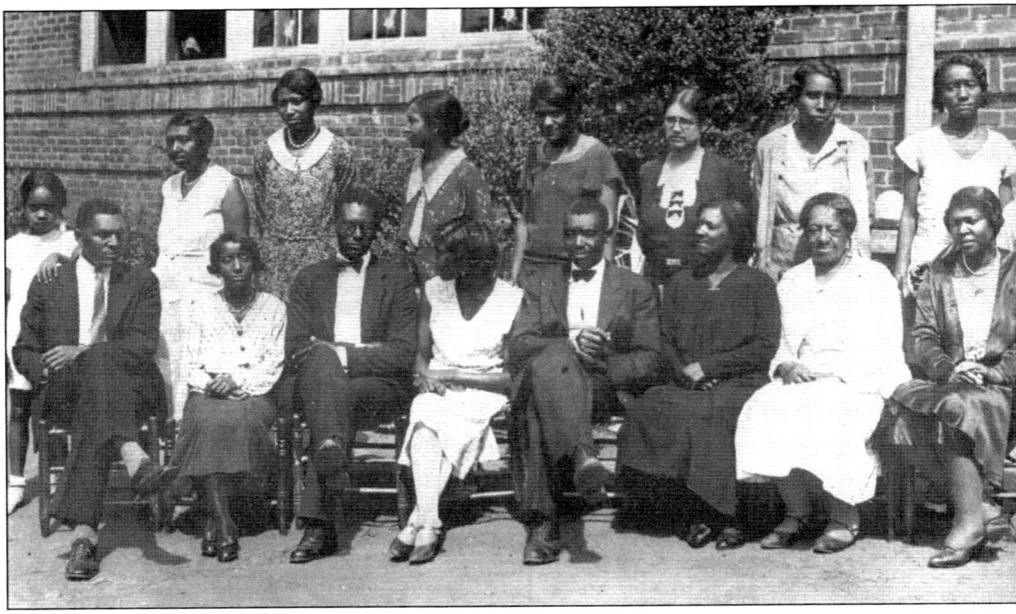

[Faculty, Drayton High School, 1932.] The faculty of Drayton High School are, from left to right, (front row) E. Gladden (child), R.F. Gladden (principal), E.H. Allen, P.B. Brooks, H.E. Nance, S. Allen, N. Gallman, A. Long, and N.P. Singleton; (back row) J.K. Gilliam, L.A.S. Graham, V. Golson, E.L. Bianchi, B.S. Henry, C. Gallman, and E.H. Guess.

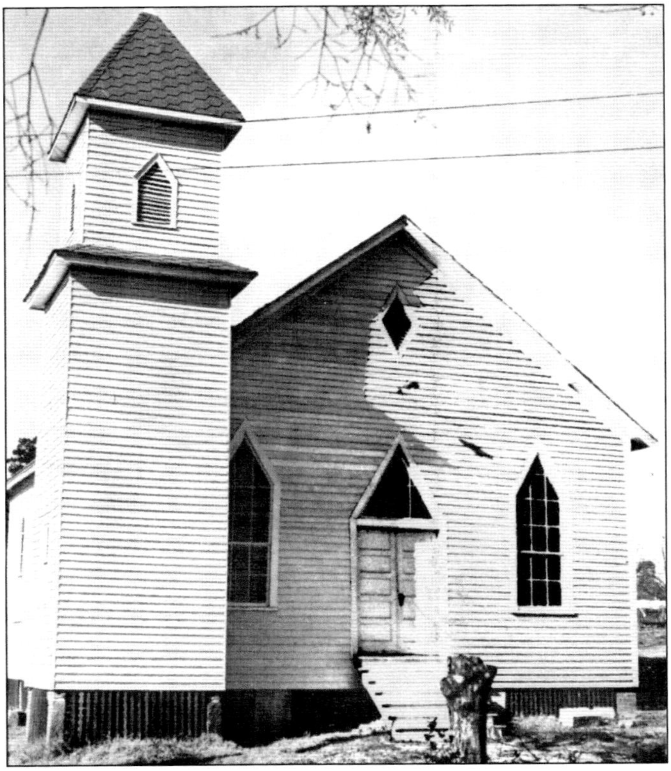

[St. Monica's Episcopal Church, 1930s.] The Protestant Episcopal Church established St. Luke's the Physician Mission in 1894. Property was bought on Lindsay Street in 1899 and a private school for blacks was begun in 1899 with 100 students and continued there for decades. In the 1930s the mission's name was changed to St. Monica's and a new church was built on South Street. St. Monica later merged with St. Luke's Episcopal Church.

GREETINGS FROM NEWBERRY [*c.* 1907]. This popular novelty flower montage includes several Newberry College buildings. The Lutheran Synod of South Carolina's college moved several times before the second ballot of 1877 when the Synod selected the town of Newberry as the final site for its Newberry College. It reopened in 1877. Tuition fees were $25 for the Junior Department, $35 for the Middle Department, $40 for the Senior Department, and $50 for the College level. Incidental expenses were $5, while room and board were $13 a month.

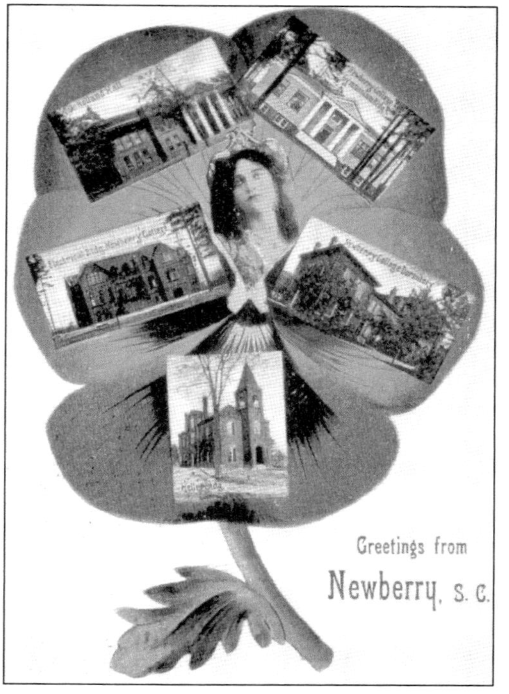

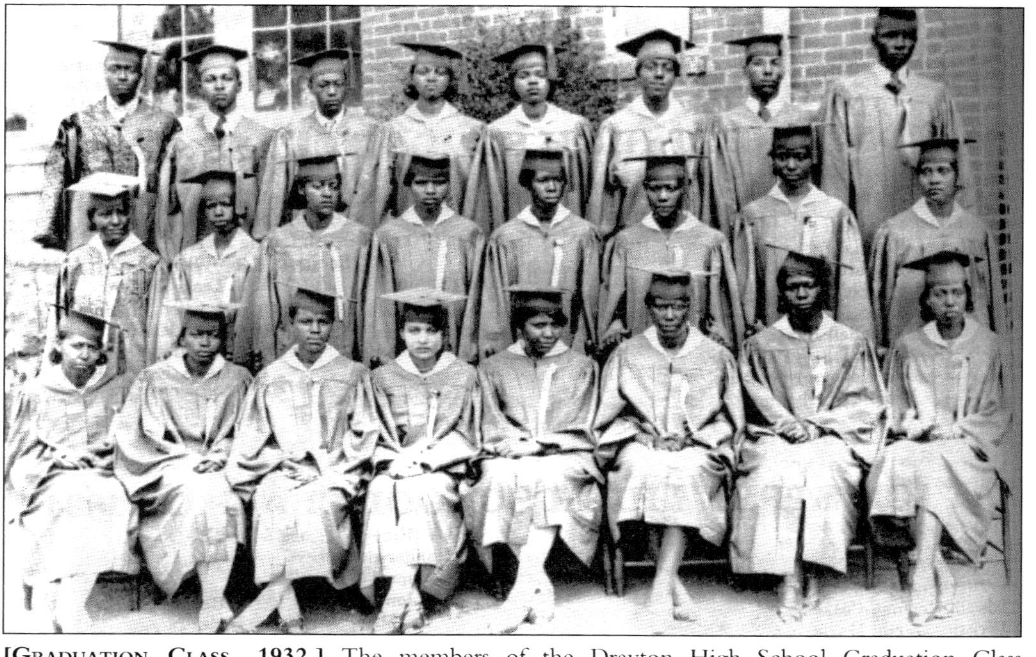

[GRADUATION CLASS, 1932.] The members of the Drayton High School Graduation Class of 1932 are, from left to right, (front row) M. Mobley, E. Simpkins, E. Wilson, O. Miller, V. Mobley, E. Ruff, E.M. Johnson, and D. Gilliam; (second row) B. Bradley, S. Ruff, C. Cromer, E. Clark, M. Gary, V. Miller, B. Jones, and B. McMorris; (third row) F. Peterson, J. Robinson, U. Gallman, J. Morgan, L.R. Harp, M. Lyles, W.C. Henderson, and W. Boyd.

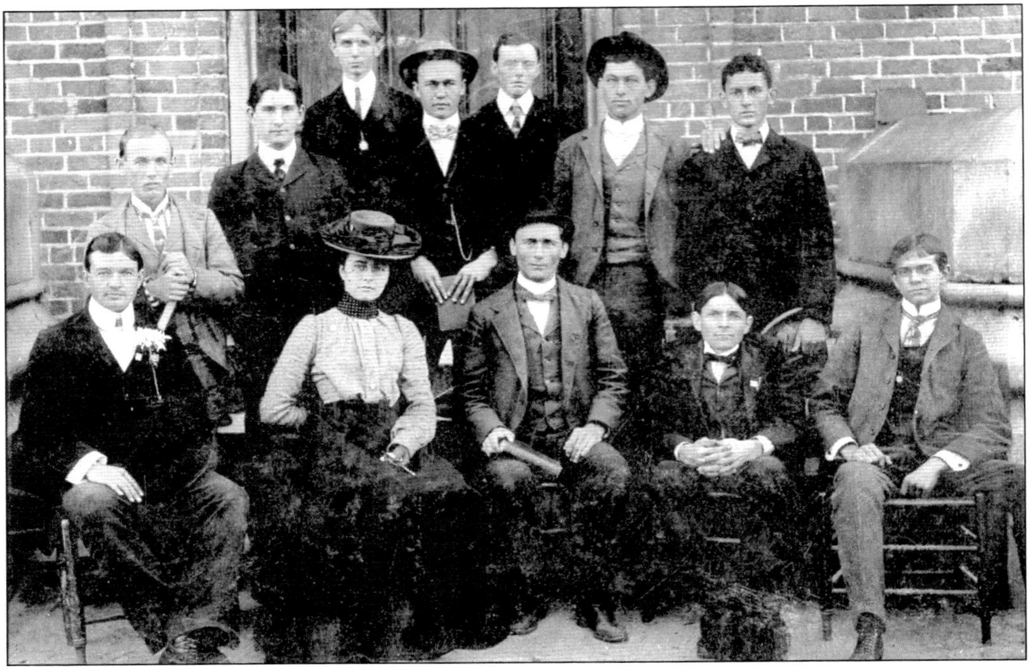

[The Newberry College Senior Class, 1902.] This class includes one of the first women, Miss Ruth Wells, to study four years and graduate with a bachelor of science from this college. In 1901 five women graduated from Newberry College after transferring into the program, or in the case of Margaret Johnstone, after being a day student for several years.

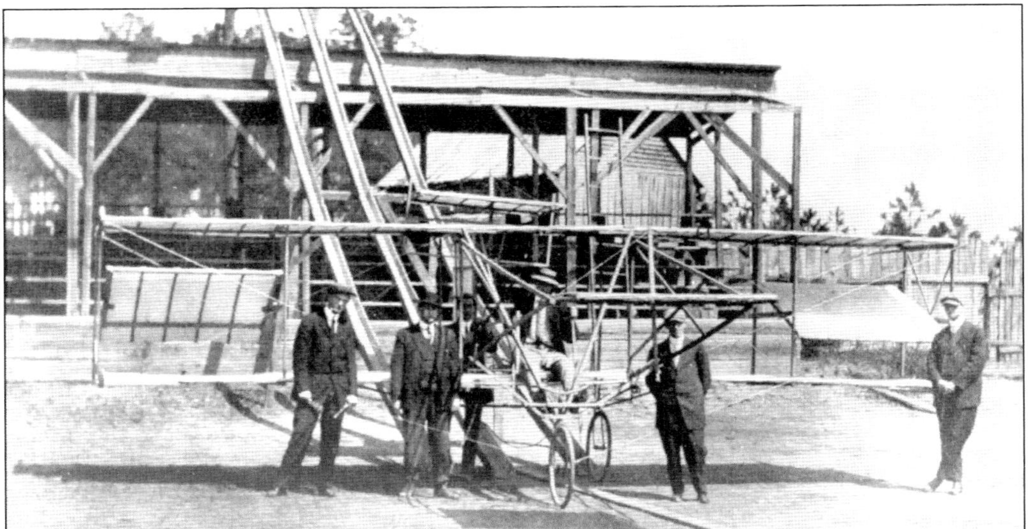

[Engineering Project, 1912.] Louis H. Wink created this airplane experiment shown above in 1912. Wink attended Newberry College from 1910 to 1912 and developed this project in the engineering department in his sophomore year. Wink fashioned this lightweight wood, fabric, and metal machine and support structure in the wood and metal shops and powered it with a small gasoline engine. However, he was not able to continue his studies at the college.

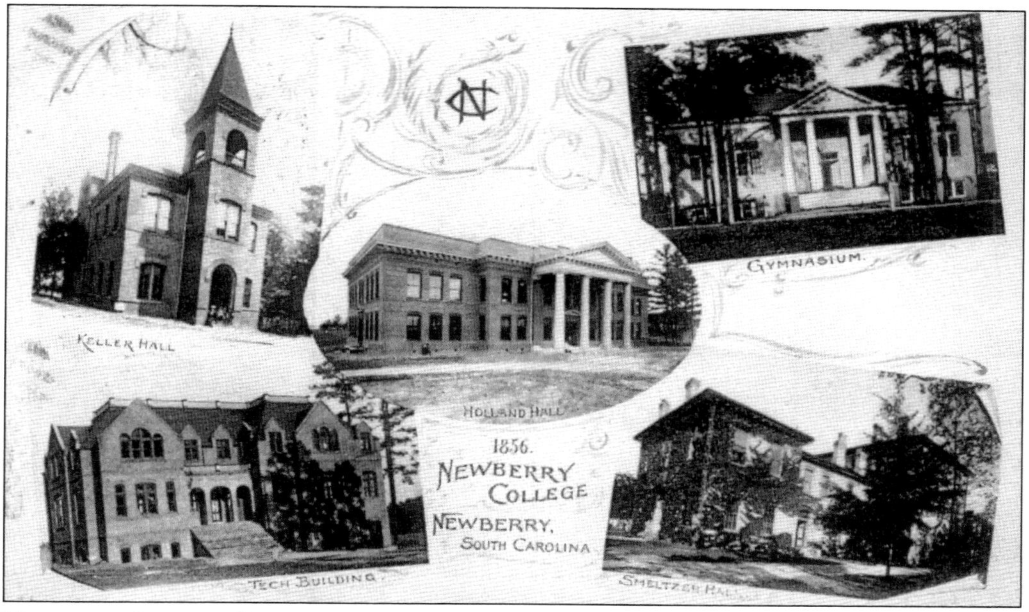

Newberry College, Newberry [*c.* 1907]. Newberry College first existed at a site near Pomaria; it then shifted to Lexington in 1834, to Newberry in 1856, to Walhalla in 1869, and finally, returned to Newberry in 1877. This postcard shows the first major buildings erected at the turn of the century. They are, upper left, Keller Hall (1895); center, Holland Hall (1904); upper right, Gymnasium (1905); lower right, Smeltzer Hall (1877); and lower left, Tech Building (Carnegie Hall) (1905).

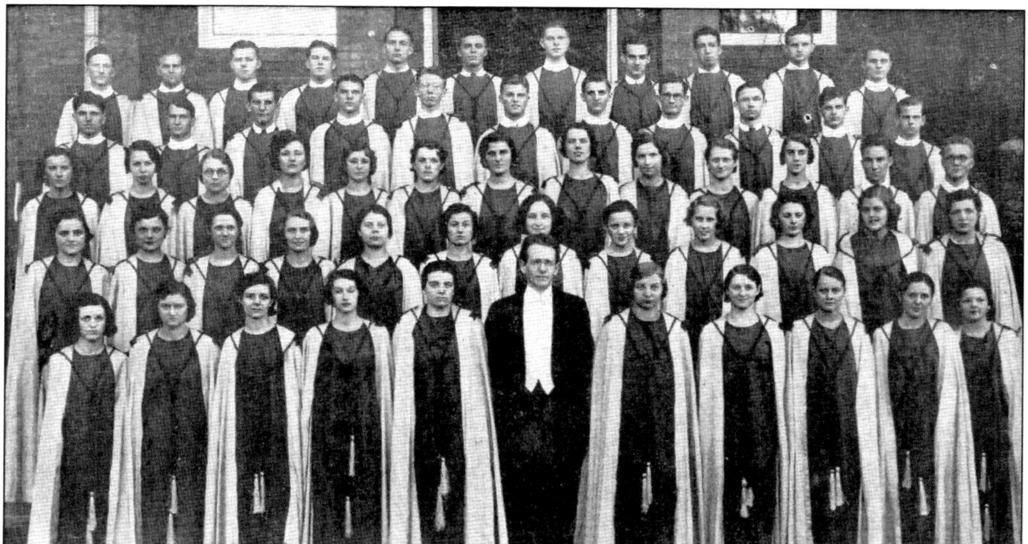

[Newberry College Singers, 1931.] This musical group was organized in 1931 by Professor Paul Ensrod and sang a repertoire of secular and sacred music. The 50 to 60 voices made annual tours to the Midwest—Illinois, Iowa, Minnesota, Nebraska and Wisconsin—the Northeast, and the Southeast. In order to expand their coverage the singers gave concerts that were broadcast by WIS nationwide.

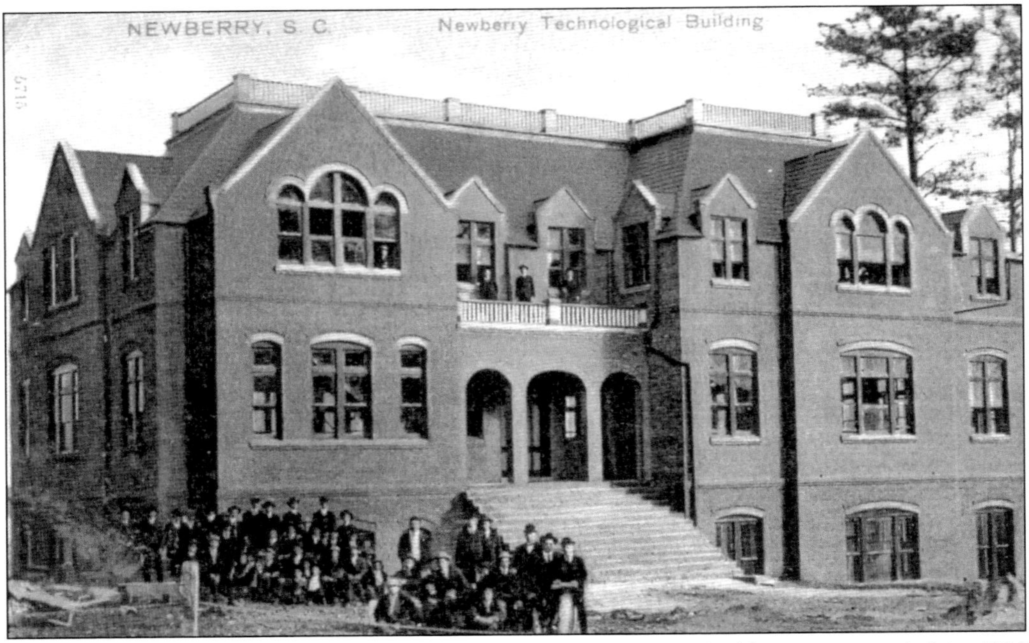

NEWBERRY TECHNOLOGICAL BUILDING, NEWBERRY [1907]. This building was occupied in 1906 and expanded Newberry's curricula into engineering studies. Courses in the areas of mechanical and electrical engineering were established and supported by shops for wood, welding, foundry, machine, electro-chemistry, telephone and telegraph, electrical power distribution, steam and turbine engines, pumping, drafting, and blue print work. These studies were discontinued in 1917.

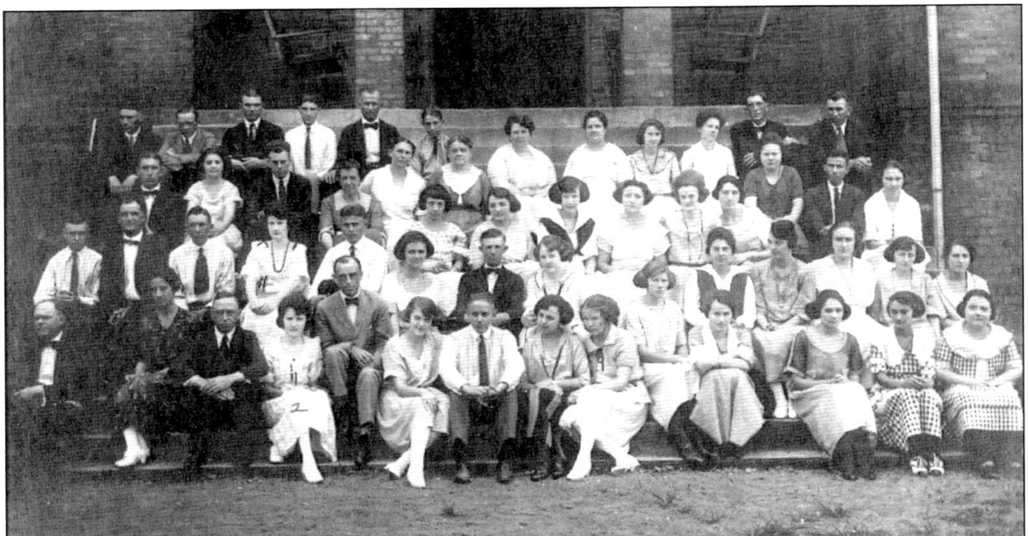

[SUMMER SCHOOL FOR TEACHERS, 1922.] Concerned by the level of education in the county and state, Newberry College created a Summer School for Teachers in 1922. Elementary to high school teachers and college students attended these classes. About 150 attended the 1922 two-month session from July 10 to August 18 for a $10 fee and $5 a week board. Both subject and teaching methods were offered in the basic academic courses, music, agriculture, and athletics.

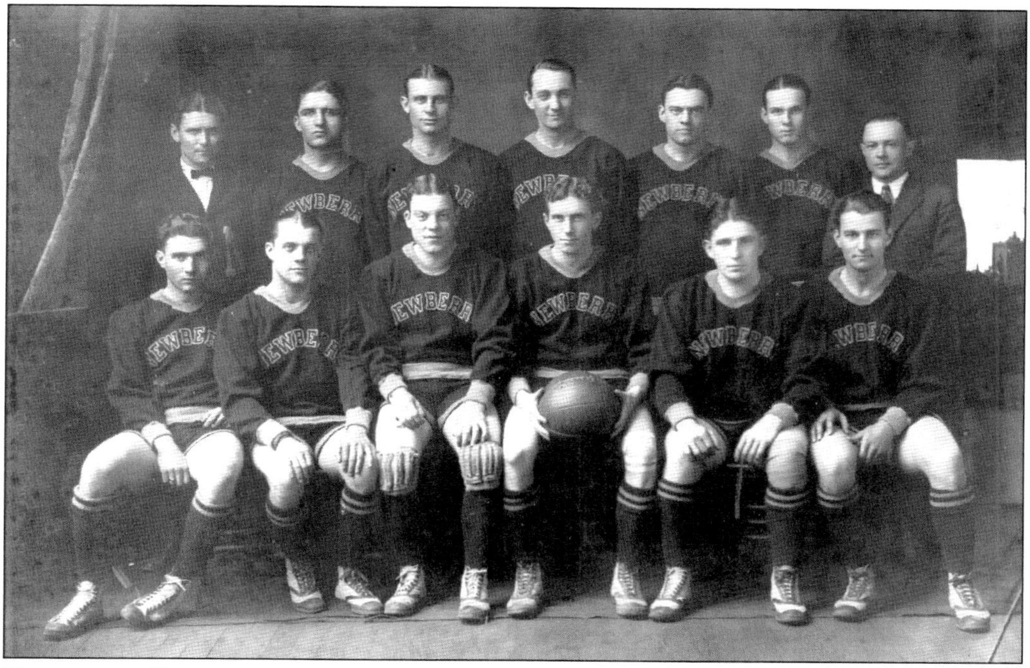

[BASKETBALL TEAM, NEWBERRY COLLEGE, 1922.] This team was one of a series of basketball championship teams. They played in the Southern Intercollegiate Athletic Association, which had a 24-team membership, and in the Intercollegiate Athletic Association of South Carolina, in which they were the state champions during the years of 1912, 1915 to 1917, and 1922 to 1924.

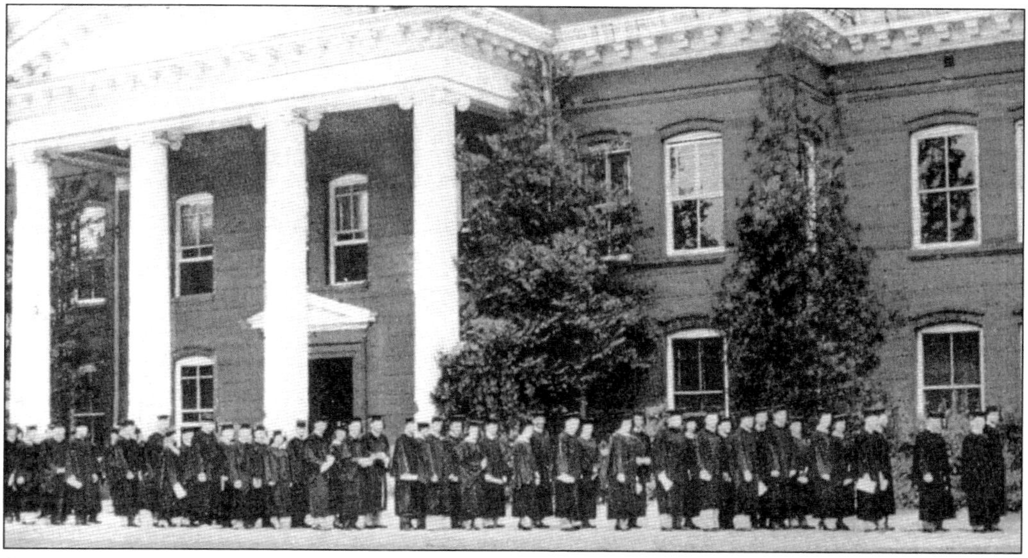

SENIORS IN ACADEMIC PROCESSION, NEWBERRY COLLEGE [1930s]. This postcard view portrays the annual promenade of the professors and graduating seniors after they have left the staging area, filed past Holland Hall, and continued onto the football field for the official program. Holland Hall designed by F.P. Milburn was named after Rev. G.W. Holland, Doctor of Divinity, the school's president from 1877 to 1895.

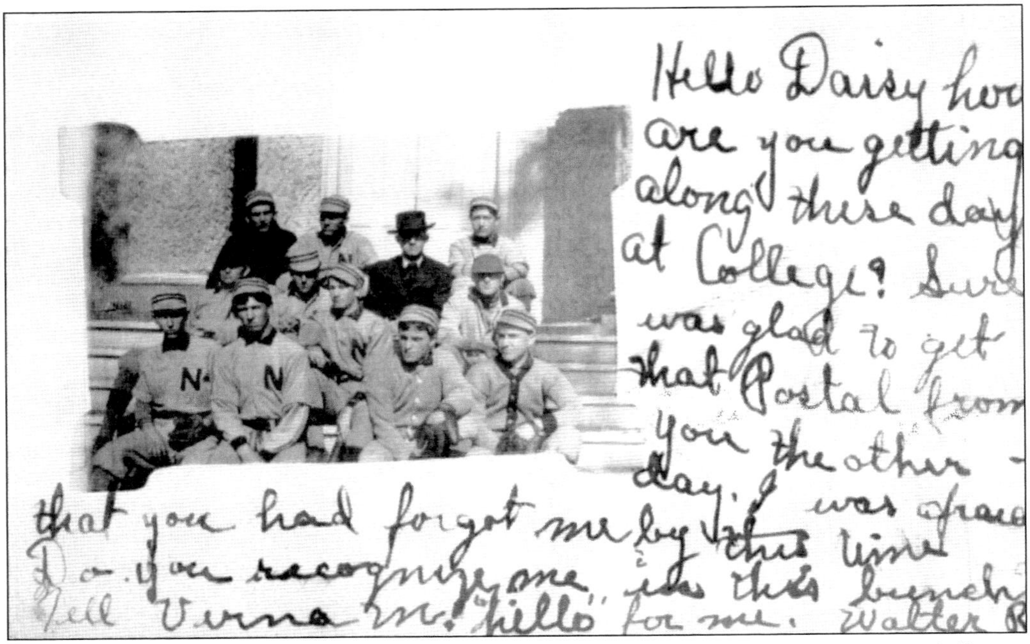

[Baseball Team, Newberry College, c. 1907.] This Kodak snapshot of the 1907 baseball team of Newberry College is typical of team postcards. The cards were processed and mailed to say a quick hello. Newberry's baseball team was established in 1895 and began playing in the Intercollegiate Athletic Association of South Carolina in 1899. They won first place in 1905, 1912, and 1917.

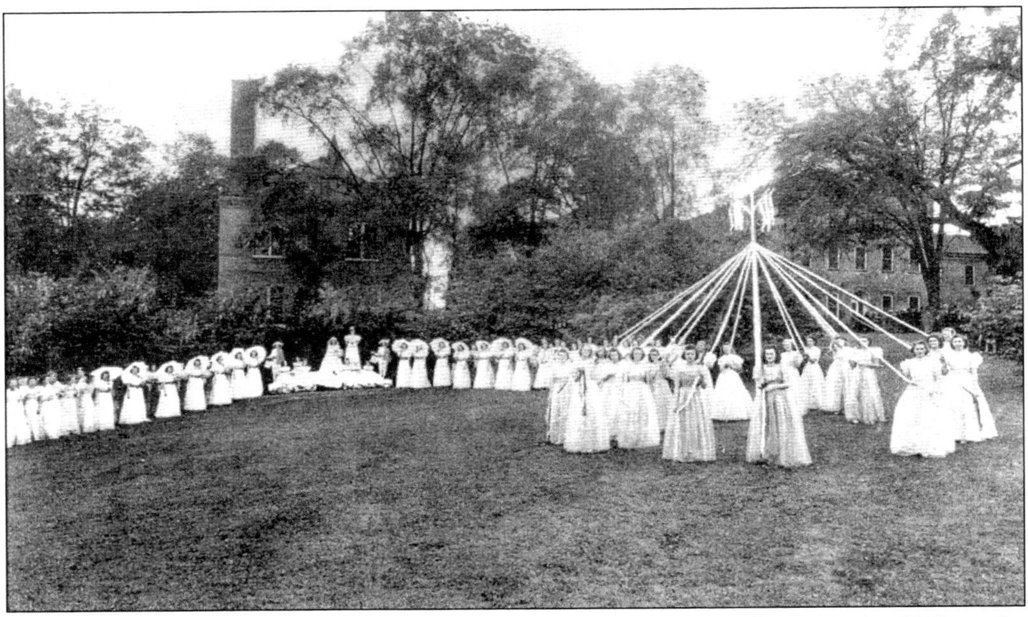

May Day, Newberry College [1930s]. The May Day events were begun in the 1930s as the major social activities held near the end of the spring semester. The May Queen and her court were usually elected and often wore formal dresses for garden activities, teas, and dances. Most colleges discontinued these events in the 1970s.

Two

Newberry Mills

The creation of the three city mills, one after the other, gave tenant farmers and others an opportunity for steady employment, merchants and builders an economic boost, and bankers new investment opportunities. The town grew in all directions. The 1889 population was 4,000. The three mills employed over 1,400 operatives with the 1902 wages per day being 72¢ for carding, 60¢ for spinning, and 50¢ for weaving with an average two-week paycheck totaling $2.25 to $2.50. Most of the paychecks went either to the company store for food, clothing, and medicine, or to the mill for rent. When the three mills were operating, their annual payroll was $345,000. One of this town's stabilizing factors was that every major financial and industrial enterprise had a board of directors with various combinations of the same entrepreneurial financiers sitting on each board. Every company knew what the others were planning to do.

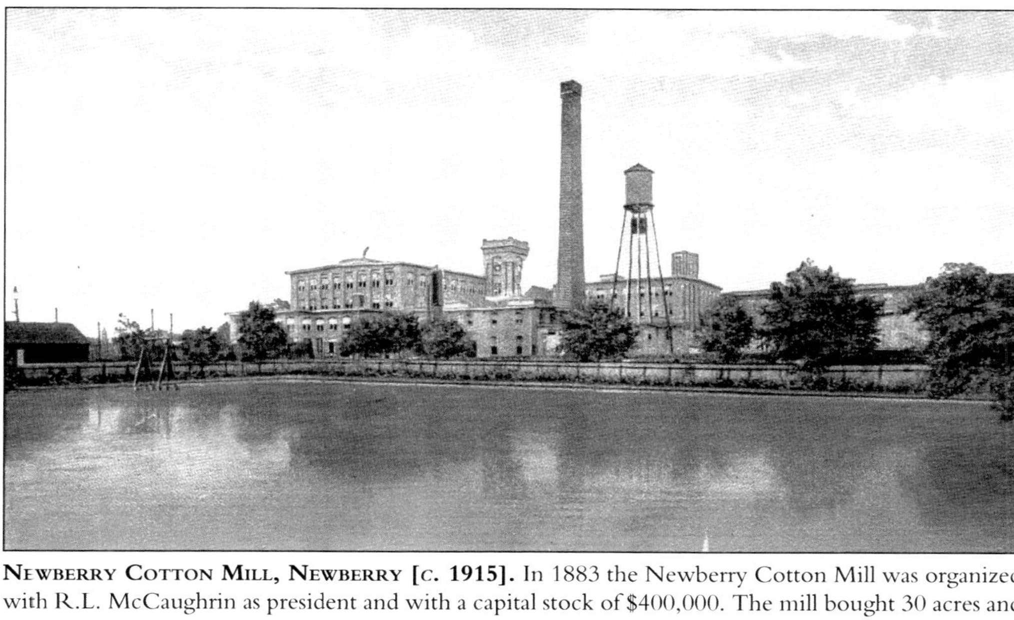

Newberry Cotton Mill, Newberry [c. 1915]. In 1883 the Newberry Cotton Mill was organized with R.L. McCaughrin as president and with a capital stock of $400,000. The mill bought 30 acres and selected architects Lockwood and Green and contractor W.T. Davis. This innovative mill was the first to run on steam. Z.F. Wright (1869–1949) was president from 1905 to 1946. The mill office was at 1017 Tarrant Street and, in 1903, had 28,000 spindles, 900 looms, 582 operatives, and a $145,000 pay roll. The company consumed 15 bales of cotton a day and made heavy sheeting and drills. The village had 81 one-story and 26 two-story homes that were built between 1884 and 1910 for a population of 1,000. There were 287 children in the village with 125 attending school. The mill closed in early 1980s and was torn down by the early 1990s.

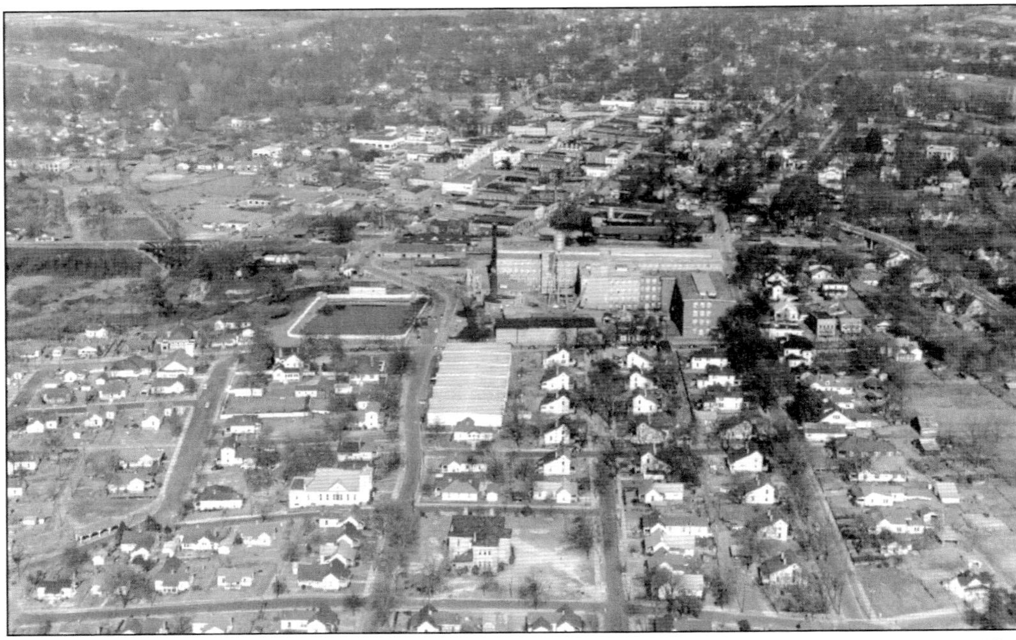

[Aerial View of Newberry Cotton Mill's Village, 1930s.] This aerial view of West End has the mill and pond in the center, the town's business section above it, and the vertical rows of identical mill houses below. In the lower center is the West End Graded School with the white frame West End Baptist Church diagonally to its left.

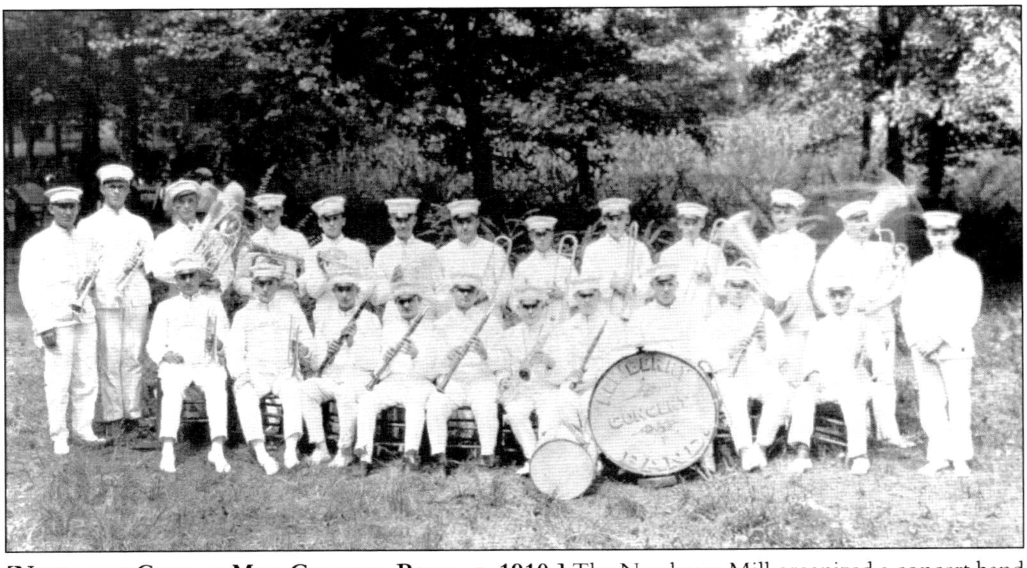

[Newberry Cotton Mill Concert Band, *c.* 1910.] The Newberry Mill organized a concert band in 1906 and furnished the band instruments and uniforms. The band was under the direction W.A. Wherry (1878–1923) for 15 years and played weekly concerts at the Band Stand in Willowbrook Park on selected nights and Sunday afternoons for 60 years. The concert band had the longest continual record in the history of the Southern Textile Band Association of South Carolina. They also played at special events, parades, and socials in the town, county, and state.

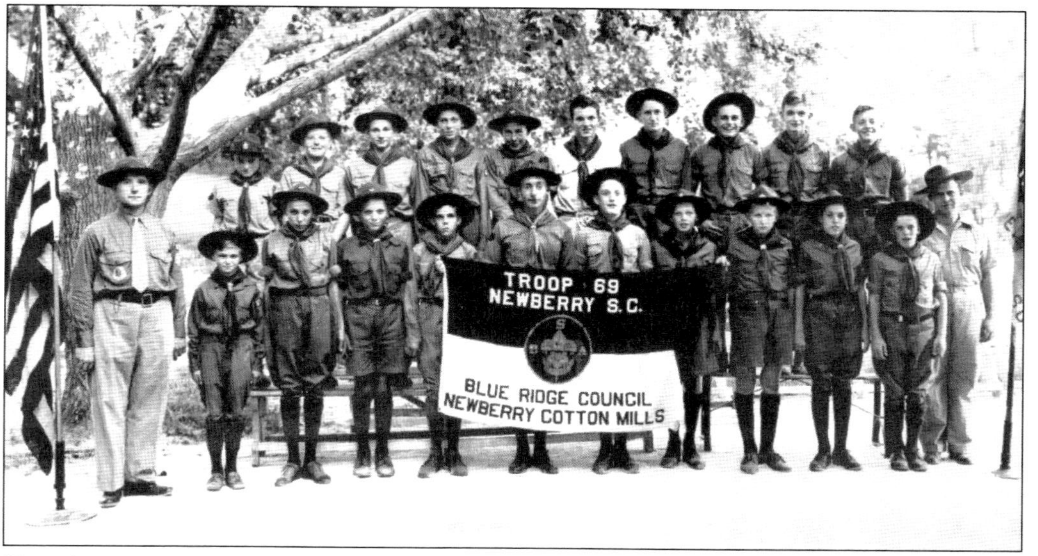

[Boy Scout Troop #69, 1940s.] Newberry Cotton Mill's Boy Scout Troop #69 of the Blue Ridge Council is shown above. Its troop leader was Dewey Kinard, standing on the far left. The scouts, from left to right, are (first row) K. Thompkins, C. Dodgen, B. Corley, E. Gruber, C. Leopard, N. Kinard, F. Ward, E. Vines, J. Danielson, R. Sanford, and L. Pitts; (second row) D. Bradley, J.G. Shealy, K. Cook, T. Ward, M. Powell, H. Corley, H. Jay, B. Hughes, F. Jones Jr., and C. Pruitt.

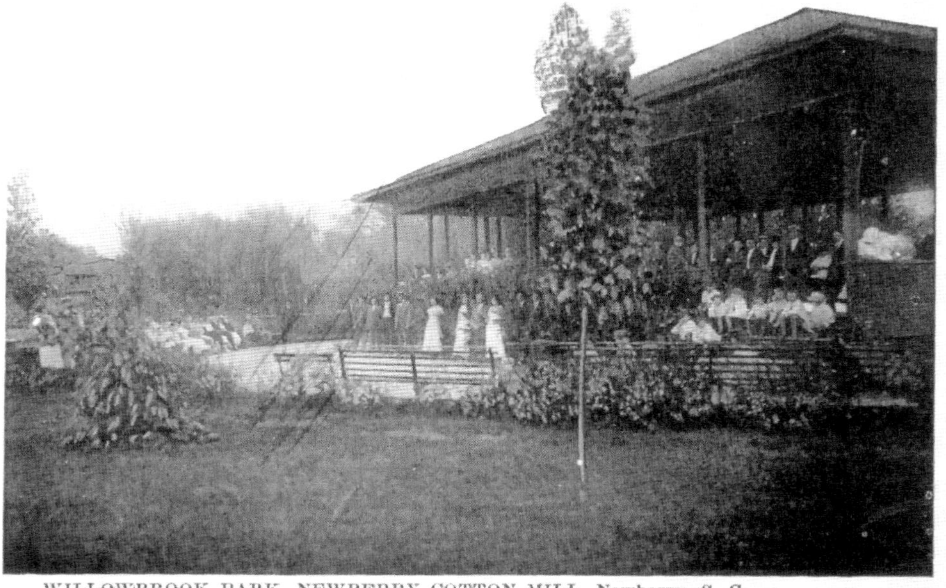

WILLOWBROOK PARK, NEWBERRY COTTON MILL, Newberry, S. C.

Willowbrook Park, Newberry Cotton Mill, Newberry [1910]. The Willowbrook Park was dedicated in 1909 and became a beautiful recreational site. The Newberry Cotton Mill band gave concerts twice a week. The postcard image above documents a full concert at the pavilion, which was also used as a skating rink. Swings and playground equipment were set up for children and others to use.

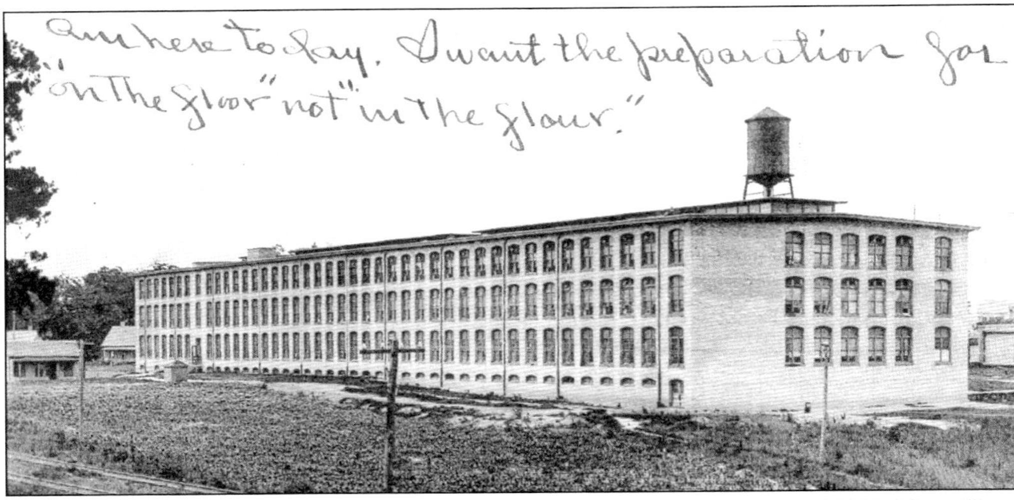

FRONT VIEW OF THE MOLLOHON MANUFACTURING COMPANY, NEWBERRY [*c.* 1907]. The mill was incorporated in 1901 with capital of $300,000. The initial officers were G.W. Summer, president; Z.F. Wright, vice president; and E.B. Wilber, general manager. J.F. Grandy built the mill on the south side of the railroad tracks at 401 Glenn Street. It began operation in July 1902 with 300 looms and 1,100 spindles to make cotton shirting, pajama checks, dimity, and quilting. Later it expanded to 60,000 spinning spindles and 1,540 looms, and it then employed 600 operatives with a payroll of $100,000. It was sold to Kendall Company in 1926, closed in 1986, and torn down in the late 1980s.

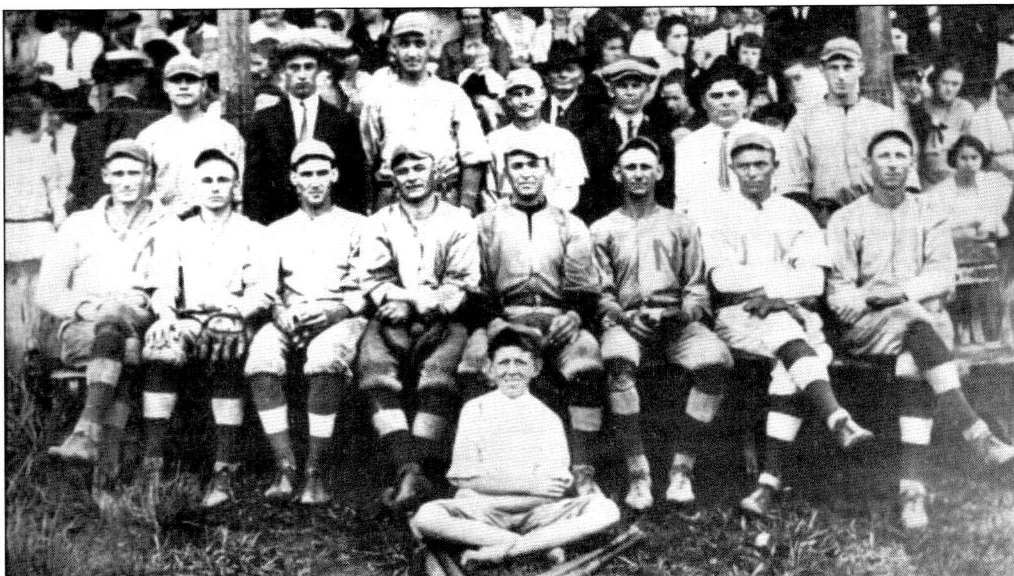

[NEWBERRY MILLS' BASEBALL TEAM, *c.* 1910.] The Mills' management considered sports and other recreational activities excellent diversions that could keep workers healthy and happy. The mills took great pride in competing with other mills in nearby counties that were a part of the Mid-State League. The players, from left to right, are (front row) J. Werts, J. Taylor, T. Livingston, T. Cromer, unidentified, E. Thompson, E. Hiller, and R. Jones; (back row) H. Hardeman, unidentified, H. Crooks, A. Bowers, H. Franklin, B. Corley, and unidentified.

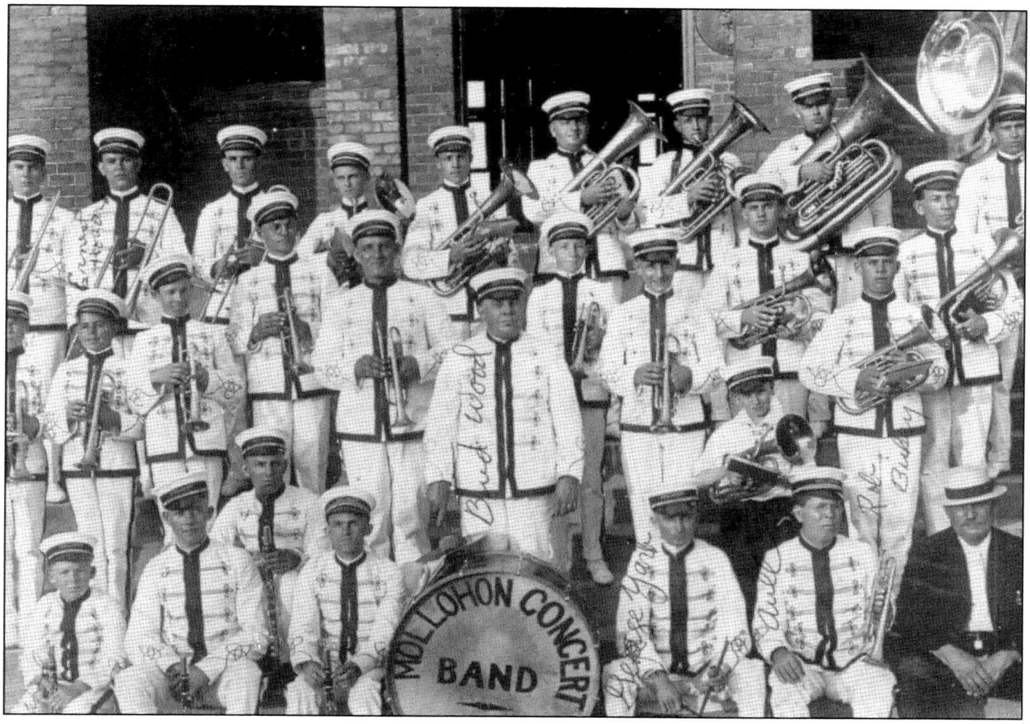

[MOLLOHON MILL CONCERT BAND, 1920s.] The Mollohon Concert Band was organized in the summer of 1919. P.R. Hallman was the band's teacher and W.A. Wherry became their director in 1920. The mill also opened a two-story brick elementary school with four classrooms, an auditorium, and a library that cost $30,000 in 1921. The 105 Mollohon children were taught by Miss R. Hipp and two other teachers.

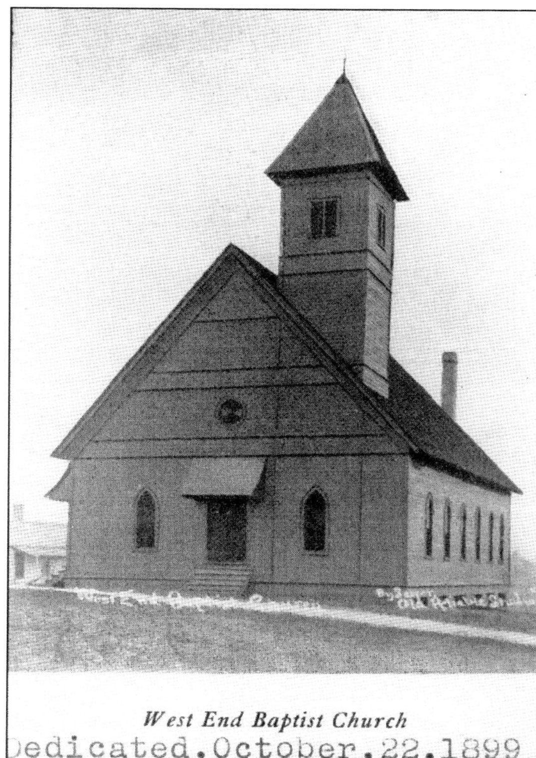

[WEST END BAPTIST CHURCH, 1890s.] The First Baptist Church assisted the operatives living in the Newberry Mills village to organize a union church in 1887, which later became the West End Baptist Church, at 615 Davis and Academy Streets. The photography at right was taken by J.Z. Salter's Old Reliable (Photo) Studio. In June 1916 lightning struck the building and burned it to the ground. It was later rebuilt.

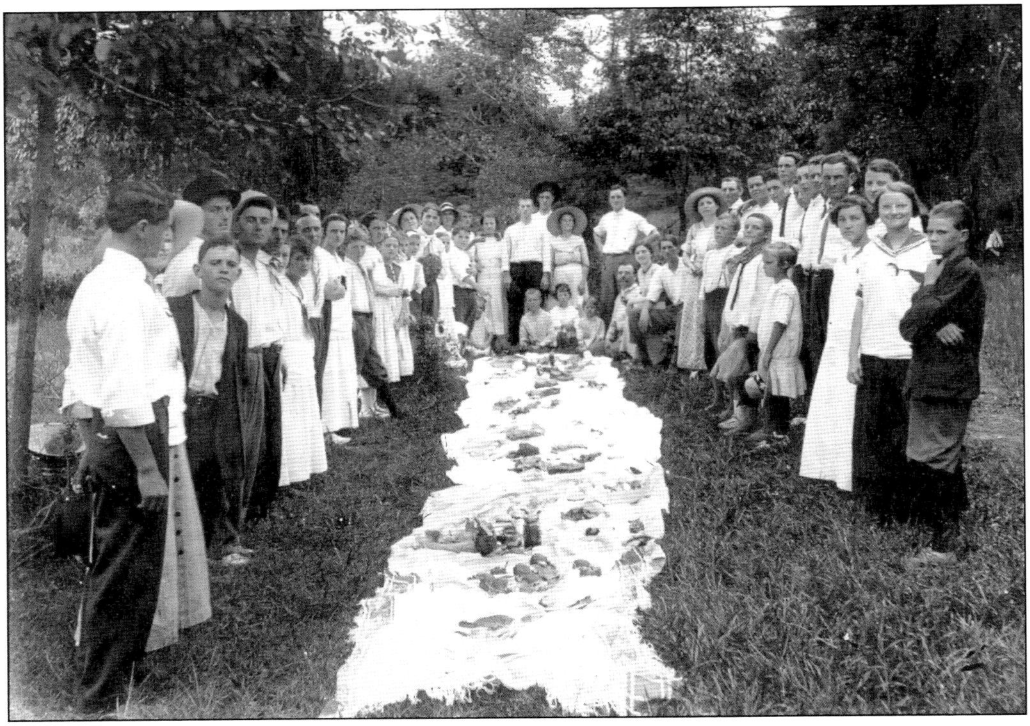

[Oakland Mills' Operatives at a Picnic, c. 1920.] On special occasions the mills' operatives would bring prepared foods and have a lunch in the grove near the mill. Parents and children were dressed in their best clothes and enjoyed visiting with fellow workers, while they shared stories, family news, and good food in a relaxed and friendly atmosphere.

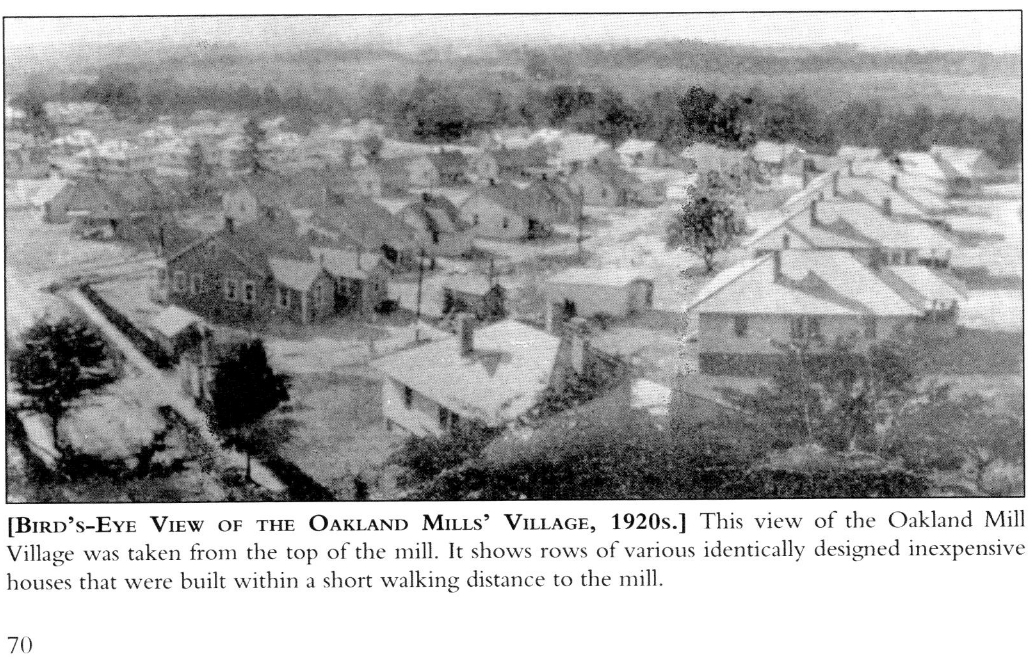

[Bird's-Eye View of the Oakland Mills' Village, 1920s.] This view of the Oakland Mill Village was taken from the top of the mill. It shows rows of various identically designed inexpensive houses that were built within a short walking distance to the mill.

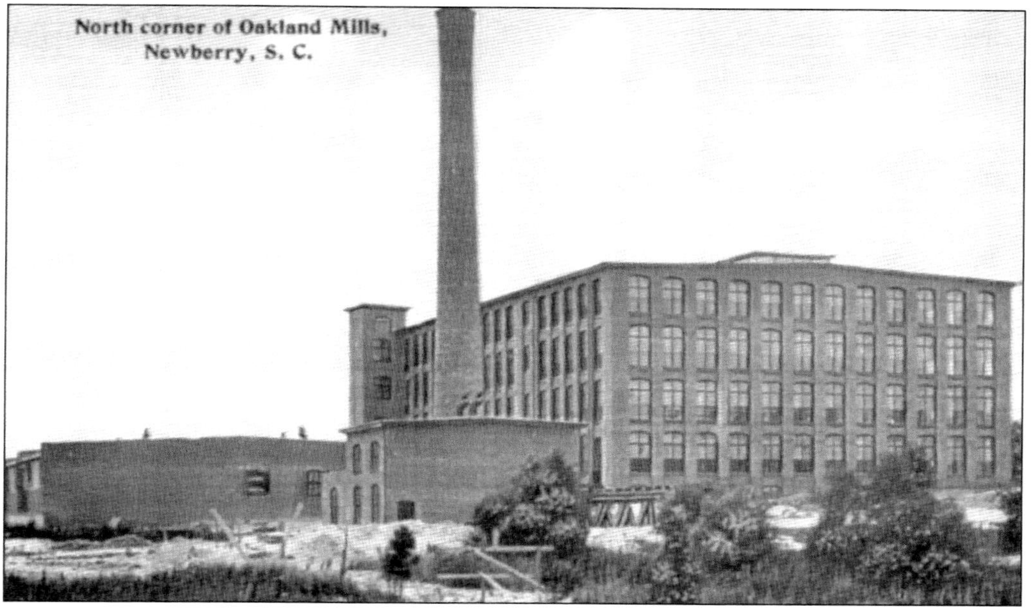

NORTH CORNER OF OAKLAND MILLS, NEWBERRY [C. 1908]. The Oakland Mills was established in 1904 with $335,000 capitol stock and built on Fair Place (2802 Fair Avenue) north of Newberry College. W.H. Hunt (1861–1927) was president, J.M. Kinard vice president, and F.N. Martin secretary. In 1912 the mill had 20,160 spindles and 542 looms, consumed 4,000 bales of cotton a year, and made wide sheeting and printed clothes. It had 226 operatives who worked three different shifts for a 55-hour work week and had a village of 75 houses with 50 additional ones added in 1925.

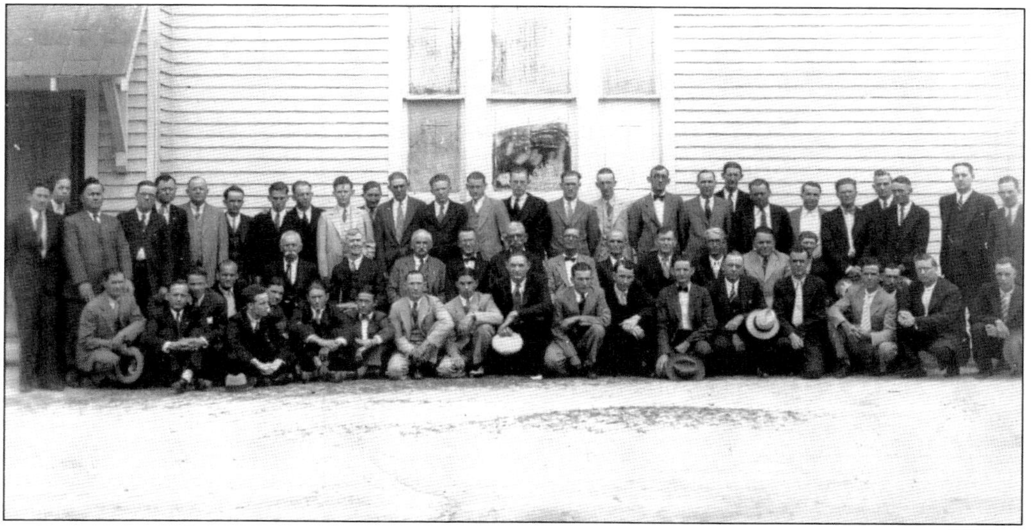

[MEN'S MEETING, C. 1920.] A joint meeting of Oakland's Methodist and Baptist men's groups was held at the union church, 1401 Second Street, which initially served both the Methodist and Baptist denominations until the Baptist built their own sanctuary. Many of the Baptist men returned to the union church building for continued fellowship and to continue work on past projects. The building later became Lewis Memorial Methodist Church.

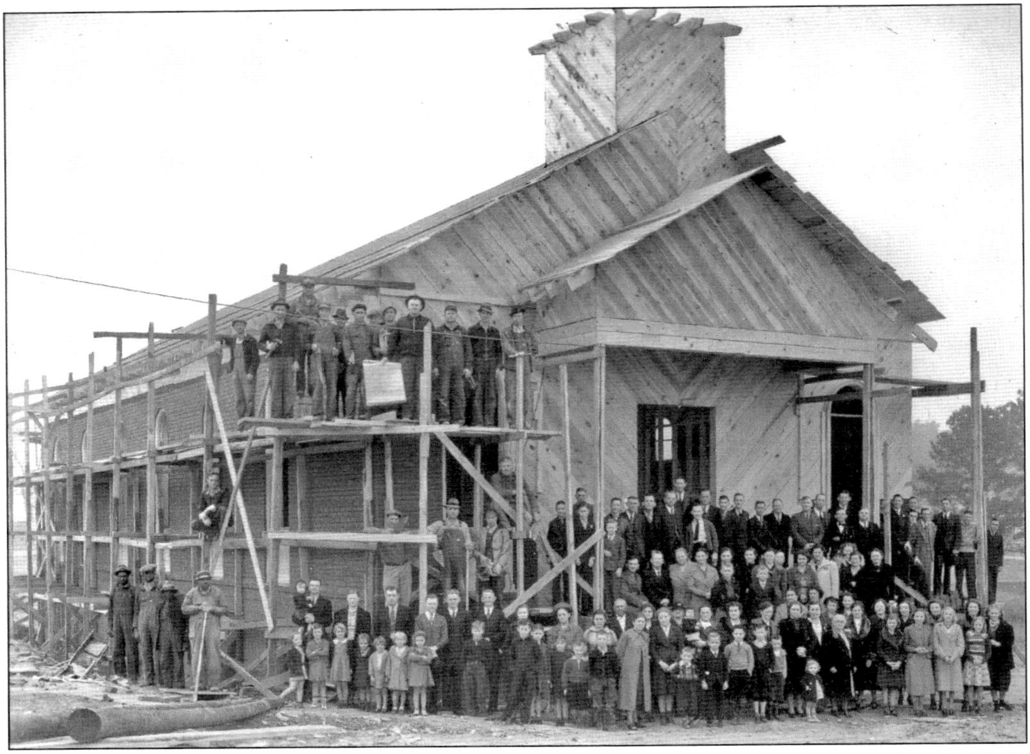

[Erecting the Baptist Church, c. 1913.] The Oakland Mills' workers established this church in 1913 and members and friends volunteered to work on weekends to build it. The view above shows families standing in front of the construction. In 1937 the church was renamed Hunt Memorial Baptist Church for W.H. Hunt, president of Oakland Mills.

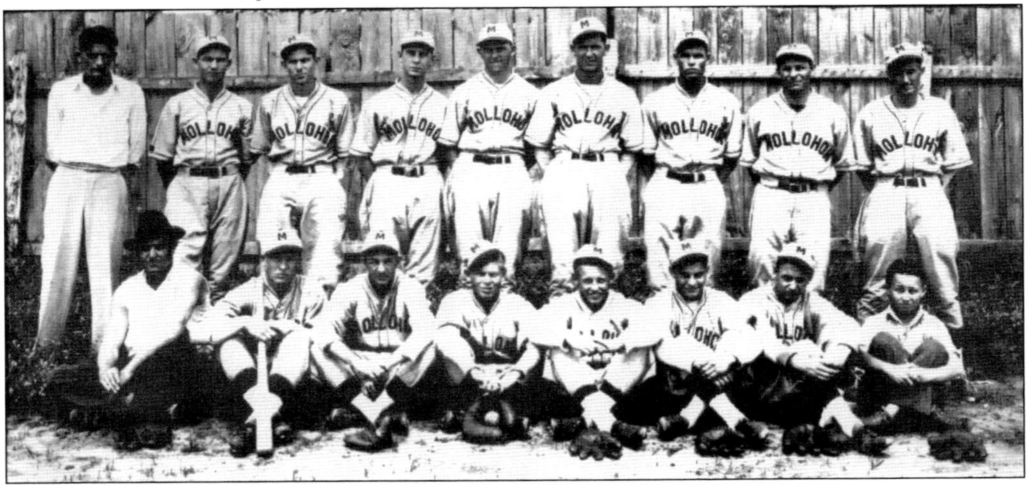

[Baseball Team, Mollohon Mills, c. 1910.] The Mollohon Mills' teams played in the Mid-South League. The players pictured here are, from left to right, (first row) C. Duncan (manager), J. McCartha, J. Martin, W. Cromer, P. Smith, E. Edwards, G. Harmon, and unidentified; (second row) C. Gowan (scorekeeper), H. Mills, T.D. Shealy, P. Rinehart, R. Shealy, B. Rollins, W. Huffstelar, H. Moates, and C. Miller.

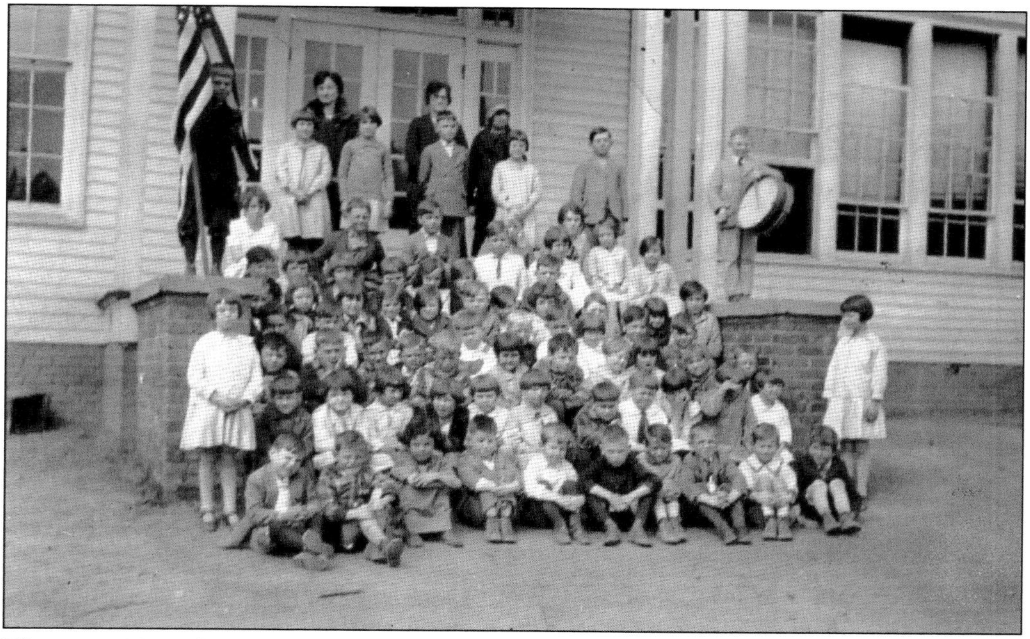

[Oakland Mills Schoolchildren, c. 1921.] The Oakland School students are photographed in front of their new (1921) four-room frame schoolhouse on First Street near Vance Street. During that year G.G. Sale and one teacher taught 78 students.

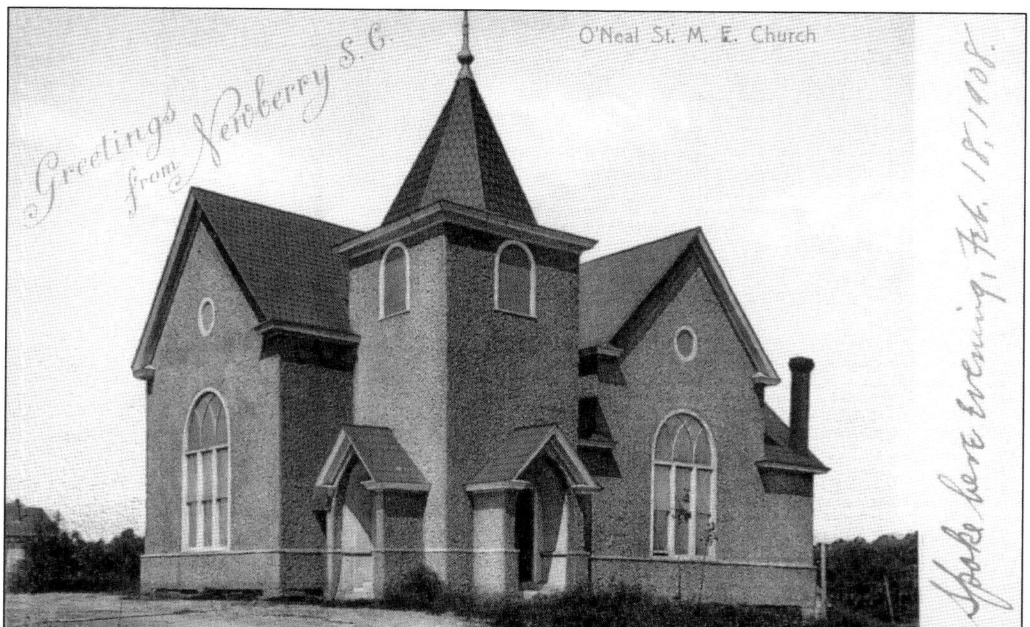

O'Neal Street M.E. Church, Newberry [c. 1907]. An 1884 tent meeting for the operatives of the Newberry Cotton Mills, West End, was the catalyst in the development of this village church, initially called the Second Methodist Church. The church's name was changed in 1895 to O'Neal Street Methodist Episcopal Church because its site was at 501 O'Neal Street.

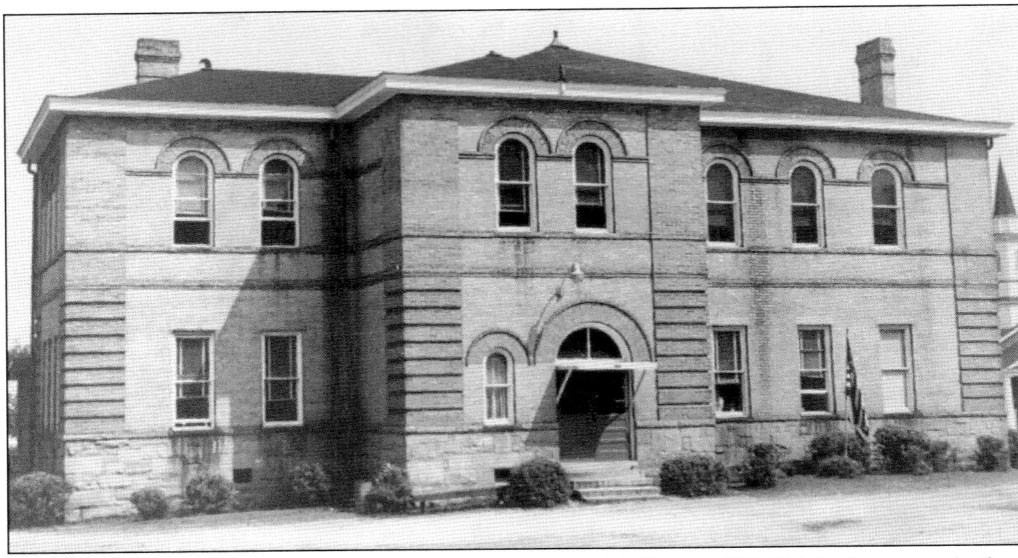

West End School, Newberry [*c.* 1910]. The West End School at 605 Wright Street was built to teach the children of the Newberry Mills. The mill built a brick, two-story, six-classroom structure with an auditorium *c.* 1885 that cost $10,000. Two rooms were added at a later date. In 1902 the village had 287 children with 125 attending the West End School. Mrs. B. Martin, principal, and three teachers taught 200 students in 1921.

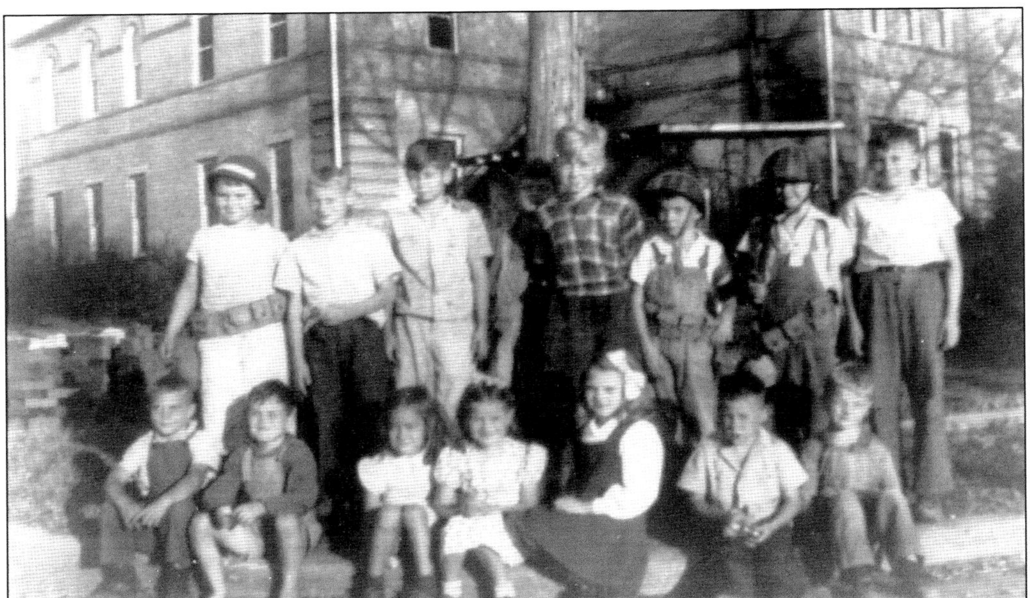

[West End Schoolchildren, *c.* 1920.] As soon as the mill was constructed and in production, a school was built in the village to educate future operatives. Mill officials wanted to break the cycle of illiteracy that handicapped the rural and village laborers. The students would take their first through fourth grade classes in the West End school. When students desired to take fifth to eleventh grade courses they would transfer to the town's public schools. In 1920 the school had four teachers and 200 students.

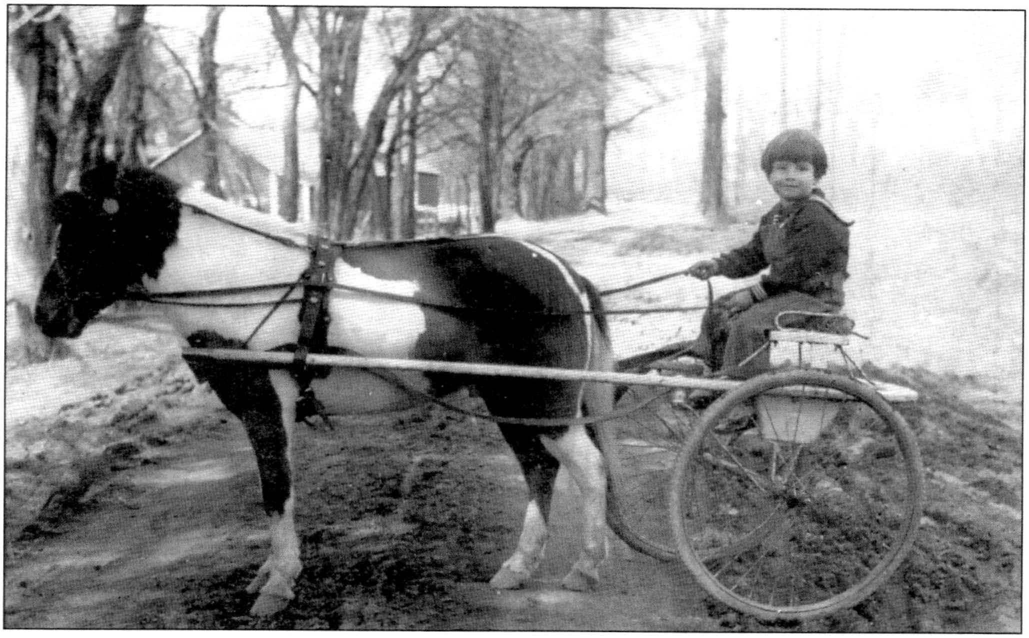

[**Boy on Pony Cart, Oakland Mills, c. 1910.**] The local photographers of many communities created a way of making small change during slack work periods by going to the mill villages and taking a pony cart to photograph the operatives and their children sitting in the cart. These postcard pictures cost the family 5¢ each, and often, photographers could take 20 to 30 pictures per trip.

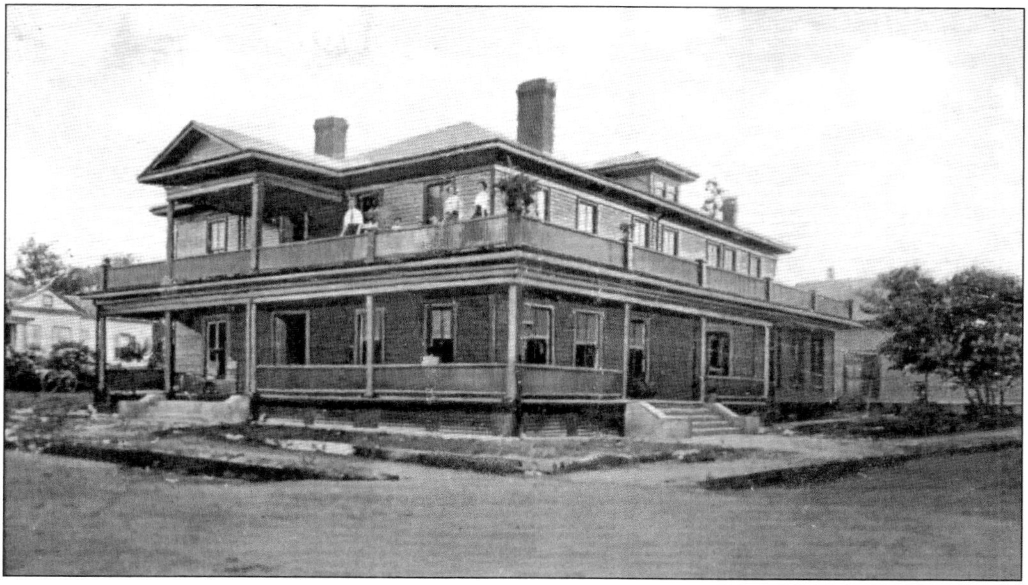

West End Hotel, Newberry [**c. 1908**]. This boarding house at the corner of O'Neal and Drayton Streets—originally the J.B. Carwile's residence—served single operatives of the Newberry Cotton Mills and those needing temporary housing. It was just a short walking distances to the mill, village churches, and YMCA centers. This structure still stands in an altered condition without the porches that encircle the building.

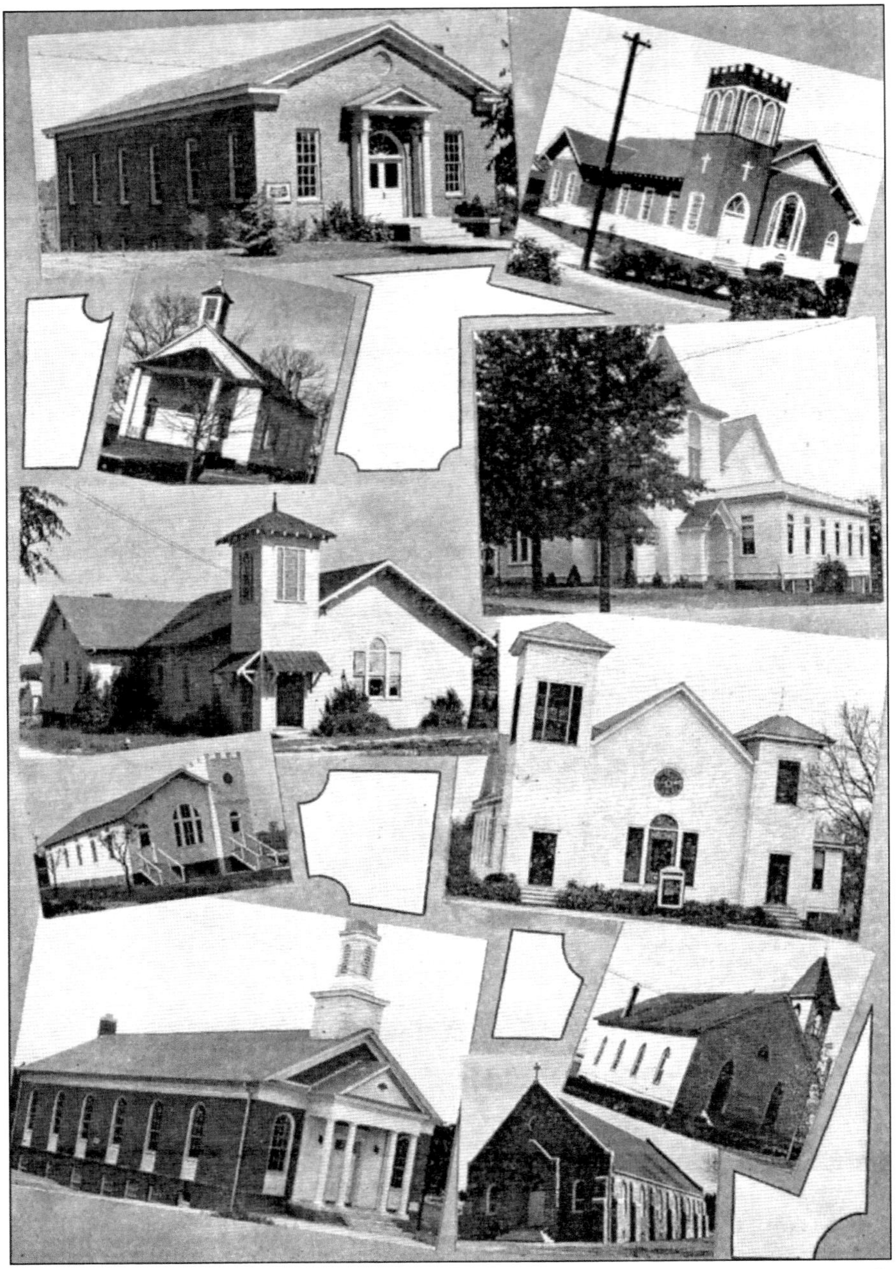

[Mill Churches, 1930s.] Many mills built union church (nondenominational) buildings so that small core groups could evolve into an independent church. The locally established congregations often assisted in the organization of the mills' churches. The Newberry Mill villages' churches, beginning at the top, from left to right, were Epting Memorial Methodist (Mollohon), Mayer Memorial Lutheran (West End), Glenn Street Baptist (Mollohon), O'Neal Street Methodist (West End), Lewis Memorial Methodist (Oakland), West End Baptist, First Pentecostal Holiness (High Point), Summer Memorial Lutheran (Mollohon), Hunt Memorial Baptist (Oakland), and Bethany Lutheran (Oakland).

Three

THE DUTCH FORK AREA

The "Dutch Fork" designation is an anglicized derivative of "Deutsch," the Germans' name for their ethnic group, and "fork" for the fork of the Saluda and Broad Rivers. This southeastern territory in Newberry, adjacent Lexington and Richland Counties, was mostly settled by German immigrants who established Lutheran Churches. Newberry County annexed two areas: Little Mountain (1902) and Peak (1920) from Lexington County. Education was important in the rural area; schools were established in Prosperity in 1873, Pomaria in 1869, and Little Mountain in 1892. Other schools were created by the congregations of various churches. One of the prominent sites in this area was Little Mountain, at 800 feet above sea level, the highest point in the Lower Piedmont region. The picture below of Little Mountain friends in a wagon illustrates this era's means of transportation in small rural communities. It also ties into the Little Mountain Reunions that began in 1882 as mass meetings of Lutherans who traveled by wagon or train to this site. The reunion of 1908 featured a big barbecue dinner that consisted of 40 hogs, 5 sheep, 500 chickens, and 2,000 loaves of bread.

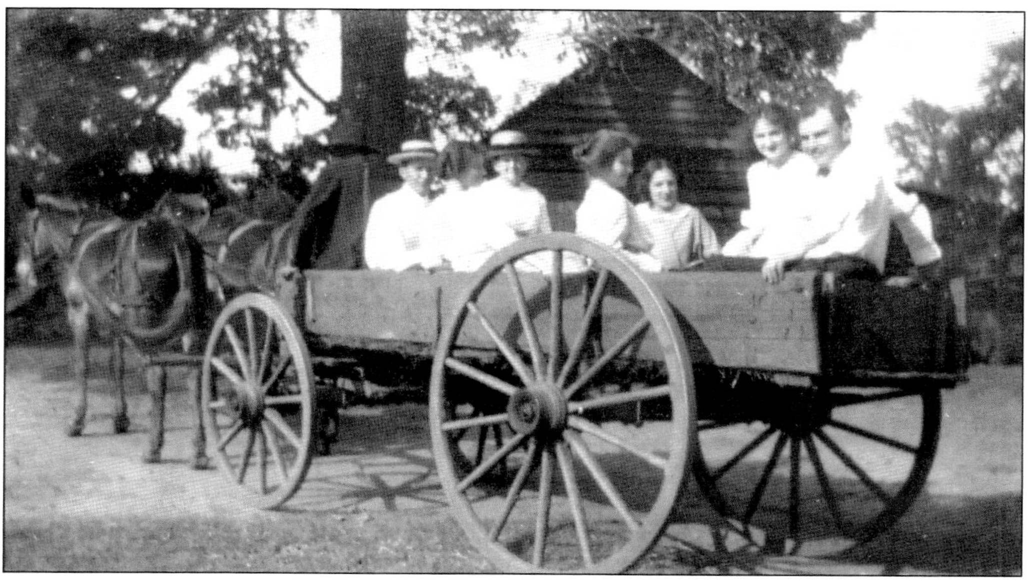

[RURAL TRANSPORTATION, *c.* 1910.] Initially horses and wagons were the transportation that served rural citizens of villages such as Little Mountain, Pomaria, and Peak, as well as numerous townships. With the paving of county roads in the 1930s and the shift from buggies to automobiles, rural customers began to travel to larger business centers such as Newberry, Prosperity, and Whitmire for greater selection, better prices, and the latest styles.

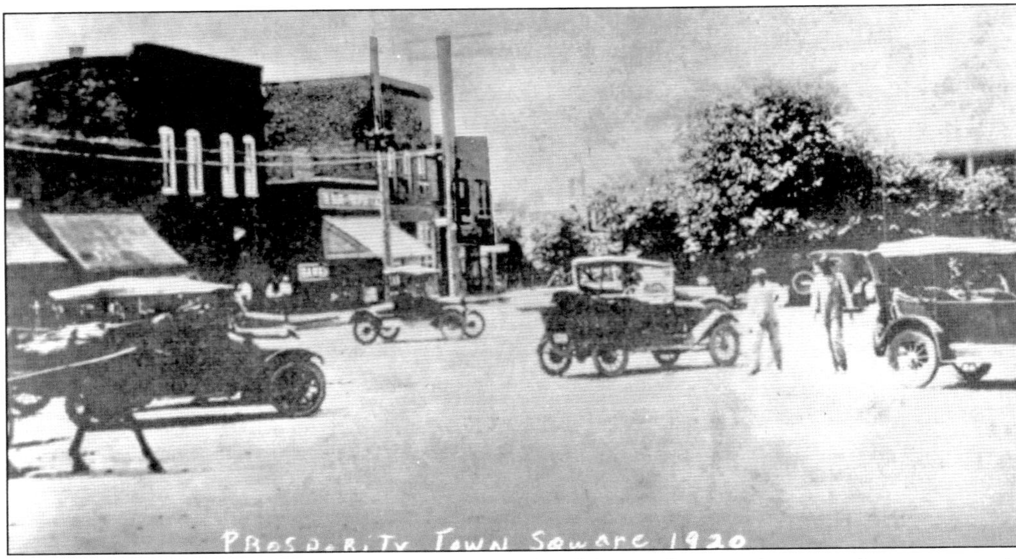

[Town Square, Prosperity, 1920.] With two railroad depots the town became a busy commercial center and the second largest town in the county at the turn of the century. Professional men including doctors, dentists, bankers, and lawyers resided in Prosperity. It also had retail stores and two banks, the Peoples National Bank and the Bank of Prosperity, which closed during the Depression. When Whitmire's mill was established, Prosperity's size in the county shifted to third place.

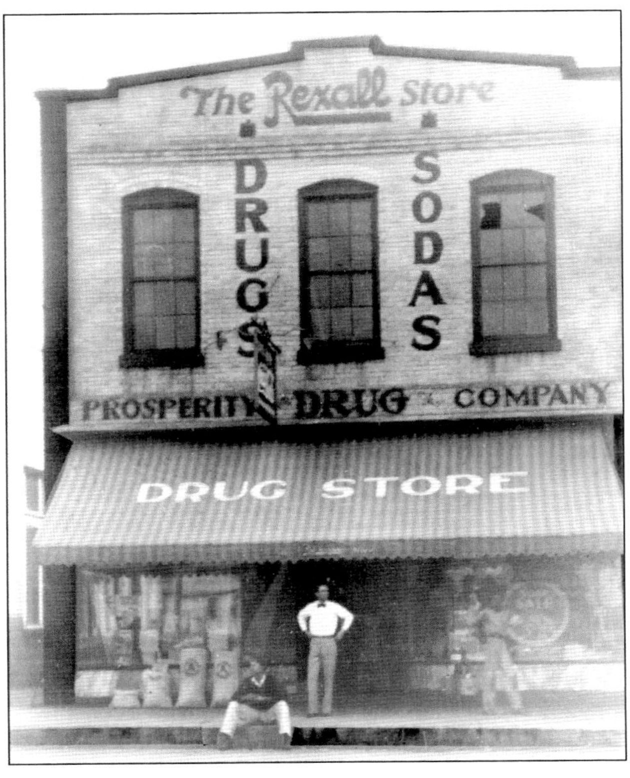

[Rexal Drug Store, Prosperity, c. 1910.] The Prosperity Drug Company was owned and operated by several local physicians. They were Dr. G.Y. Hunter (*c.* 1869–1936); Dr. J.I. Bedenbaugh (1874–1960), who at one time was president, secretary, and treasurer; and Dr. J.S. Wheeler (1872–1927). The pharmacist was initially Dr. C.K. Wheeler (1891–1968) and then his son Dr. C.K. Wheeler Jr., who ran it until 1978.

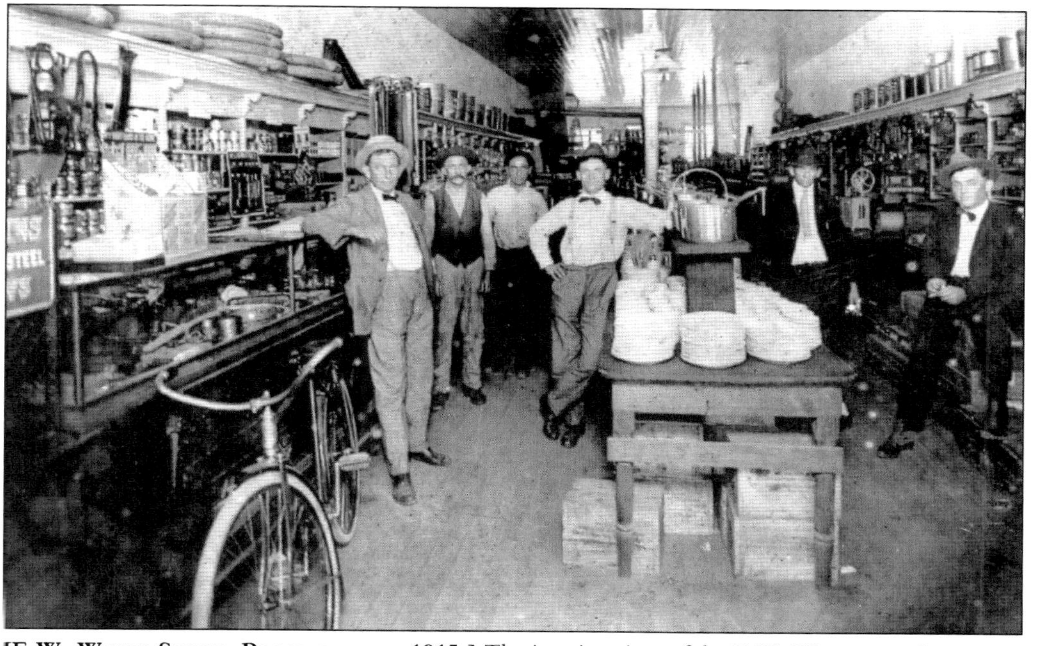

[E.W. WERTS STORE, PROSPERITY, *c.* 1915.] The interior view of the E.W. Werts store documents the diverse stock of a small town general store. Their ads in Newberry's *The Observer* listing house furnishings, bicycles, and hardware were published to encourage potential rural customers to come to Prosperity and shop in the Werts store when they needed something special.

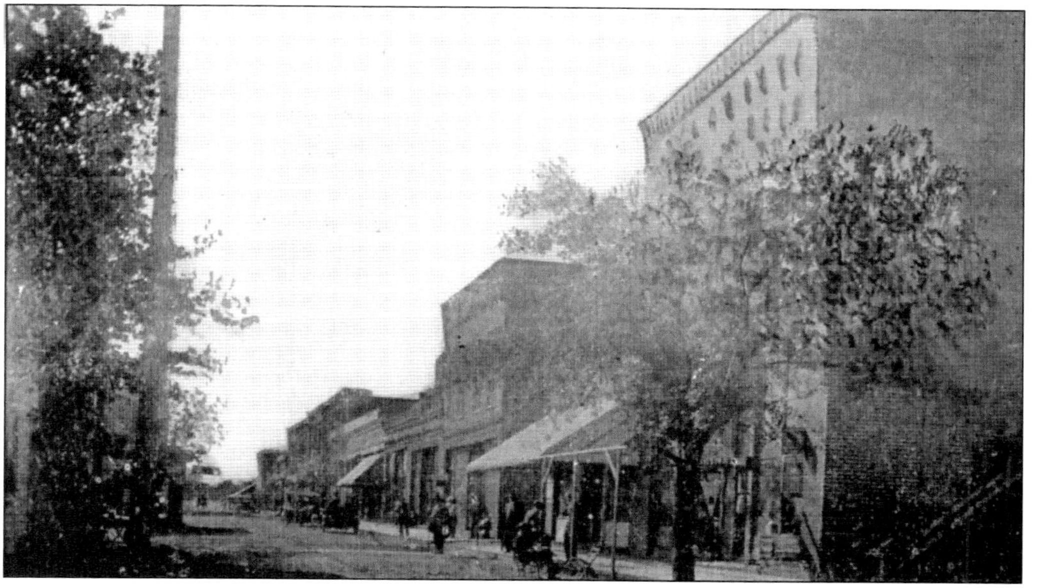

MAIN STREET, PROSPERITY [*c.* 1908.] The 1812 Mills Atlas inscribed Prosperity M.H. [A.R.P. Meeting House] at the location of Prosperity. When a village began to evolve at this site it was called Frog Level but later called Prosperity beginning in 1873. Rural Free Delivery mail service began in 1899 from Prosperity with Frank V. Capers serving on alternate days. This view of Main Street starts with the Wheeler and Moseley Store on the right.

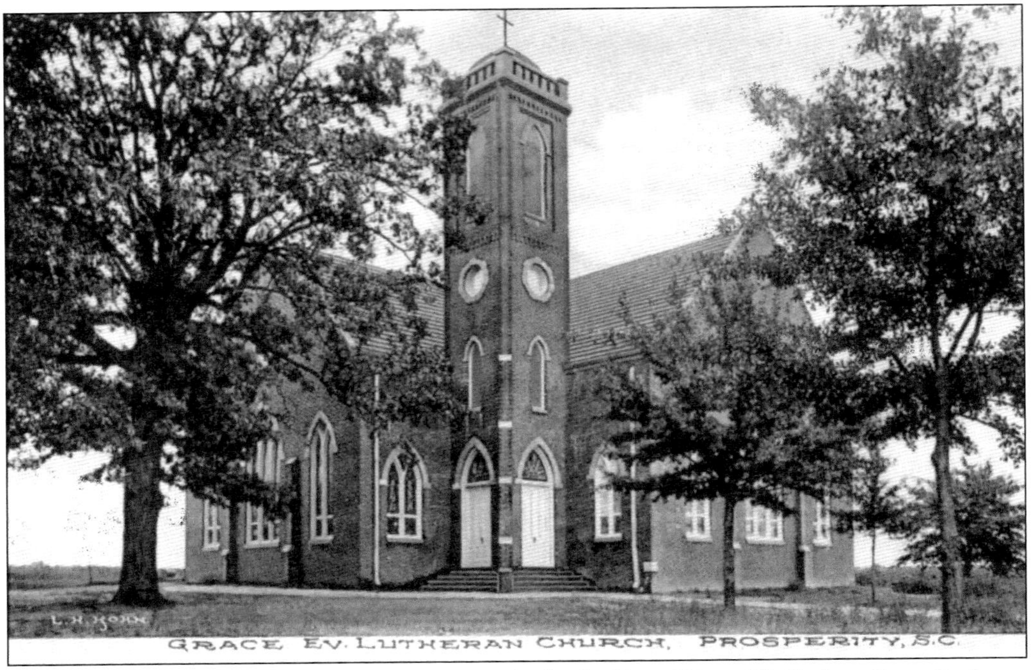

GRACE LUTHERAN CHURCH [*c.* 1907]. Under the leadership of Rev. W. Berley, Grace Lutheran Church was organized and a simple structure built in 1859. The church was initially called Newville at Frog Level. In 1878 a new sanctuary was raised at a cost of $850 and the name was changed to Grace. The town's name became Prosperity. The church shown above is the third and present Gothic edifice, which was begun in 1907 and dedicated in 1910.

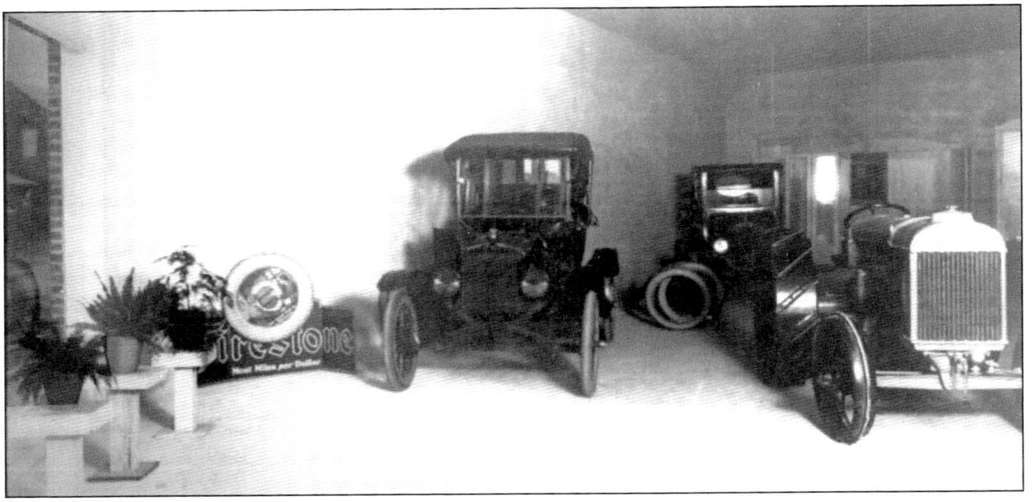

[FORD SHOWROOM, PROSPERITY, C. 1920.] The Shealy Motor Company was granted the Ford franchise for Prosperity in 1920. Before the paved roads, the county's dirt roads were uneven, rutted, and sometimes washed out. Several counties used prison labor to repair them; however, in the Prosperity District, the town relied on conscription labor where every able bodied man was obliged to either volunteer to repair the roads or to send a substitute laborer. This was a minor problem for slow moving horse and wagons but a major nuisance for motor car travel.

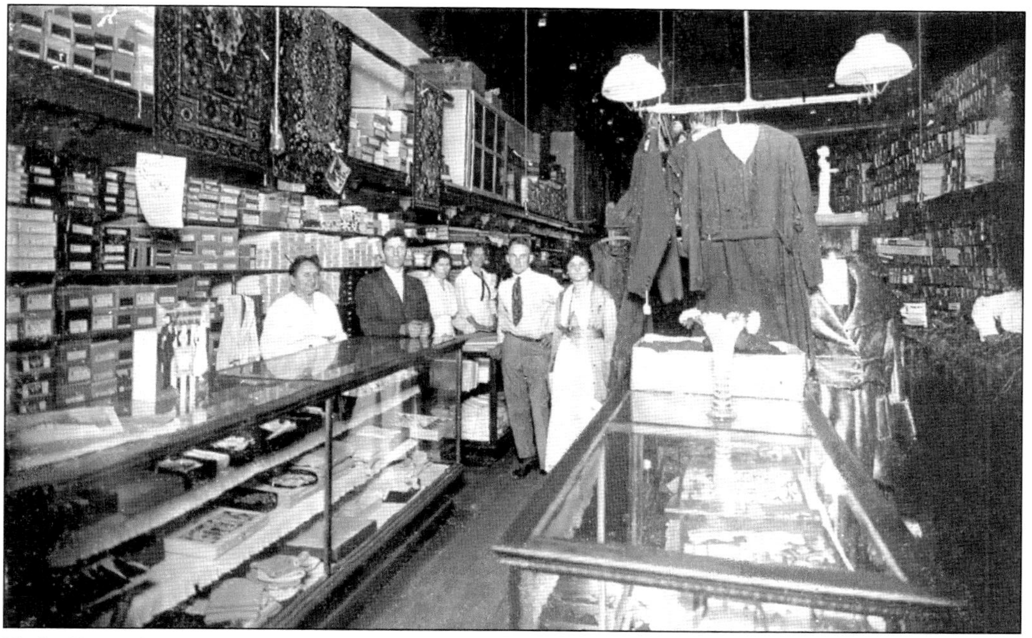

[L.A. Black's Dry Goods Store, *c.* 1910.] The Interior of L.A. Black's (1878–1969) Dry Goods store indicates a well-stocked establishment. L.A. and Mrs. L.D. Black moved to Prosperity in 1908 and set up shop on Main Street with an inventory that included a full line of dry goods, men's and ladies' suits, dresses, coats, overcoats, shoes, and millinery. During the first two decades Prosperity's merchants, including Black's store, published ads in Newberry's *The Observer* with great regularity.

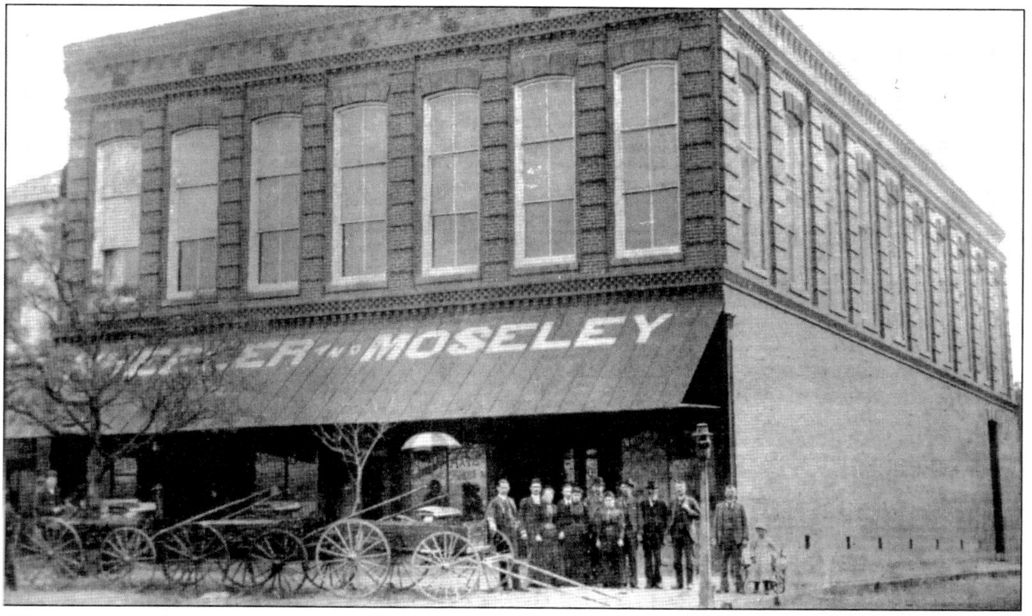

[Wheeler and Moseley Store, Prosperity, *c.* 1907.] The Wheeler and Moseley Store, established by 1873, was a combination dry goods, millinery, and grocery store. Newspaper ads were found in Newberry's *Herald and News* and *The Observer* from 1907 until they closed in January 1916.

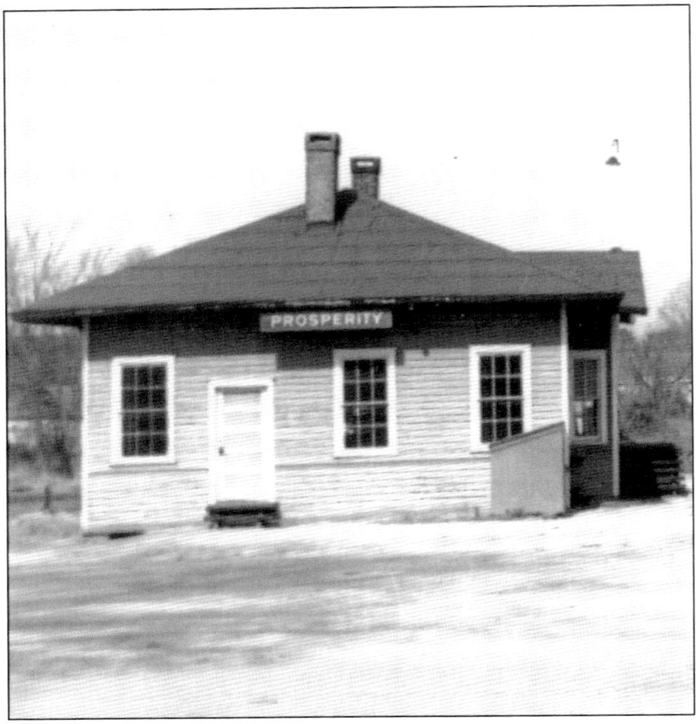

[Depot, Prosperity, c. 1908.] The Greenville and Columbia (G&C) Railroad placed a depot in Prosperity in 1851 and the Columbia, Newberry, and Laurens Railroad's station came in 1886. The G&C schedule had Prosperity as the first stop after Columbia. Both lines scheduled freight and passenger service twice a day. Passenger service ended when the CN&L discontinued it in 1952.

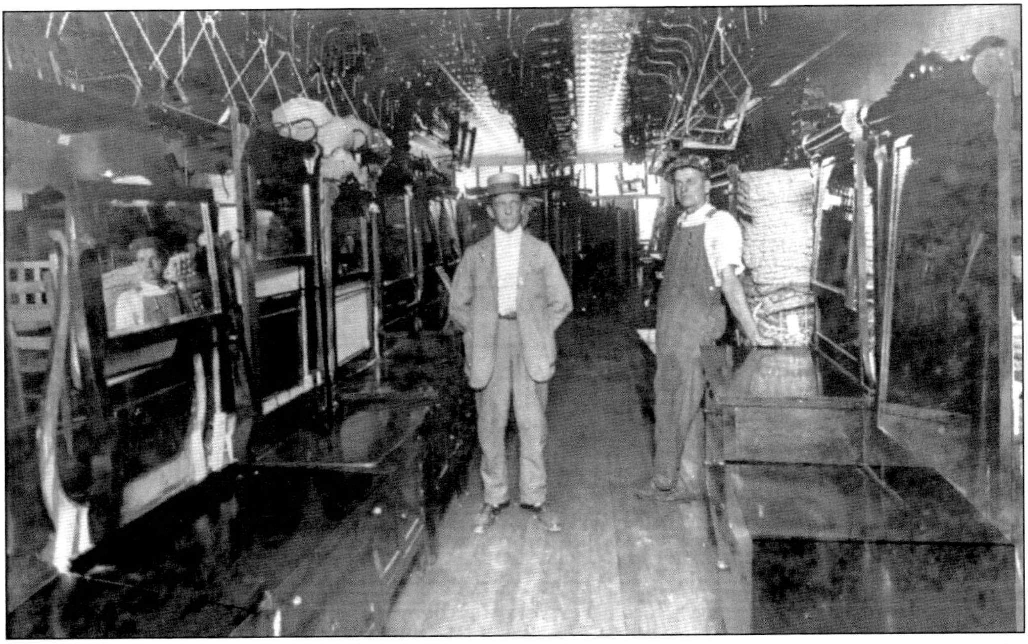

[Prosperity Furniture Store, c. 1910.] The interior of Prosperity Furniture Store illustrates the popular furnishings of that era. The store was established by Dan Hamm Sr. and Allen Hamm at the turn of the century with Dan Hamm's sons, Dan and Walter, continuing to run the business until 2000. This picture shows Dan Hamm Sr. (left) and Ben F. Dawkins (right).

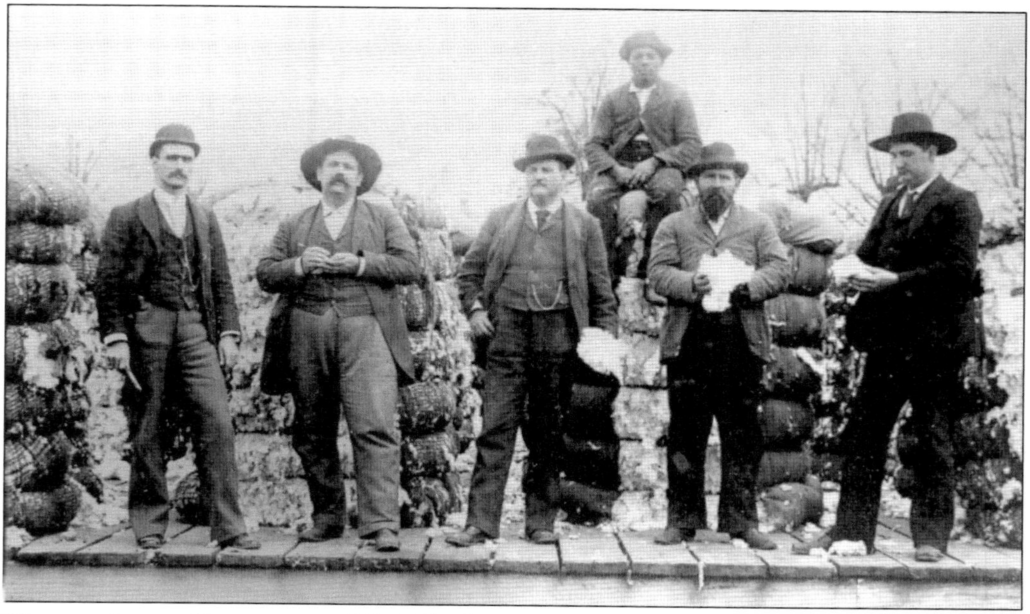

[Cotton Scene, Prosperity, 1892.] The Prosperity cotton buyers in 1892 were K. Baker, A.G. Wise, L.S. Bowers, J.L. Wise, and A.K. Hawkins. Cotton sales were the lifeblood of Prosperity and each of the towns and villages across the county. In 1920 Newberry County raised 35,000 bales of cotton, which sold for 32.7¢ a pound. Soon after, the boll weevil damaged or destroyed a large portion of the crops and the price fell radically, causing many merchants and farmers to face bankruptcy.

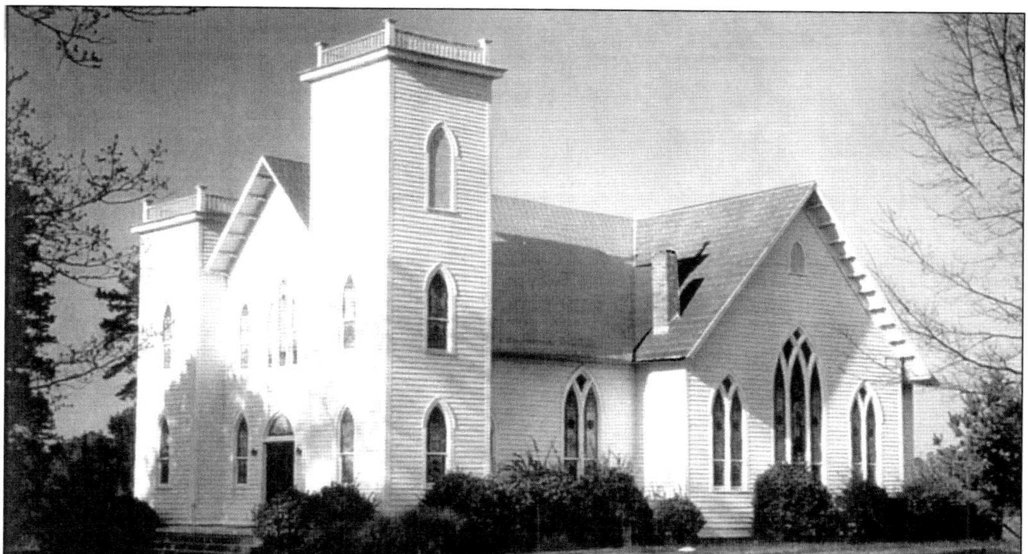

[Corinth Lutheran Church, Prosperity, *c.* 1927.] About 1842 a congregation of 27 people that had settled in the fork area of the Big and Little Saluda Rivers organized and built a church called Corinth. In 1872, after the Civil War, Rev. P. Derrick led a movement to build a larger building. Solving the need for more space, the present sanctuary was erected in 1927 for $2,100. Members furnished the materials and J.J. Seastruck furnished the labor.

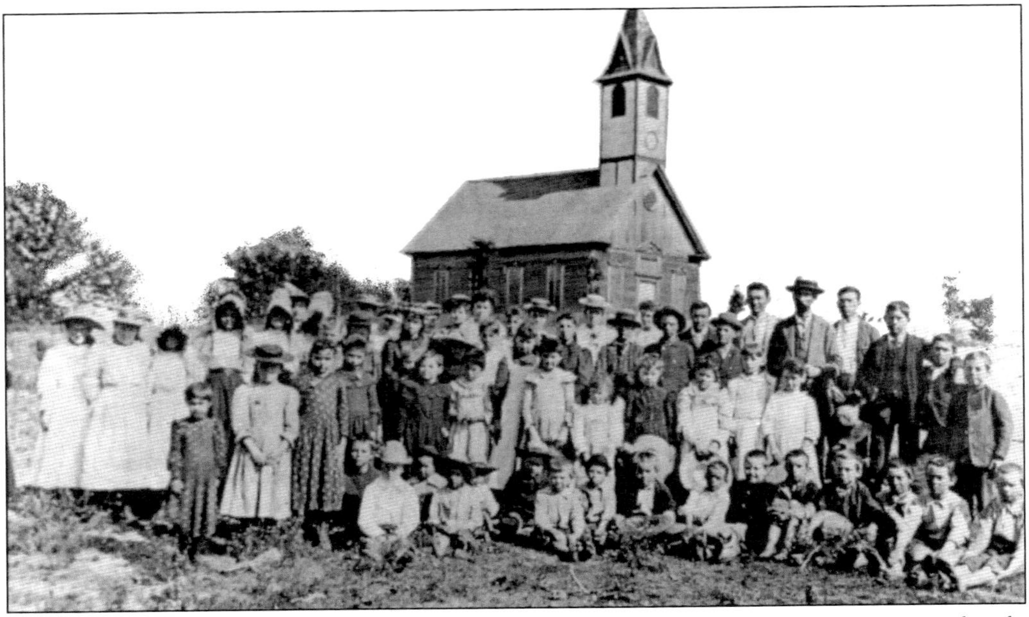

[Associate Reformed Presbyterian Church, Prosperity, 1890s.] The A.R.P. Church, established by the Scotch-Irish settlers in 1802 under the guidance of Rev. J. Rogers, was Prosperity's first church. The initial Prosperity Meeting House—located inside the current city's cemetery—was placed on the 1825 Mills' map. Reverend Rogers was the pastor of three other congregations, so this church was without a regular pastor for its initial 14 years. The second Prosperity Meeting House was erected *c.* 1840 on the same cemetery site.

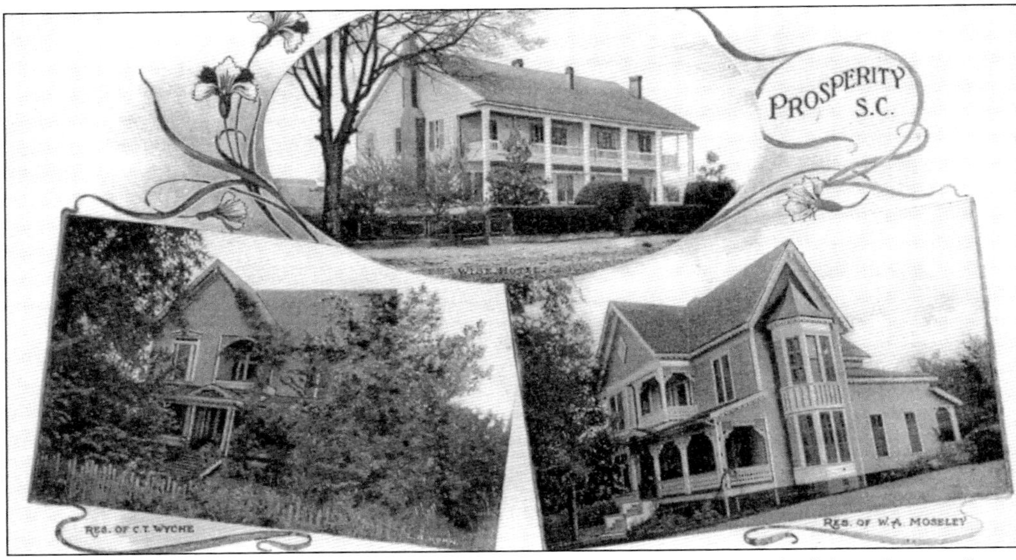

[Early Frame Buildings, Prosperity, c. 1907.] This montage postcard of three houses shows, on the left, the residence of Dr. C.T. Wyche (1857–1930), who practiced medicine from 1882 and also served in the state legislature; in the center, the J.H. Wise Hotel that was described as a charming country hotel for traveling men at a cost of $2 a day; and on the right, the home of W.A. Moseley, a Prosperity merchant.

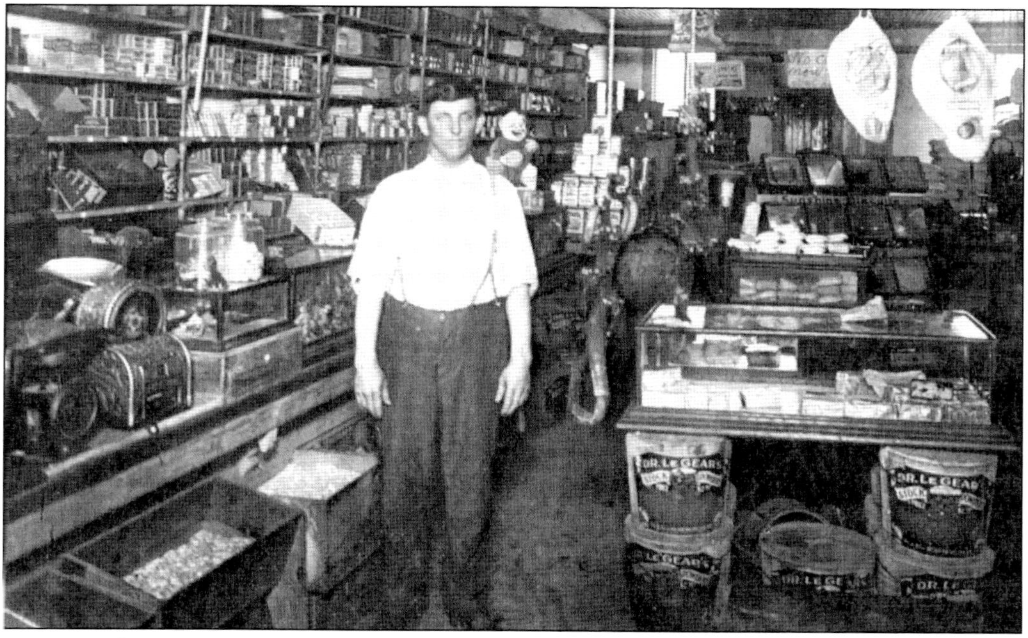

[Mathis' Grocery Store, Prosperity, *c.* 1910.] Mathis' grocery store is a typical example of a small town store. The merchant served customers that planted, harvested, consumed, and preserved their crops. The grocer stocked the necessities of coffee, sugar, flour, spices, meats, and other goods. Some patrons would barter foodstuffs for needed supplies.

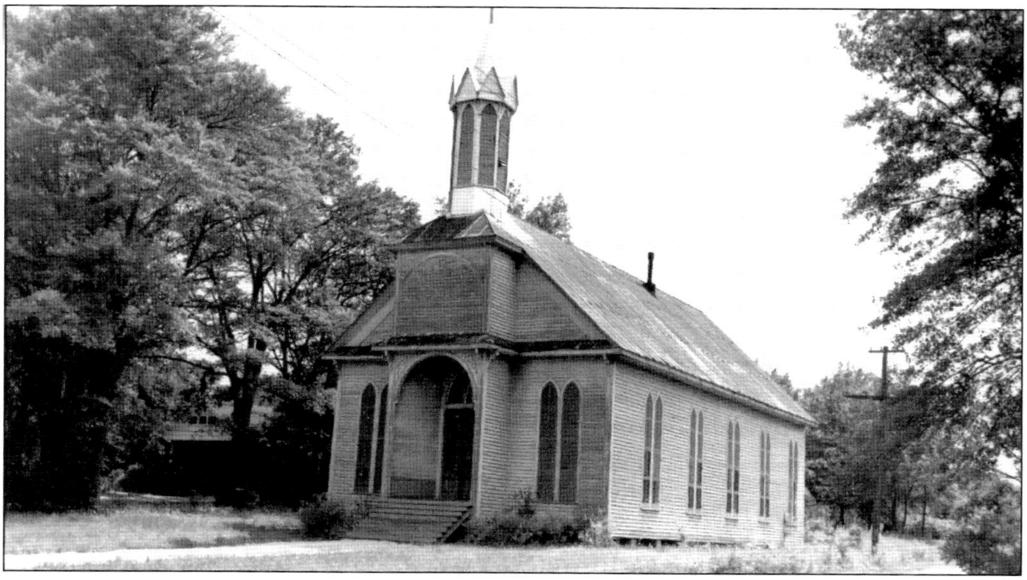

[A.R.P. Church, Prosperity, *c.* 1908.] In January 1889 a site inside the city limits was given to the congregation by Rev. J.C. Boyd, and a third sanctuary was built on the corner of McNary and Church Streets. In 1959 this congregation united with the nearby old A.R.P. Cannon Creek Church congregation and built a new brick church on the Newberry to Prosperity Highway. This structure was torn down *c.* 1996.

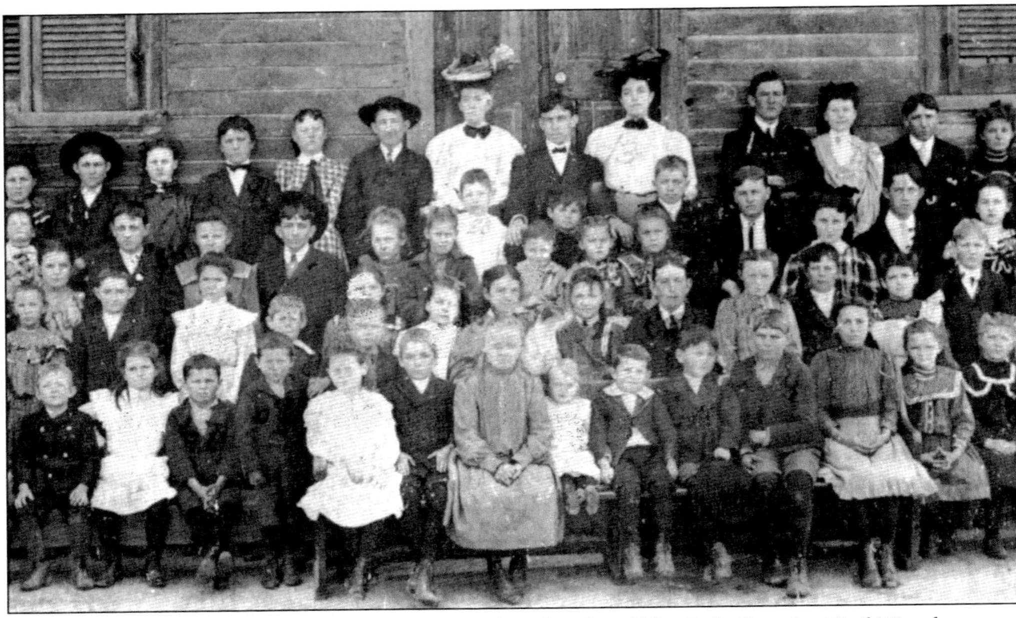

[Prosperity Academy Students, 1890s.] Public schooling did exist before the Civil War; however, the first roots of Prosperity's evolving school system can be traced back to the 1873 Prosperity Academy with its two-room wooden school house near the cemetery. C.W. Welch was the teacher of 97 students in six grades. The picture above shows the students of that school.

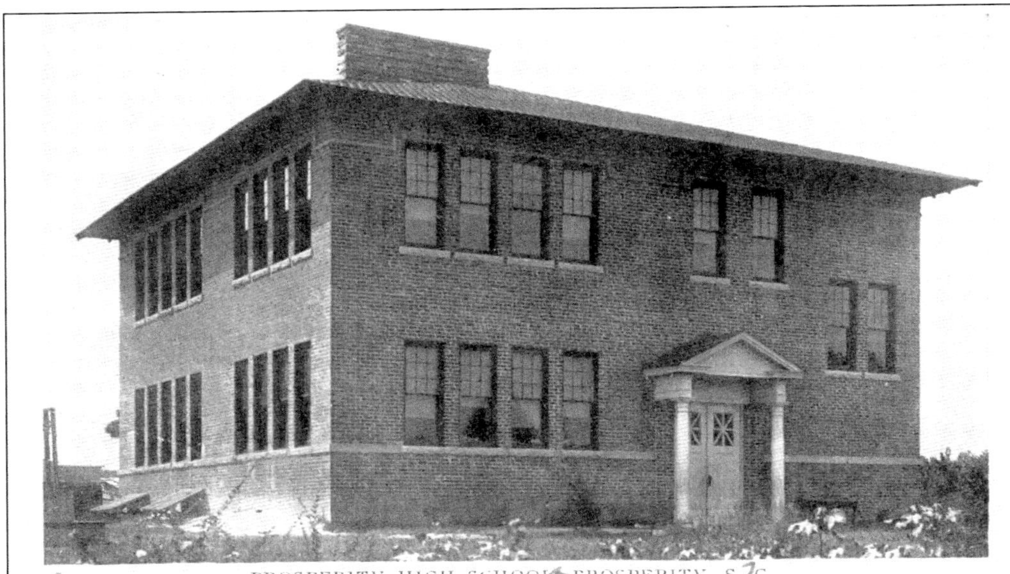

Prosperity High School [c. 1908]. This new brick high school was built in 1907 and had 67 students enrolled in the upper grades. The older frame building was then used by elementary students. In 1925 the high school could award state-accredited diplomas since their students had completed a 16-unit state-approved program. This building later became an elementary school after the high school and Mt. Pilgrim's school were consolidated.

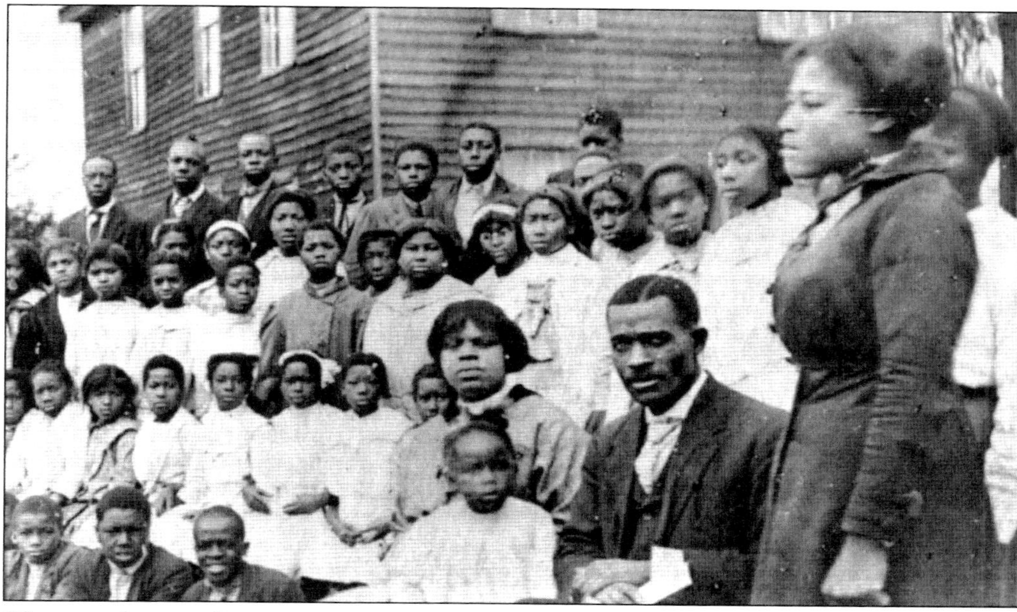

[Howard School Students, c. 1890s.] The Shiloh A.M.E. Church's one-story frame sanctuary also served as a school, with the preacher also acting as the teacher. The church built both a frame school and a new church building before 1899 and changed the school's name to Howard. Neither county nor the state funded the school. The 1900 state superintendent of education's report listed Prosperity as having one black school with two teachers and 137 students in a 20-week school term. Howard's students are shown above.

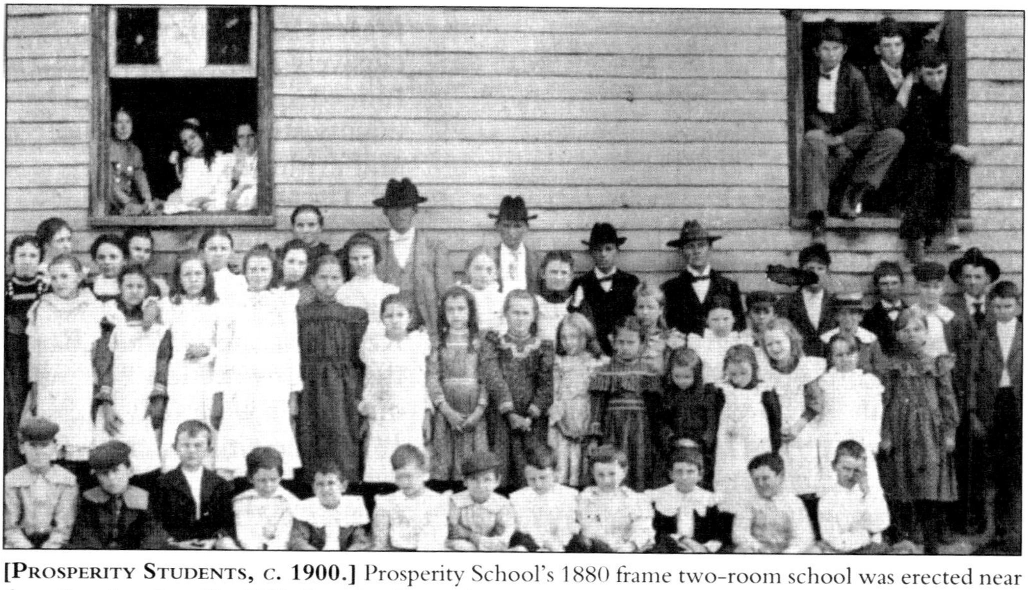

[Prosperity Students, c. 1900.] Prosperity School's 1880 frame two-room school was erected near the railroad station. By 1889 the school's employees were Rev. A.J. Bowers, principal; J.E. Edwards, teacher; and Miss L. Luther, teacher, and 100 children attended. The curriculum included the standard subjects and Latin, Greek, advanced mathematics, physiology, and music. The school picture above was made outside this school.

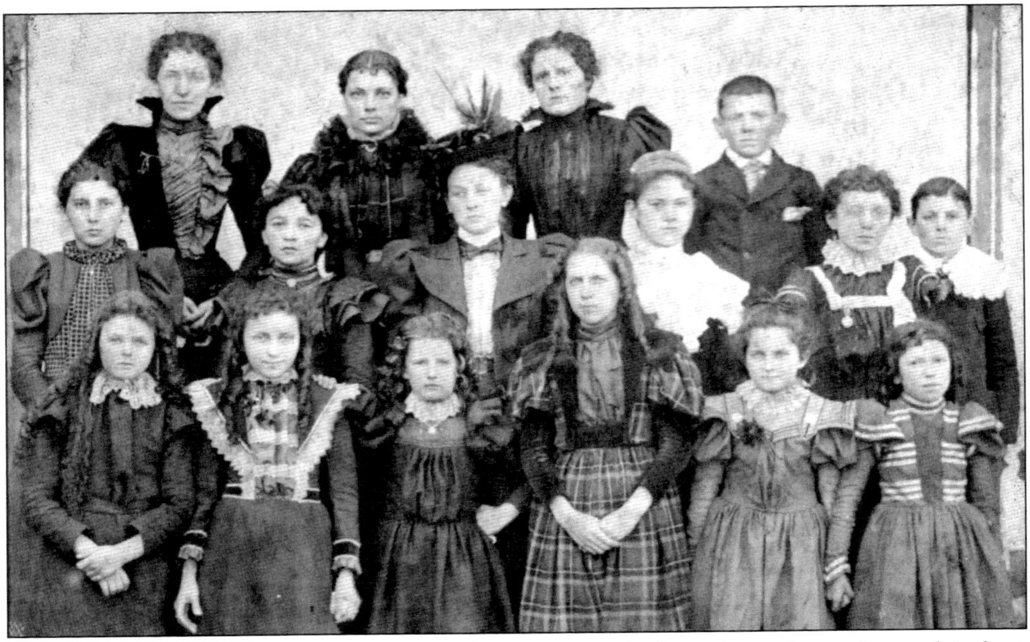

[Music Students, Prosperity, c. 1900.] The group portrait above shows the teachers and students of the music class that was included in the curriculum of the 1880 to 1900 era. In 1900 the South Carolina Superintendent of Education Annual Report listed this school district as having one white school with three teachers and 149 students in a 28-week school session.

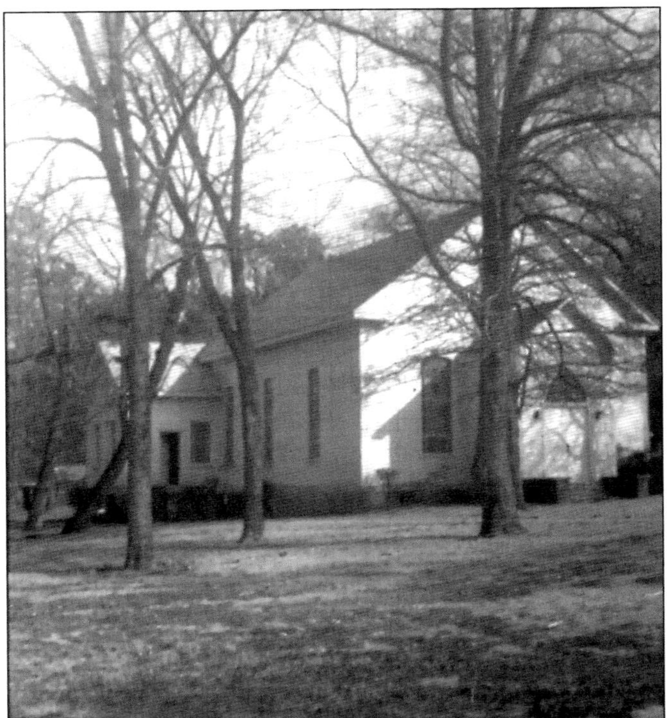

[St. Matthew's Lutheran Church, Pomaria, c. 1920.] Heller's Church, which was organized by Rev. J.D. Scheck organized in 1827, was built at a site ten miles northwest of Pomaria near the Broad River. The first building was destroyed by a cyclone in 1844 and was rebuilt two years later. The second sanctuary was dedicated in 1885. During the ministry of Rev. E.K. Counts from 1934 to 1943, memorial windows and six Sunday school classes were added.

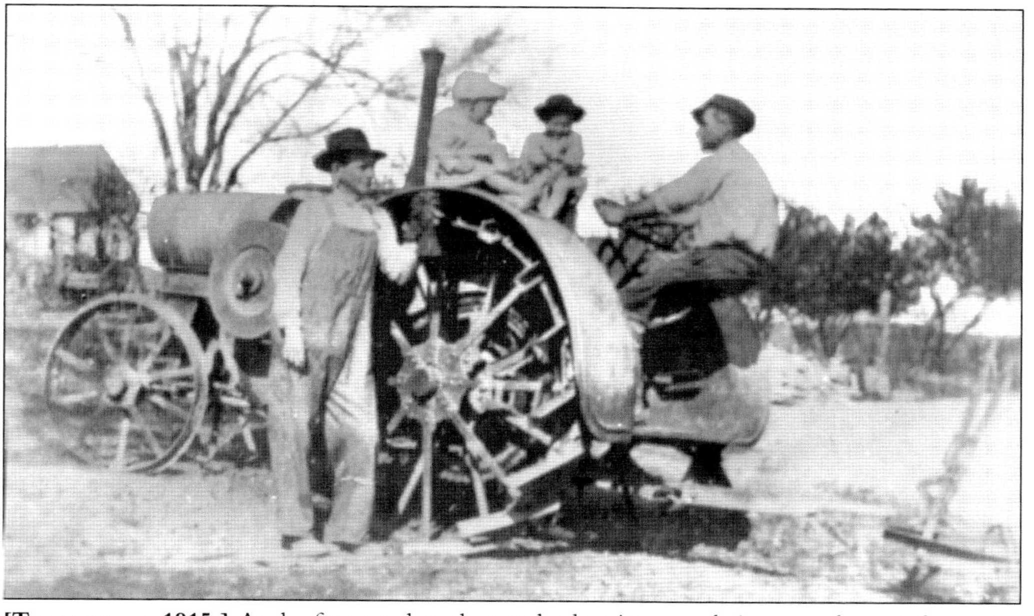

[Tractor, c. 1915.] As the farmers cleared more land to increase their cotton harvest the tractor began to replace oxen and mules so that the planting and harvesting of crops could be accomplished more quickly and efficiently. This also meant that a farmer's income could be increased and harvest liens (the loan of seed and other farming necessities by merchants that was to be repaid when the crop was sold) could be settled. Unfortunately, during the 1920s and 1930s, the cotton crops failed. Many farmers could not pay their liens and, as a result, lost their mortgaged farms; many merchants and bankers could not repay their loans and went bankrupt.

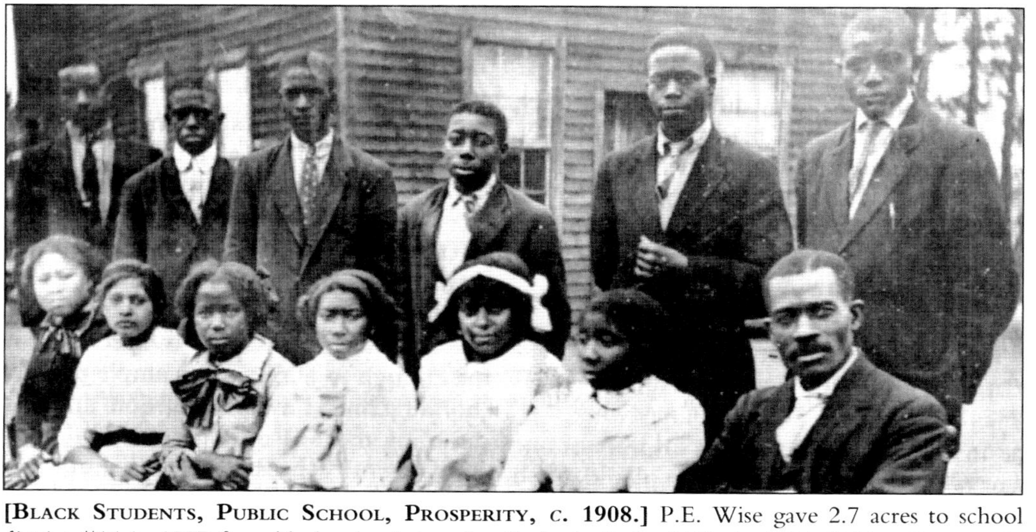

[Black Students, Public School, Prosperity, c. 1908.] P.E. Wise gave 2.7 acres to school district #14 in 1907 for a black school that the district built for $100. In 1924–1925, a Rosenwald school was built. The Rosenwald grants—given to Southern states to build standard schoolhouses for black students—were funds that were matched by local, district, county, and state moneys. Most of these frame buildings were used until the 1950s.

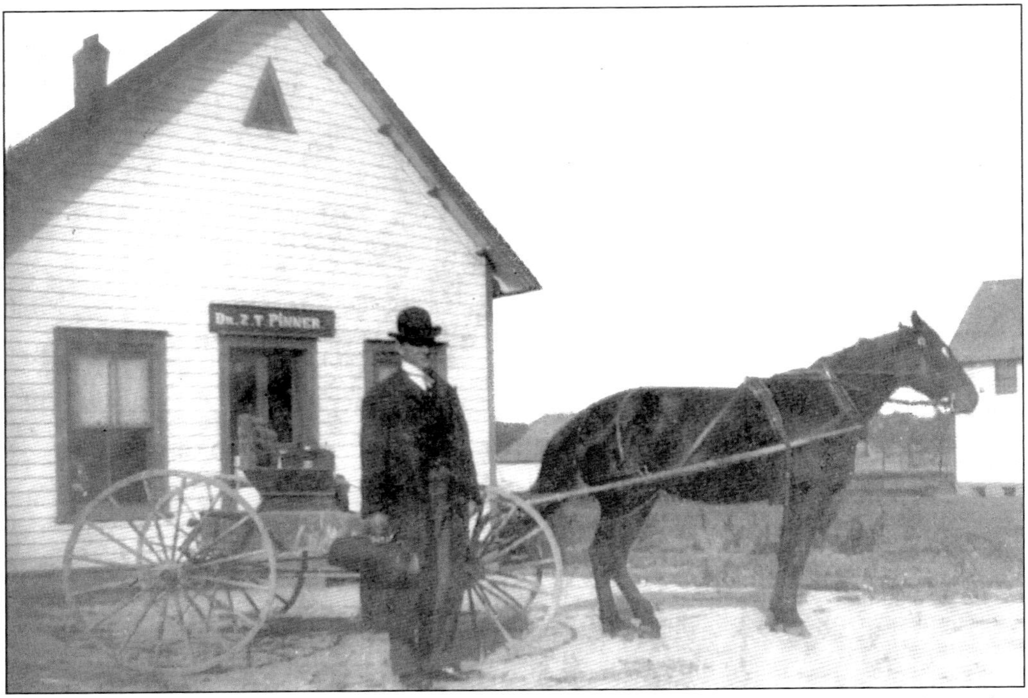

[DR. PINNER, POMARIA, c. 1910.] Dr. Z.T. Pinner [1878–1940] was born in Arden, North Carolina and graduated in medicine from the College of Tennessee before settling in Pomaria. He had an extensive practice, owned a drug store, and was elected president of the Newberry County Medical Society in 1914.

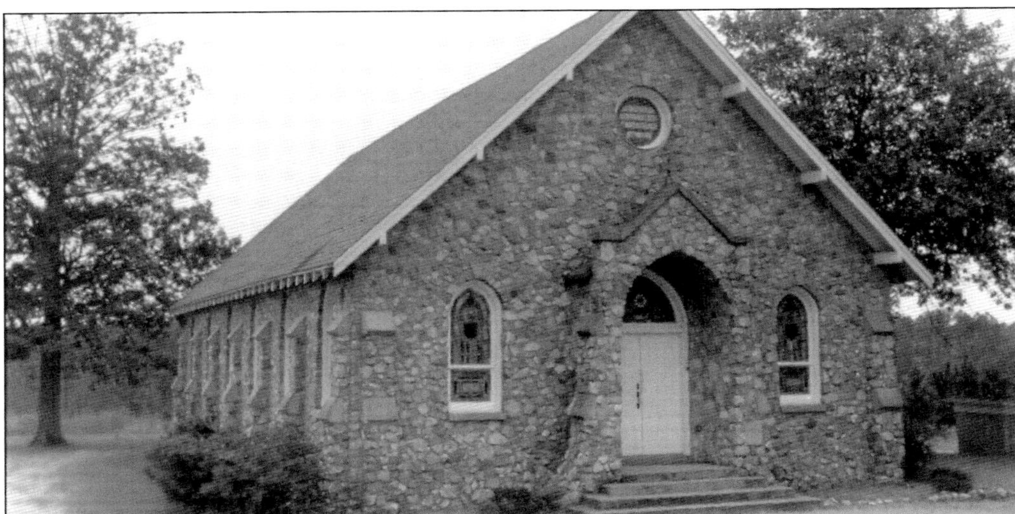

[MT. PILGRIM LUTHERAN CHURCH, PROSPERITY, c. 1934.] Rev. J.D. Bowles organized the Mt. Pilgrim Lutheran Church in 1880 with 32 charter members and dedicated the first frame building on a four-acre site donated by A.G. Miller, which was used for 40 years. In 1934 a new sanctuary was built as the congregation gave money, lumber, and labor; gathered field stones; and fashioned the stones into a Gothic structure.

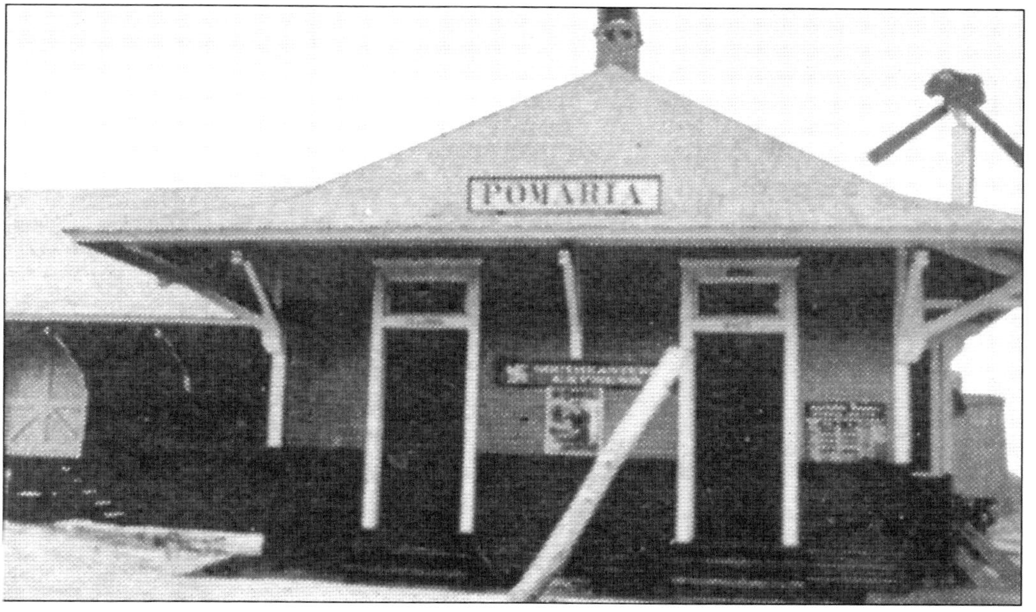

[Depot, Pomaria 1920s.] This town, first called "Countsville," had its name changed to Pomaria in 1840. By 1851 the Greenville and Columbia Railroad had completed a line through Pomaria, where they established a depot and water tank, making it a fuel and water stop. The rail service permitted freight and commerce to arrive in Pomaria and cotton to be sent to outside markets. In 1902 T.W. Holloway, a merchant and assistant postmaster, filed a charter to incorporate Pomaria. The depot has since been razed.

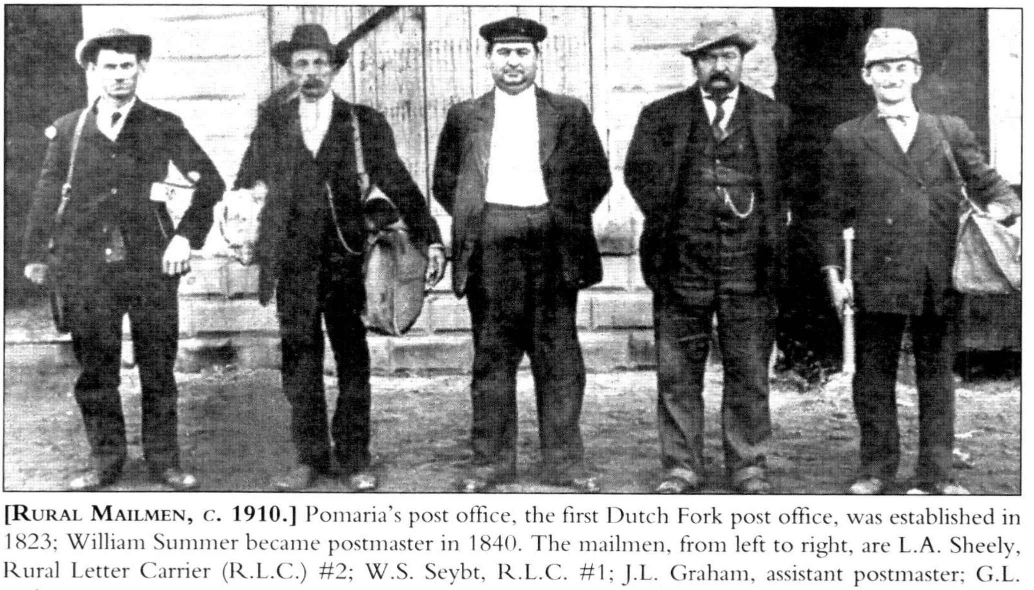

[Rural Mailmen, *c.* 1910.] Pomaria's post office, the first Dutch Fork post office, was established in 1823; William Summer became postmaster in 1840. The mailmen, from left to right, are L.A. Sheely, Rural Letter Carrier (R.L.C.) #2; W.S. Seybt, R.L.C. #1; J.L. Graham, assistant postmaster; G.L. Wilson, postmaster; and G.W. Setzler, R.L.C. #3. The 1910 annual convention of the state Rural Letter Carriers met in Newberry. In 1910, South Carolina's 354 post offices had rural routes, with the majority being in the Piedmont region; also, 750 carriers traveled 17,000 miles and handled 100,000 pieces of mail annually.

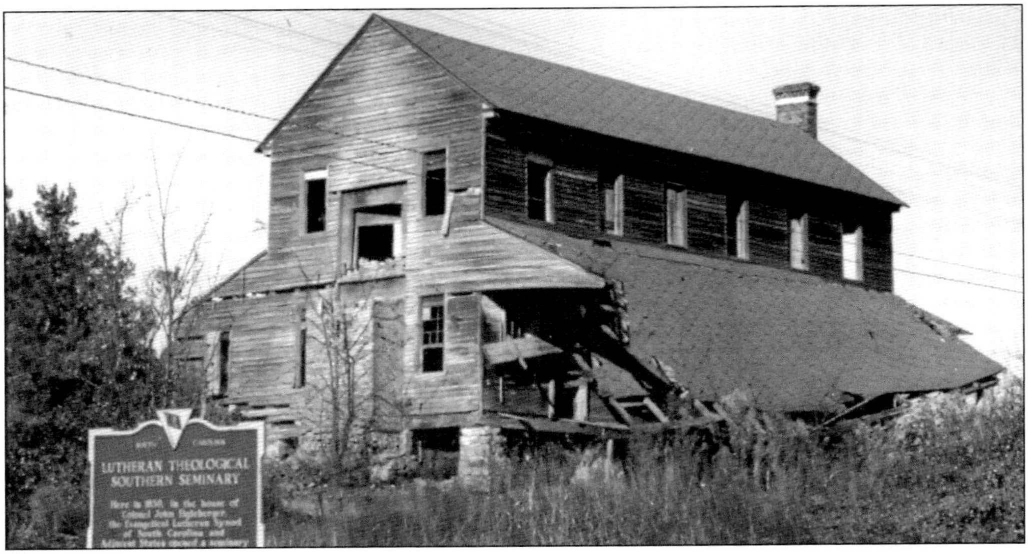

[Southern Theological Seminary, Pomaria, 1930s.] Rev. J.G. Schwartz trained men for the ministry in 1831, since a theological seminary did not exist in the South. He moved with five young men to Col. J. Eichelberger's home and began teaching; this building became the Southern Theological Seminary. When Schwartz died in 1832, the seminary moved to successive locations before coming to Columbia in 1911. It remains a significant Lutheran seminary in 2001. The home above has been razed.

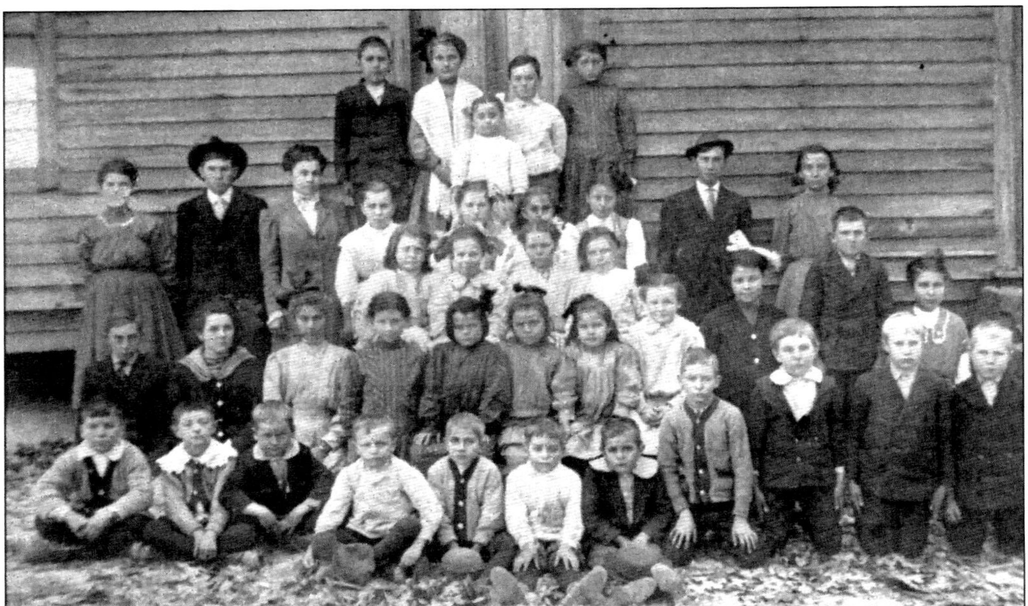

[Bethel Academy, *c.* 1900.] Bethel was established in 1869 a half mile outside of Pomaria. The 60-by-26-foot schoolhouse was built by local citizens and members of the Masonic, Knights of Jericho, and Grange Orders, who used the second floor for their meetings. The 1900 state superintendent's report lists Pomaria as having a one-room and one-teacher school for 39 white students in a 24-week term and a one-teacher school for 127 blacks in a 20-week session.

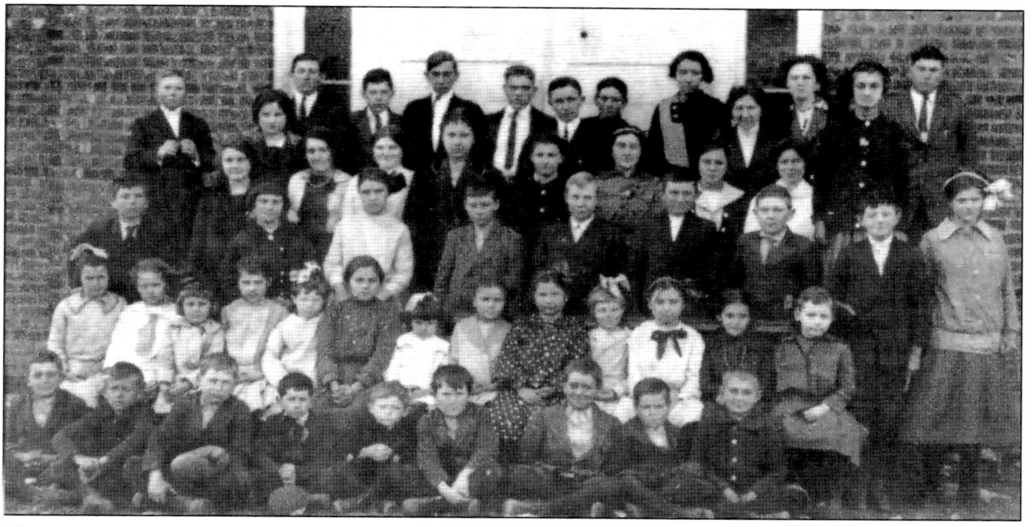

[POMARIA SCHOOL CLASS, 1913–1914.] The class above was the first group of students to attend the new school. The student distributions by classes in 1920 were as follows: first grade, 22 students; second grade, 5; third grade, 12; fourth grade, 7; fifth grade, 8; sixth grade, 7; seventh grade, 8; eighth grade, 6; ninth grade, 3; tenth grade, 2; and eleventh grade, 2, for a total of 80 students. Area schools in 1927 consolidated with the Pomaria school and the school curriculum was expanded to include the eleventh grade. Pomaria could award state-certified diplomas in 1928.

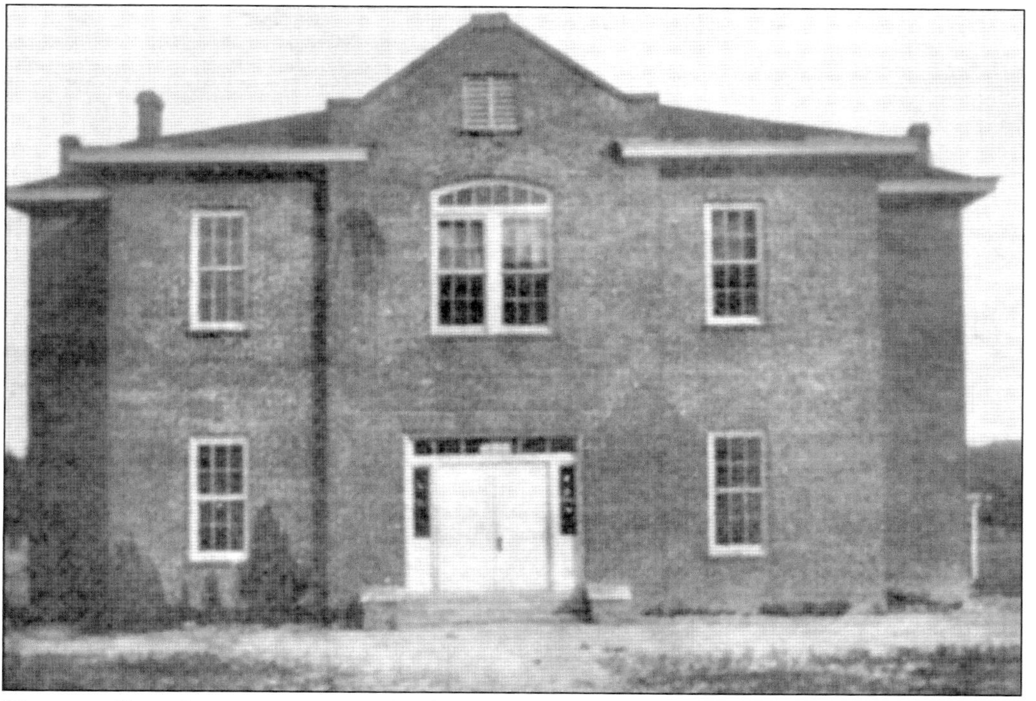

[POMARIA HIGH SCHOOL, 1914.] A sale of $3,500 worth of bonds supported the building of this new two-story brick high school in 1913. It had two classrooms, a large auditorium, and a library. W.A. Reiser was the first principal and Ms. L. Ligion was the other teacher.

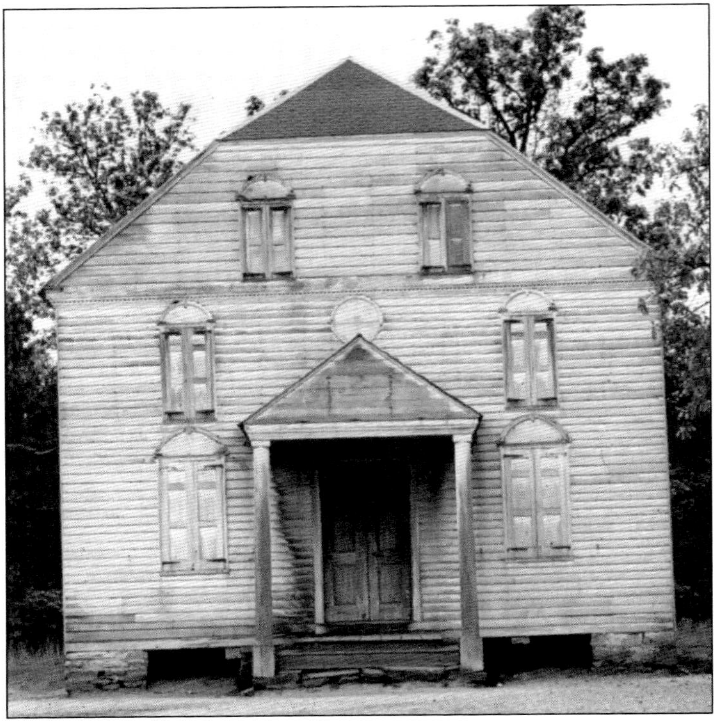

[St. John's Lutheran Church, c. 1910.] St. John's was built in 1809 and has been a house of worship for 141 years, making it the oldest frame Lutheran Church in the state. The interior has a high pulpit reached by several steps and a sounding board over the pulpit. It began as a German Reformed or Calvinistic Church where men sat on the right and women on left. A frame schoolhouse on the grounds was used until 1921.

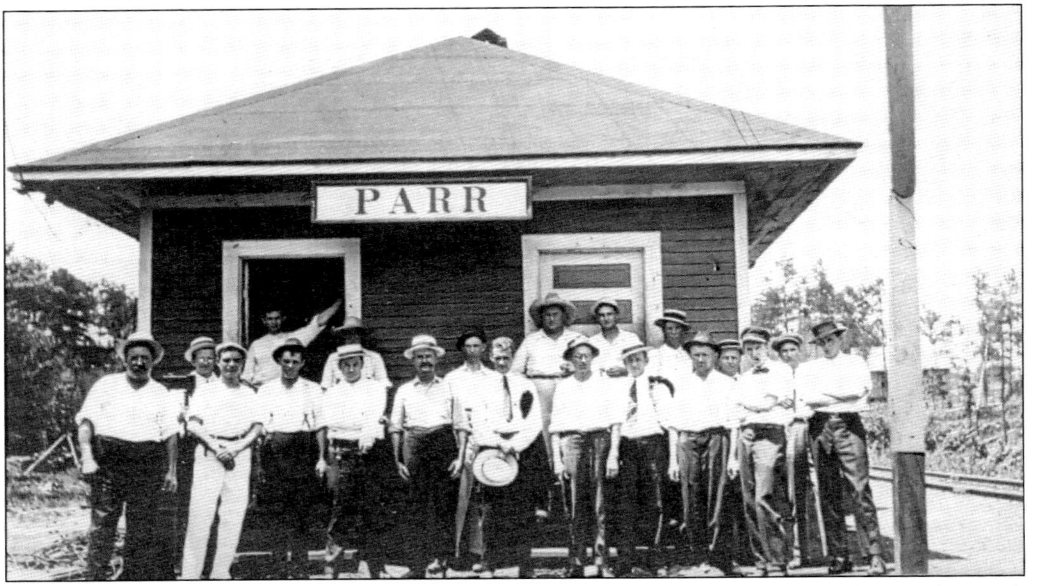

[Parr Railroad Station, c. 1914.] The Southern Railroad route from Columbia on the north side of the Broad River to Shelton had a station at Parr. On May 30, 1914, the power company invited 500 guests for a grand opening of their new facilities. They arrived by train for a barbecue lunch and a baseball game between Columbia's Boy Scouts and the McMaster School students. The officers of Broad River Power Company were E.W. Robertson, president and treasurer; H. Parson, vice president; and A. Wallace, general manager.

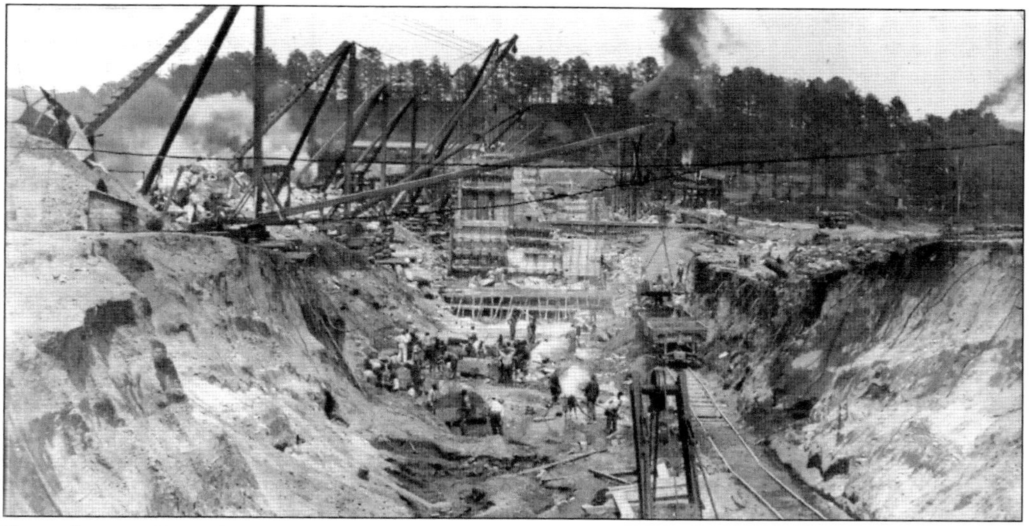

Parr Shoals Dam Construction [c. 1913]. Parr Shoals, the site of an 1800s grist mill, was located on the Broad River, 25 miles north of Columbia. The idea of a Parr Shoals Power Plant evolved in 1905 but was not funded until E.W. Robertson, president of Columbia Railway, Gas and Electric Company, developed it. The Parr Hydro Plant was constructed from 1912 to 1914 and included a 35-foot-high by 2,000-foot-long concrete dam; a 2,925-acre reservoir; a sub station containing five hydro-electric turbo-generators with a capacity of 10,000 kilowatts; and 24 miles of transmission lines supported on 70-foot steel towers between the Parr plant and Columbia.

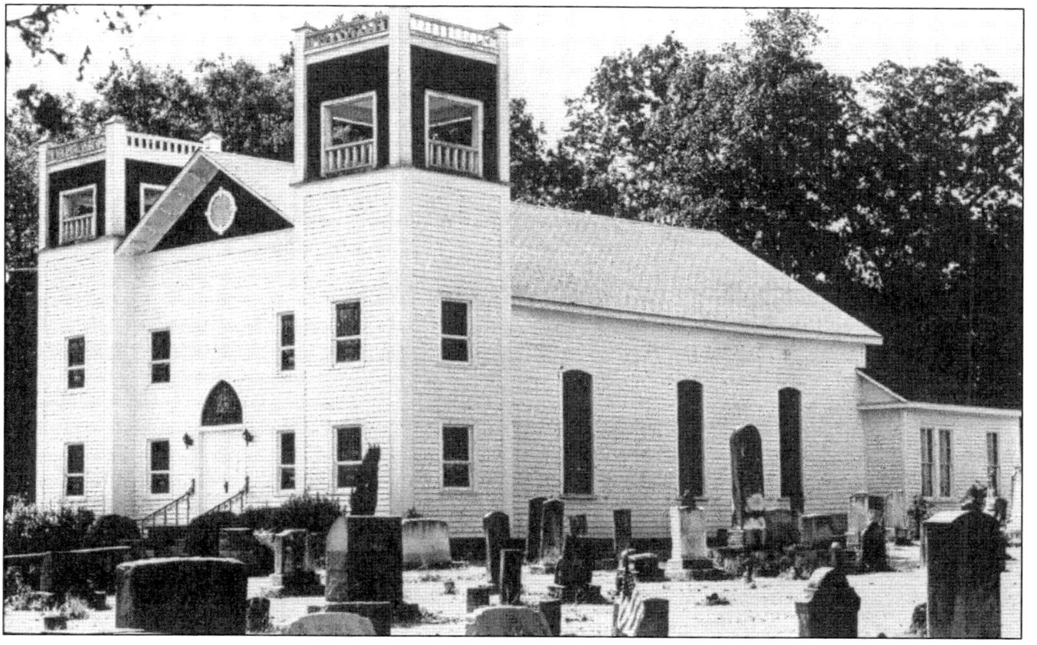

[Bethlehem Lutheran Church, Pomaria, c. 1910.] This congregation was incorporated in 1788; however, their church building was not constructed until Rev. G. Dreher led the effort in 1816 on a site two miles north of Pomaria. The present edifice was erected in 1881 with various additions and remodelings taking place throughout the 20th century.

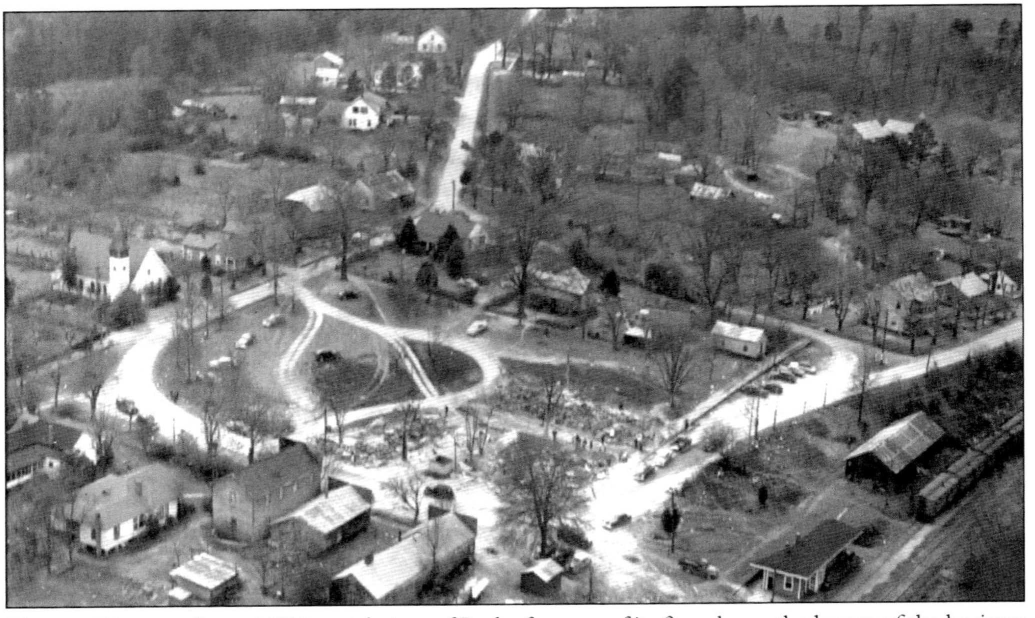

[Aerial View of Peak.] This aerial view of Peak after one of its fires shows the layout of the business district, depot, remaining stores, and the fire sites. Many of the small villages in this county developed around a depot and it became the hub for the community's limited economy. Their inexpensive frame structures were continually being destroyed by fire.

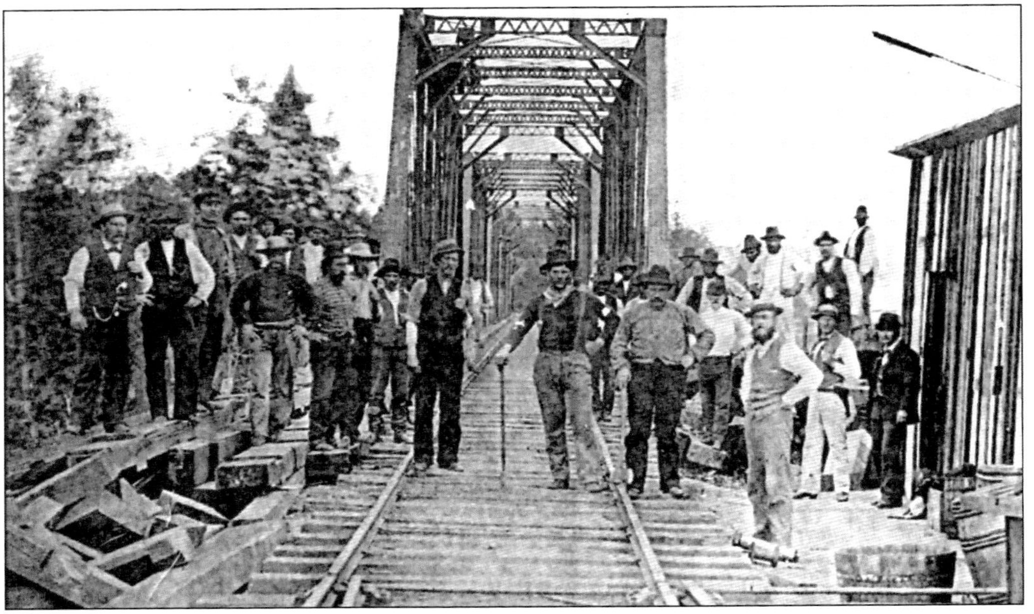

[Trestle Repair, c. 1903.] In 1865 this trestle across the Broad River was destroyed in the Civil War. Unfortunately, the repair of the Southern railway trestle was not completed until 1903. It not only provided a link between Newberry and Fairfield Counties, it also permitted traffic to move from Columbia to Newberry and beyond. Peak became the base for the following three railroad track repair crews: the Newberry team, the north Fairfield County crew, and the south Fairfield County crew.

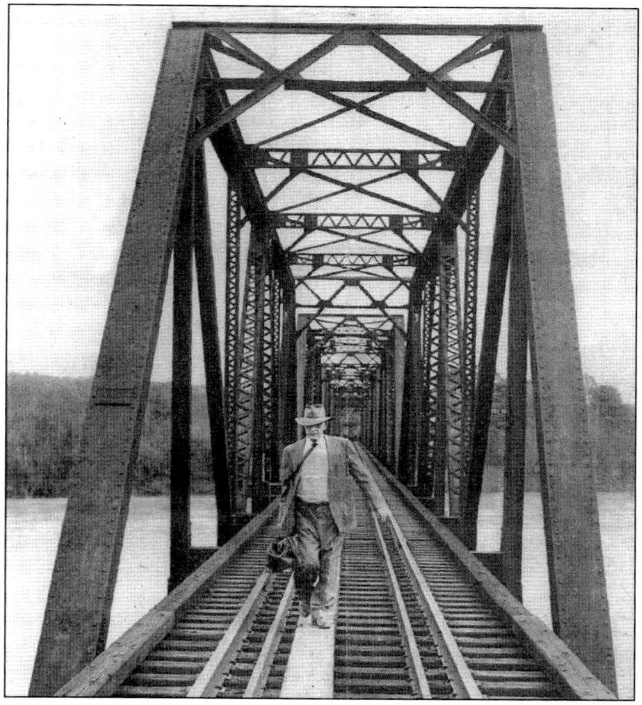

[Dr. C.A. Pinner, 1930s.] Peak, first known as Peak's Station, was named for railroad superintendent H.T. Peak in 1853 when it was established as a habitation for workers on the Greenville and Columbia Railroad. It was not incorporated, however, until 1880. Since the only crossing of the Broad River for a 40-mile stretch between Columbia and Shelton was this trestle, some residents like Dr. C.A. Pinner Sr. (1892–1962) would walk across the trestle to a car parked on the Fairfield side to get to his patients across the river.

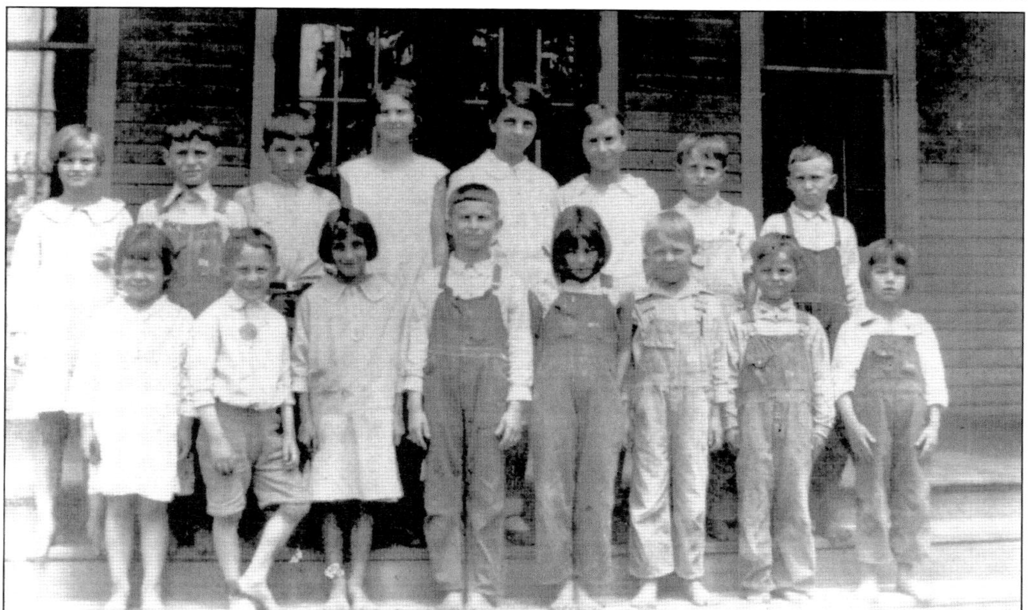

[Grammar School, Peak, 1932.] Peak's school started in the 1890s, and the 1900 superintendent report listed a one-teacher frame school for 37 white students. The class picture above was taken in front of the building that replaced the 1915 two-teacher structure described by Lueco Gunter as being an old unpainted type that housed 43 pupils. Students above were wearing dresses and shirts that their mothers made from printed cloth flour sacks. By 1920 Peak had become a part of Newberry County.

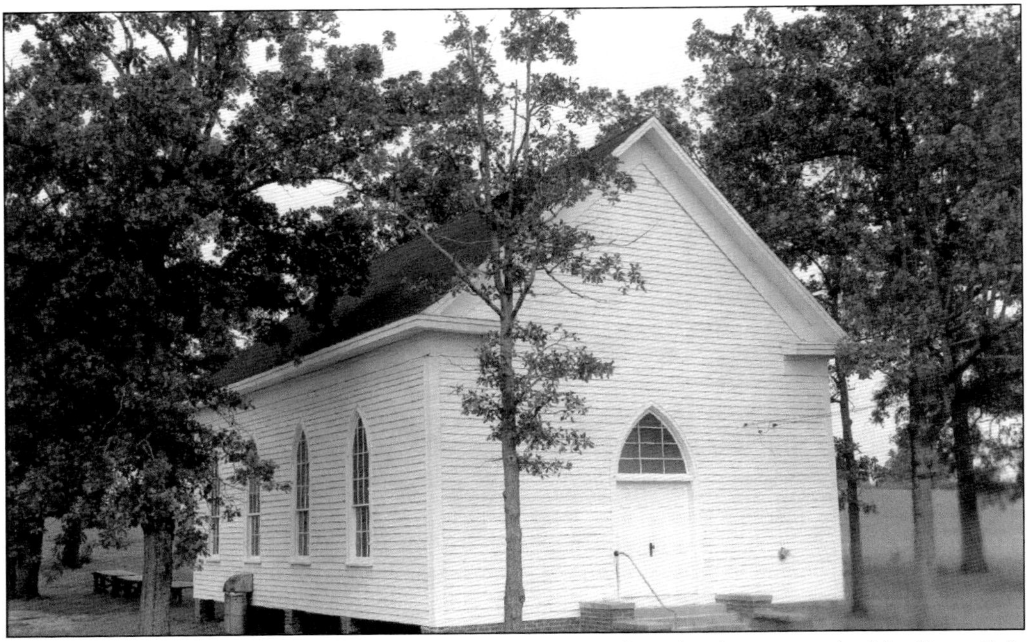

[Mt. Olivet Lutheran Church, 1920s.] In 1882 a Sunday school was organized by Rev. C.A. Marks, and it was dedicated as the Mt. Olivet Lutheran Church in 1890. The church was located in the O'Neall section of the county on a site given by Mrs. A. Cason. In 1929 the Lake Murray waters forced many families to migrate off of their land, leaving only a few original members of the church to carry on. Membership has increased in recent years.

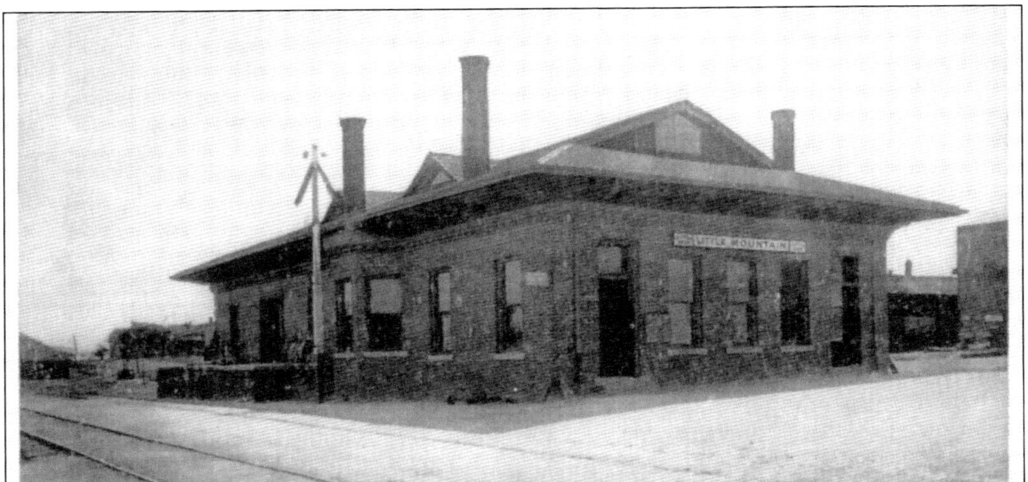

R. R, Station, Little Mountain [c. 1910]. The building of the Columbia, Newberry, and Laurens Railroad's depot in Little Mountain became the nucleus of that community, which was incorporated in 1890. The community built homes, stores, schools, and churches. The local commerce was cotton, which attracted brokers, warehouses, oil mills, banks, and hotels. Machine shops and wood-working craftsmen, blacksmiths, and livery stables related to potential railroad repair and service. The highlight of every first Saturday in August was the reunion festival participants, who came and went by the hundreds.

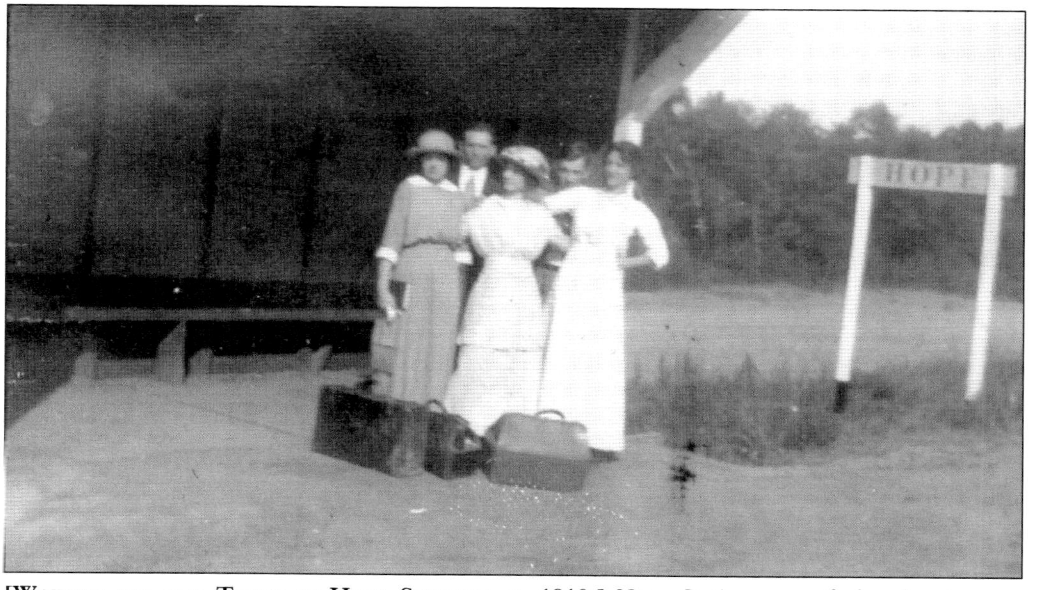

[WAITING FOR THE TRAIN AT HOPE STATION, *C.* 1910.] Hope Station was a fuel and water stop for the Greenville and Columbia Railroad that was built in 1851, and it was midway between Alston (Fairfield County) and Pomaria. The station was conveniently placed for travelers who desired to take a one-day shopping trip or visit a friend at a station up the line.

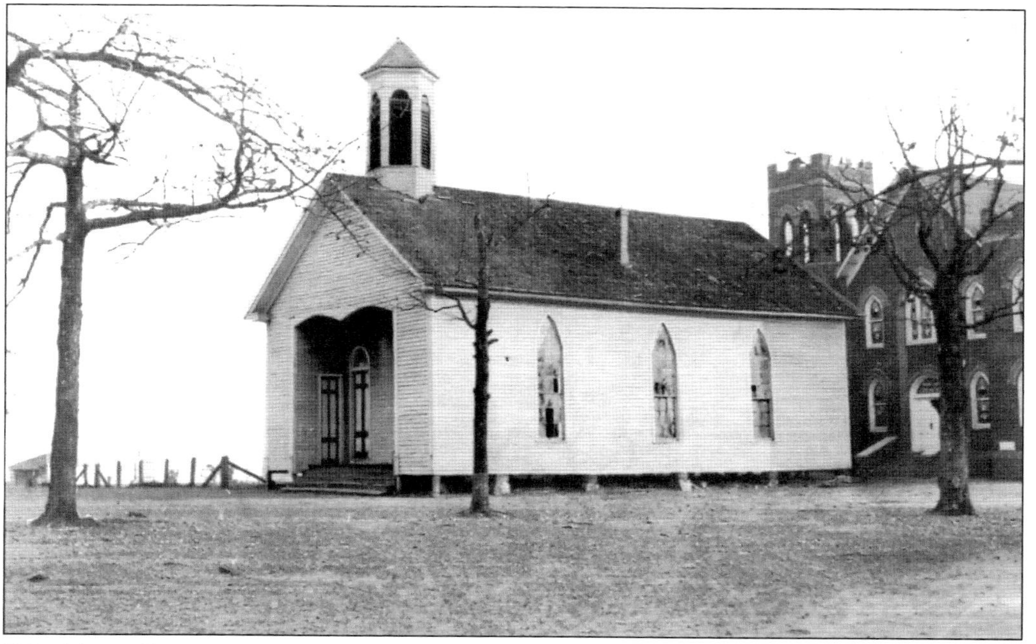

[MT. TABOR LUTHERAN CHURCH, *C.* 1924.] Mt. Tabor is located one mile north of Little Mountain. Rev. J.A. Sligh organized the congregation and had the frame edifice above erected in 1880. In 1925 Rev. J.L. Cromer began a vigorous drive to build a new brick church partially shown above. He induced the members to donate to the church all the eggs laid on Sunday. These gifts and others permitted the church to be built and free of debt in two years.

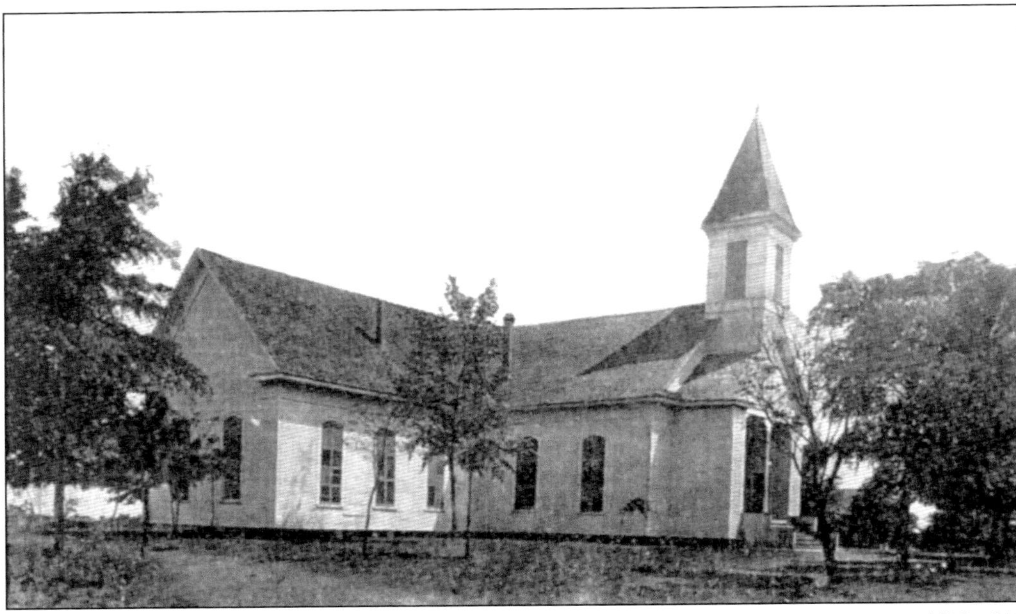

[Holy Trinity Lutheran Church, Little Mountain, c. 1905.] Holy Trinity was established in 1891 following a sermon by Rev. J.K. Efird, and the 34 charter members soon began to construct a frame sanctuary that was 35 feet by 56 feet, with a 16-foot narthex on the front. They also fashioned a homemade alter and pulpit. It was finished in October 1891 and cost $465. In 1902 they added a Sunday school room on each side at the back.

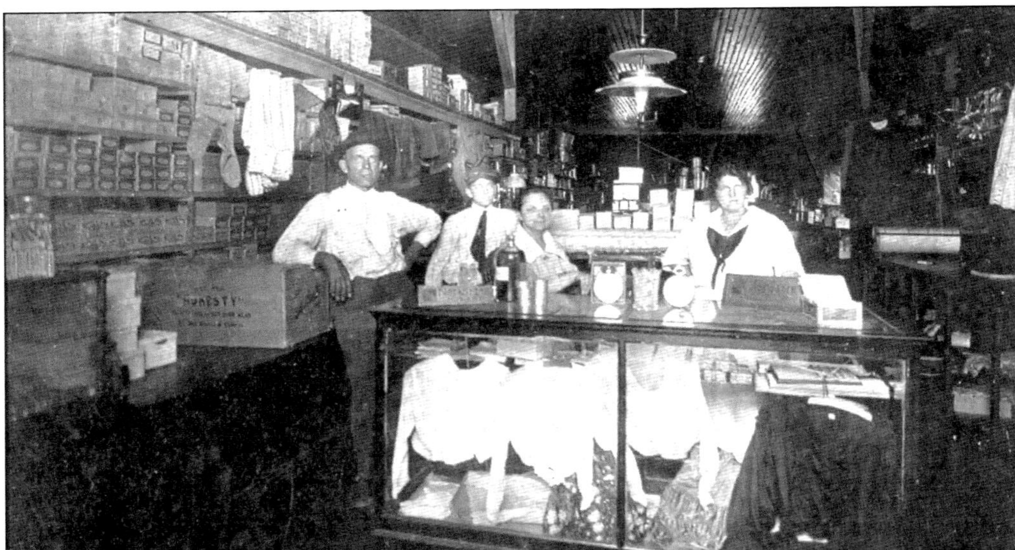

[J.K. Derrick Store, c. 1910.] J.K. Derrick and Company stocked clothing and dry goods for the customers of Little Mountain and others who saw their ads in *The Observer*. This view shows a large glass case with expensive lace blouses, hand bags, bottles of perfume, and other accessories at the entrance to the store. J.K. Derrick, his son L.C., his wife Lavinia, and a clerk are standing behind the case.

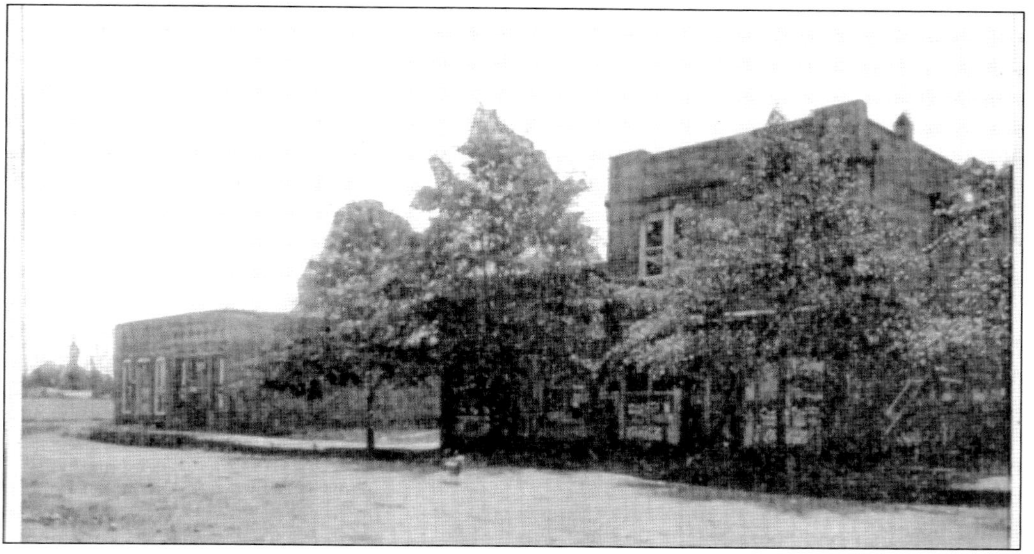

Main Street, Little Mountain [1917]. Noah Boland owned the acreage where Little Mountain is located and became the first mayor in 1890. In 1888 he was appointed postmaster and his daughter, Anna Boland, was postmistress from 1914 until her death in 1953. The first drug store was established by J.B. Lathan and Dr. John Marion Sease, and it was located on the ground floor of the Masonic building. The Farmers and Merchants bank was organized in 1907 and the Little Mountain Oil and Fertilizer Company began in 1905. Little Mountain was annexed into Newberry County in 1902. The population in 1910 was 440, in 1920 it was 399, and in 1930 it was 244.

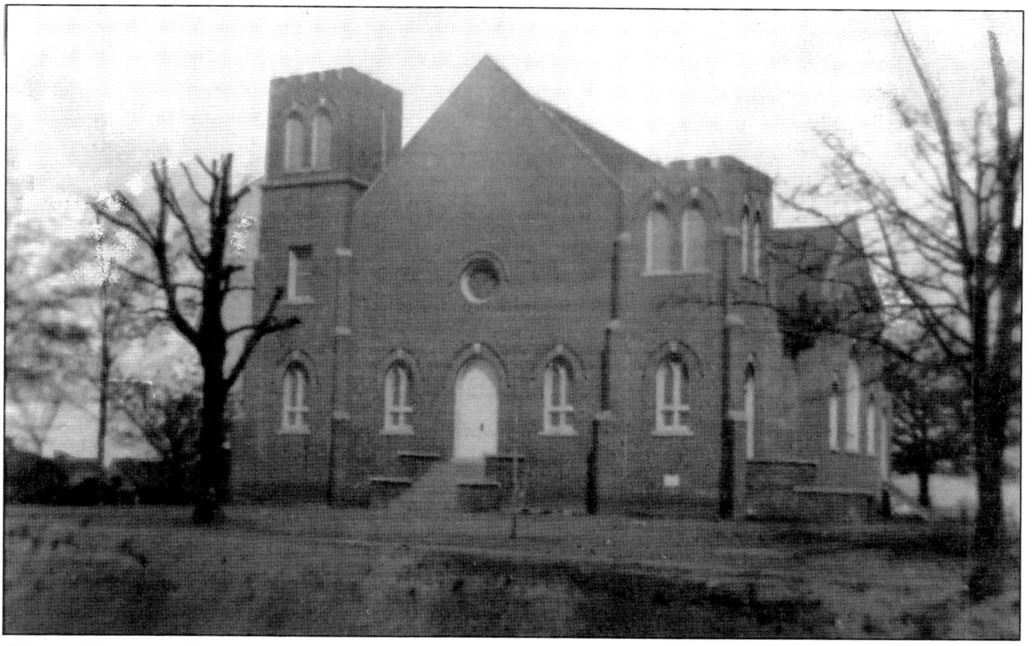

[Holy Trinity Lutheran Church, Little Mountain, *c.* 1919.] The congregation in 1913 began a building fund to erect a larger brick structure. The second brick edifice was built in 1917 at a cost of $14,000 and dedicated in 1922.

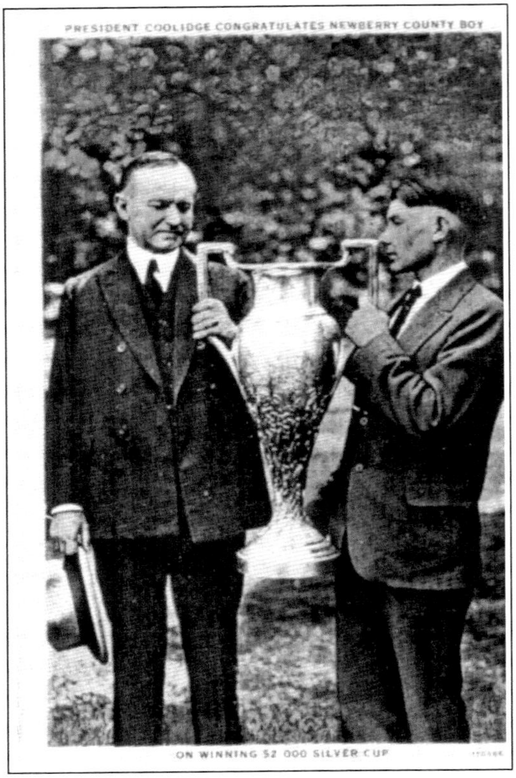

PRESIDENT COOLIDGE CONGRATULATES NEWBERRY COUNTY BOY [1926]. Willie Pat Boland, the 17-year-old son of C.F. Boland of Little Mountain, won the Southern Railroad's initial $2,000 Silver Cup for growing the best 10 ears of corn in 1925. Boland was a participant in a Southern States competition between the 450 county farm agents' entries. In May 1926 he traveled to Washington, D.C. to meet President Calvin Coolidge (1872–1933), the 30th president, where the postcard photograph above was taken. He also visited the U.S. Congress.

[LITTLE MOUNTAIN HIGH SCHOOL, *c.* 1910.] The high school shown below was complete in 1909 and cost $10,000. V.B. Sease was the principal with A. Davis, R. Summer, and W.B. Shealy as teachers. A.L. Pugh was the superintendent in 1915 when the high school had 5 teachers and 188 students. By 1924 it had become a four-year high school that could award state certified diplomas.

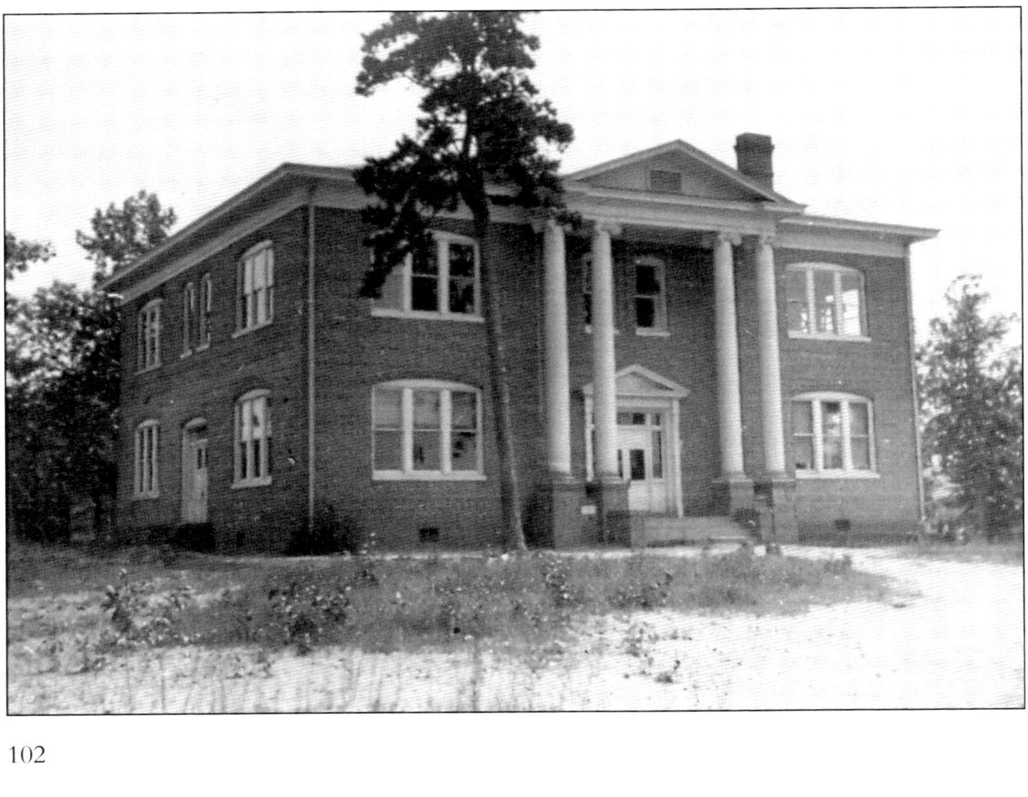

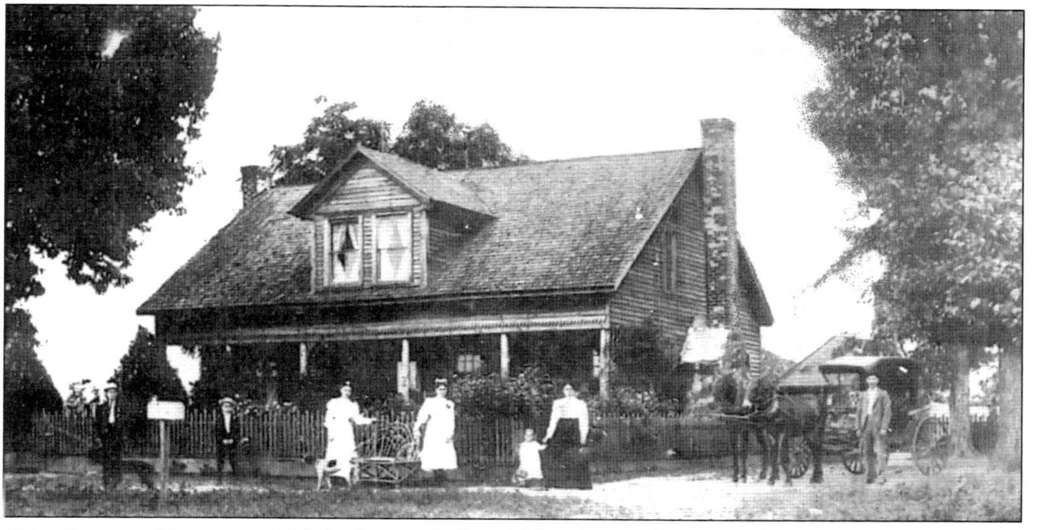

[The Taylor Home, *c.* 1908.] The Noah E. and Ellen N. Taylor home, built *c.* 1885, is located on the Counts Sausage Road (2001) near the Bush River bridge. The Taylor family, standing in front of their residence in this 1908 scene, from left to right, includes Herman N., Bernard, Ruby Lee, Hettie T. Bowers, Artie T. Hawkins, Ellen N. (mother), and Noah E. Taylor (father). This farm is about six miles west of Prosperity in the St. Luke's Community.

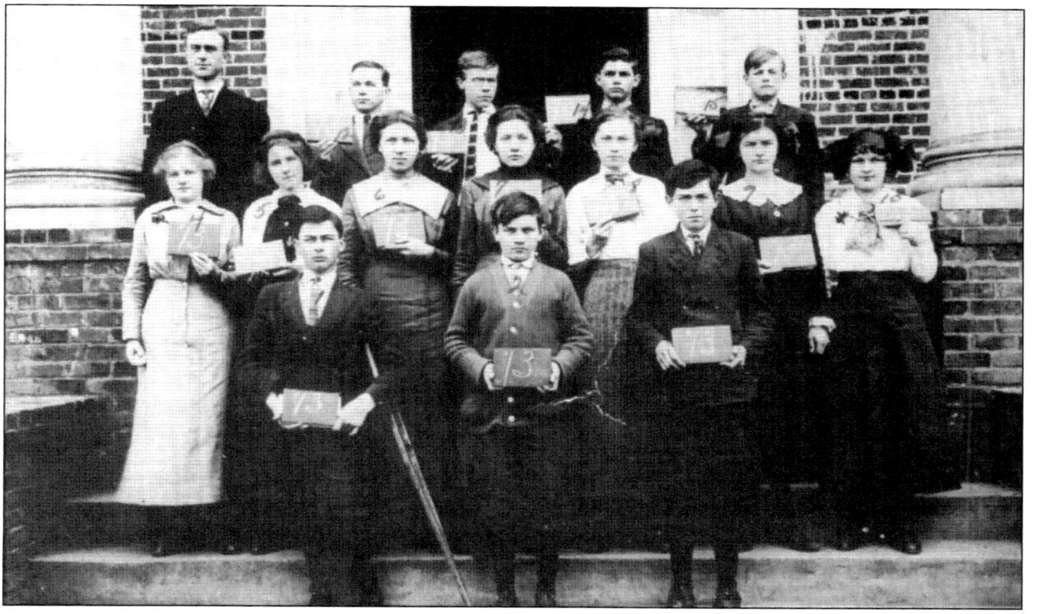

[Class of 1913.] Little Mountain's first school opened in 1892 in a tenant house and was taught by Rev. S.L. Nease, pastor of newly established Holy Trinity Lutheran Church. Later A.N. Boland gave an acre of land, and a one-room school was erected with T. Dreher as teacher. In 1900 the school had 90 students in a session of 28 weeks. J.W. Ballentine taught from 1905 to 1908. In 1920 the student classes were first grade, 18 students; second grade, 9; third grade, 13; fourth grade, 12; fifth grade, 14; sixth grade, 11; seventh grade, 15; eighth grade, 20; ninth grade, 15; and tenth grade, 10, for a total of 137 children.

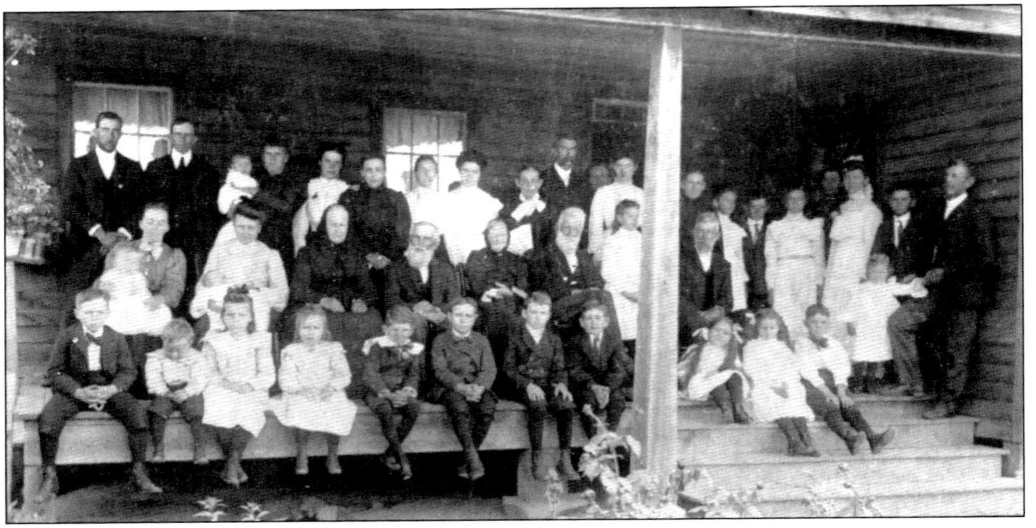

[**Boozer Family Reunion, c. 1905.**] This picture of a Thomas Boozer Family reunion in 1905 was taken on the front porch of their residence on Tode Hawkins Road (2001) in the Stoney Hill section of the county. The home was two miles from St. Luke's Lutheran Church and the children attended the St. Luke's School. The old homestead burned down in 1990.

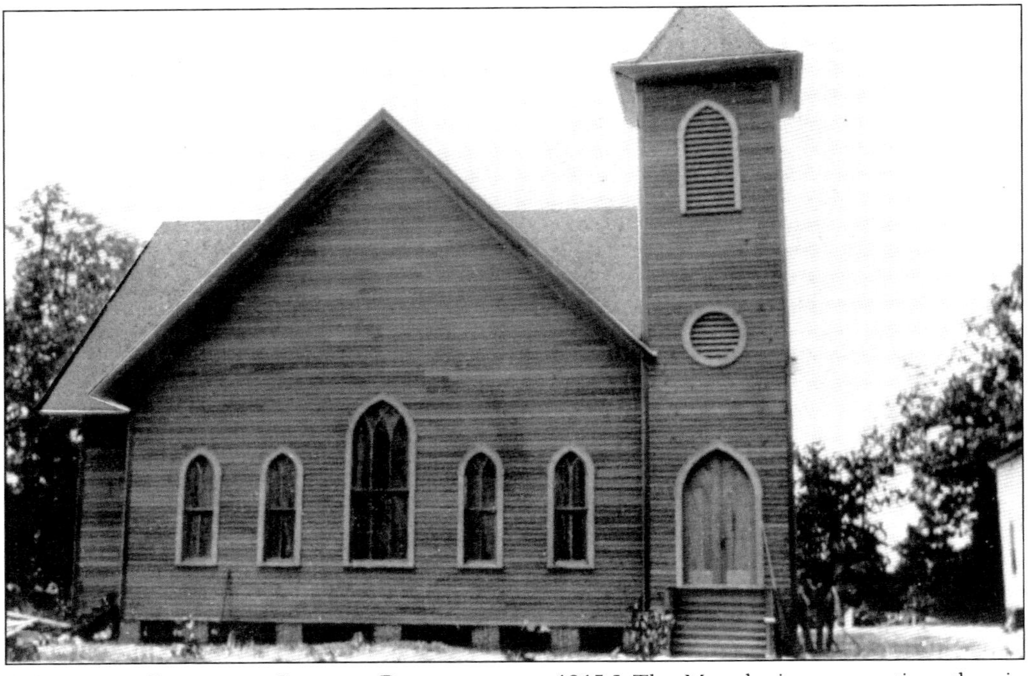

[**Macedonia Lutheran Church, Prosperity, c. 1915.**] The Macedonia congregation, then in Lexington County, was organized in 1847. The first frame meeting house *c.*1850—without heating—was used for 35 years. The second edifice, shown above, was built in 1914 at a cost of $4,000. The waters of Lake Murray (in 1928) came within yards of the church on three sides. The church lost one-third of its pre-1928 members but has rebuilt its membership by 2001. The church is now in Newberry County.

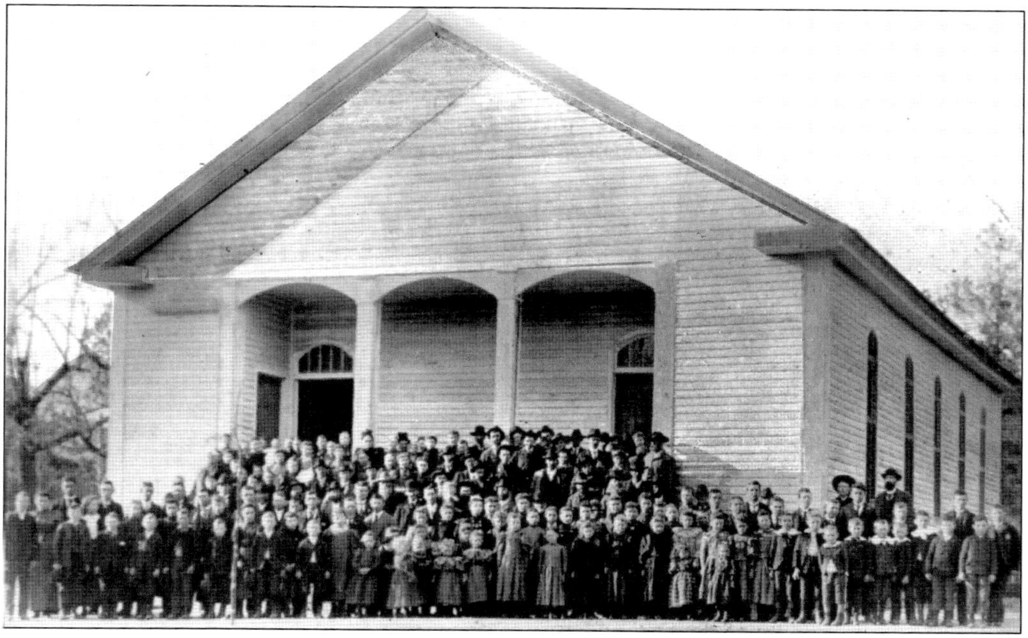

[St. Luke's Lutheran Church, 1896.] The Rev. J.G. Schwartz organized this congregation at Stoney Hill in 1828. In 1845 the initial building was razed and a larger one built on the same site, which continued in use for 110 years. This congregation became the largest rural church in the Synod. The picture above was taken in 1896. St. Luke's families also built a one-room school in the 1880s on their grounds, which had 79 students in 1900. V. Hawley, principal, and three other teachers instructed 121 students in 1923.

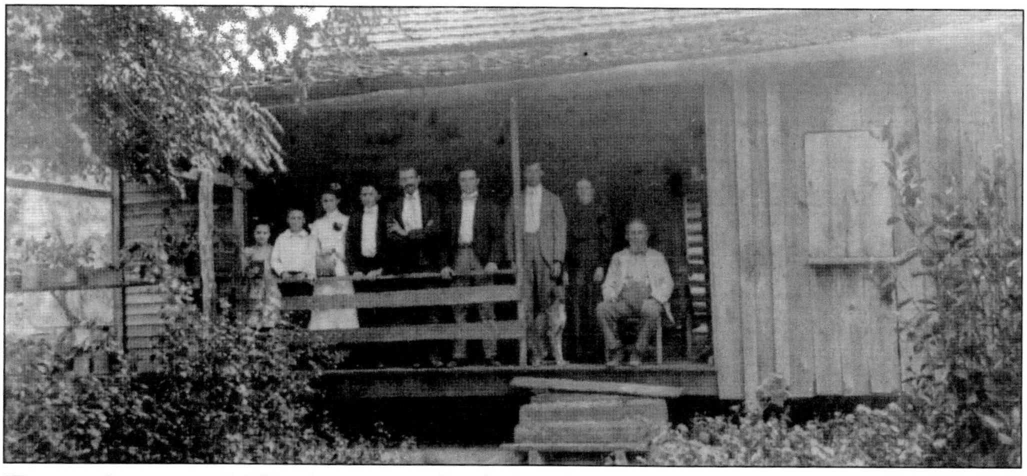

[Family Gathering.] This picture was taken before the 1880 marriage of Amanda E. Hawkins to Joseph O. Moore on the front porch of the Drayton Pinkney and Nancy Masuria Boozer Hawkins family residence (*c.* 1850). The home and farm were located on Stoney Hill Road (2001) on land behind the future Stoney Hill School. Family members on the porch, from left to right, included Emma, Paul, Amanda, Joseph O. Moore, Samuel, Henry, Ruben, Nancy (mother), and Drayton P. Hawkins (father). Later, Joseph Moore ran a community store where neighbors could barter or sell foodstuffs for needed merchandise.

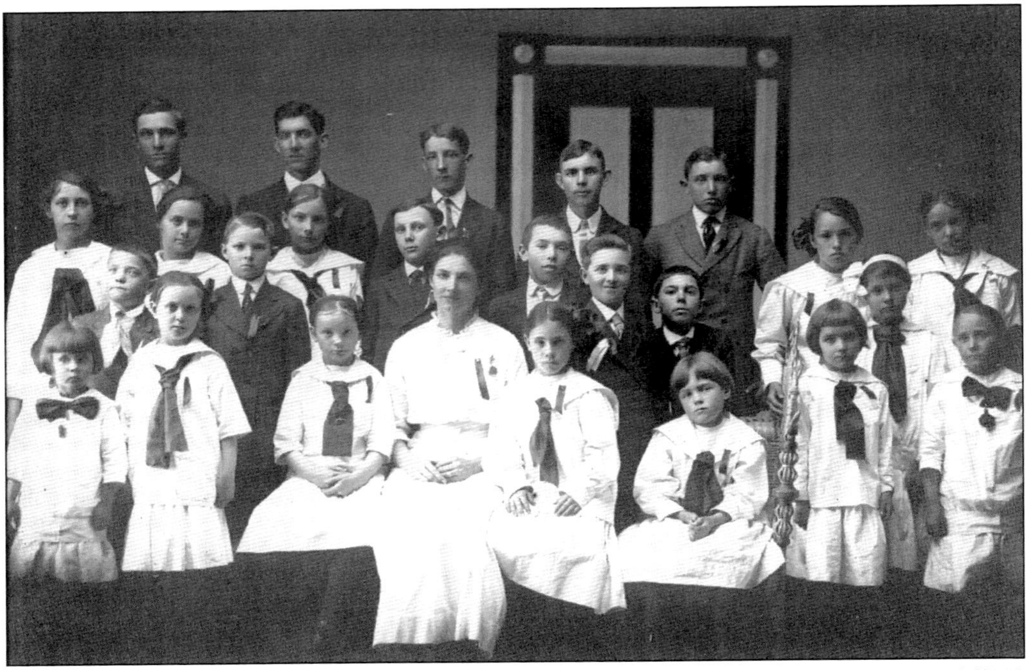

[Big Creek School, c. 1921.] Big Creek School was a one-room frame structure near Road #391 and Big Creek Road (2001), with 57 white students studying in a 24-week session in 1900. The black students had similar provisions for 53 children in a 20-week term. In 1921 Big Creek had two teachers with E. Saner acting as principal and 32 students. They were divided by grades as follows: first grade, 5 students; second grade, 0; third grade, 3; fourth grade, 8; fifth grade, 3; sixth grade, 3; seventh grade, 3; and eighth grade, 6. The picture above was probably one taken at the county fair on School Day.

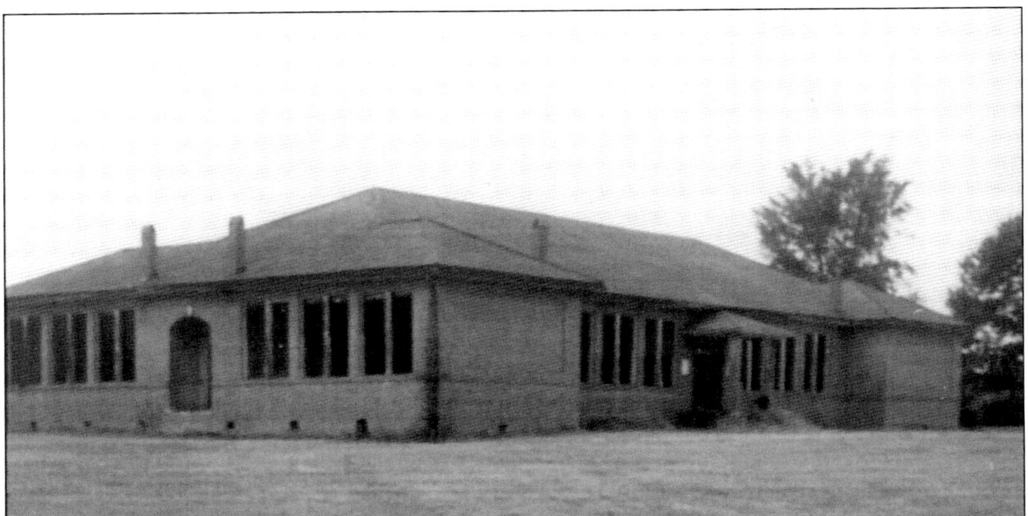

[Stoney Hill School, c. 1924.] Stoney Hill School, near St. Luke's Church, was created during the period of consolidation when the two small neighborhood one-room schools—Big Creek and St. Luke's—were joined in this brick schoolhouse in 1924.

Four

Western Newberry County

This section was settled by the English and Scotch-Irish who migrated south from Virginia and Pennsylvania. These settlers established Baptist and Methodist churches northwest of a line extending from Higgins Ferry on the Saluda River (east of Silverstreet) to the Ashford Ferry on the Broad River (near Road #34) in the upper county's upper 60% of the county. The western section had limited contact with the courthouse except for sites like Jalapa and Kinards, which had railroad depots to connect them. E.H. Aull, Newberry's Superintendent of Education, considered rural education to be the major problem for the county. In 1912 Newberry's rural white school system had 64 teachers and 51 schools serving 1,585 students, while its rural black system had 57 teachers and 54 schools that served 4,273 blacks. By 1930 consolidation had reduced the small one-room schools—56 white and 55 black—to 2 white and 23 black one-teacher schools, and 10 white and 19 black two-teacher schools. Rural education was improving.

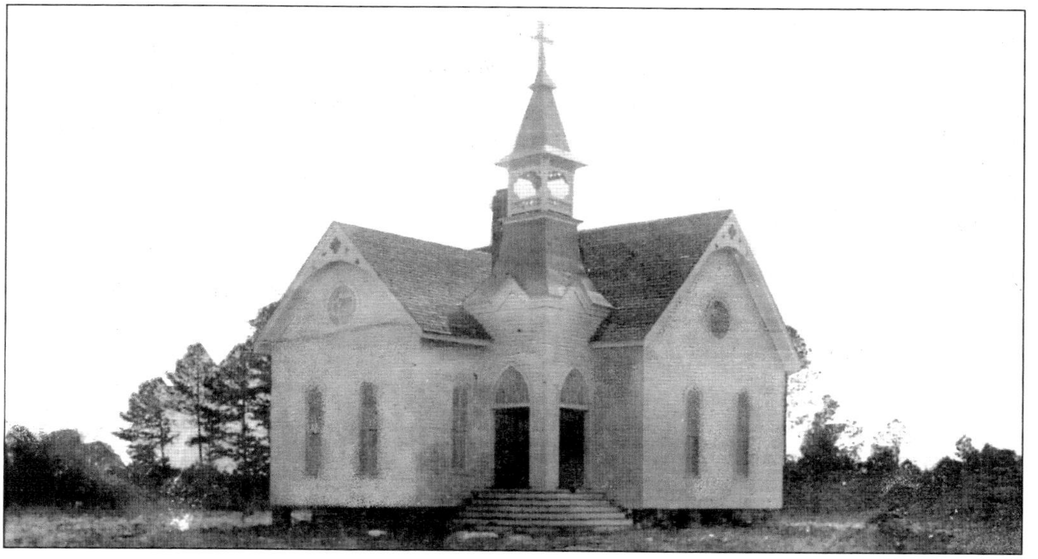

[Silverstreet Lutheran Church, c. 1910.] An interest in creating a Lutheran church in Silverstreet began as early as 1872; however, it did not occur until 1908. The church was erected in July 1909 with pastors supplied by Newberry College. A new church was built in 1951.

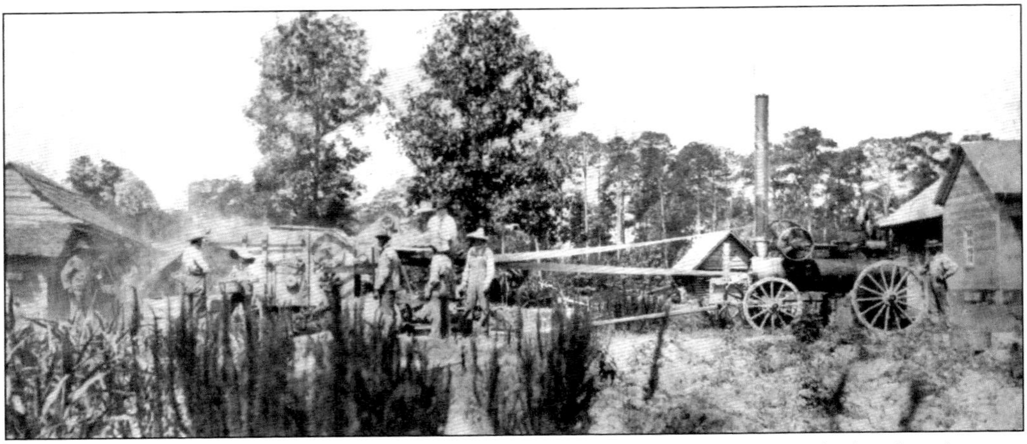

[SAWMILL, SILVERSTREET, C. 1915.] The Greenville and Columbia Railroad placed a depot at Silverstreet in 1851, which was followed by a post office, a bank, and various stores in 1865. Silverstreet, eight miles southwest of the courthouse, became a prosperous community that evolved around the depot. Farmers found that the land was rich, level, well-drained, and good for cotton, which could be shipped from the depot to markets east or west. In the scene above the Paces Derrick's saw mill, using an early steam driven tractor, is being used to thresh grain.

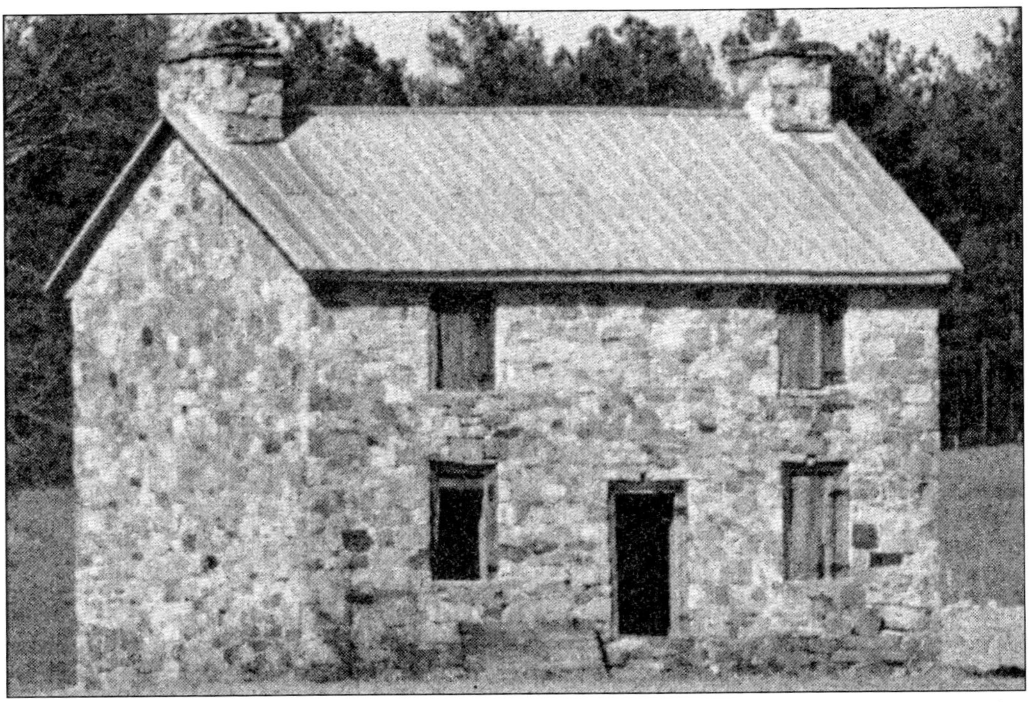

[ROCK HOUSE, 1930S.] Located about three miles south of the courthouse near Highway 395, this house was constructed in the Pennsylvania Dutch style and was built by Jacob Hofmann Sr., a Dutch Fork German, on 200 acres of land granted to him in 1758. This structure, which was created out of local stones, used very little wood an no nails. It is one of the oldest houses still standing in upper South Carolina.

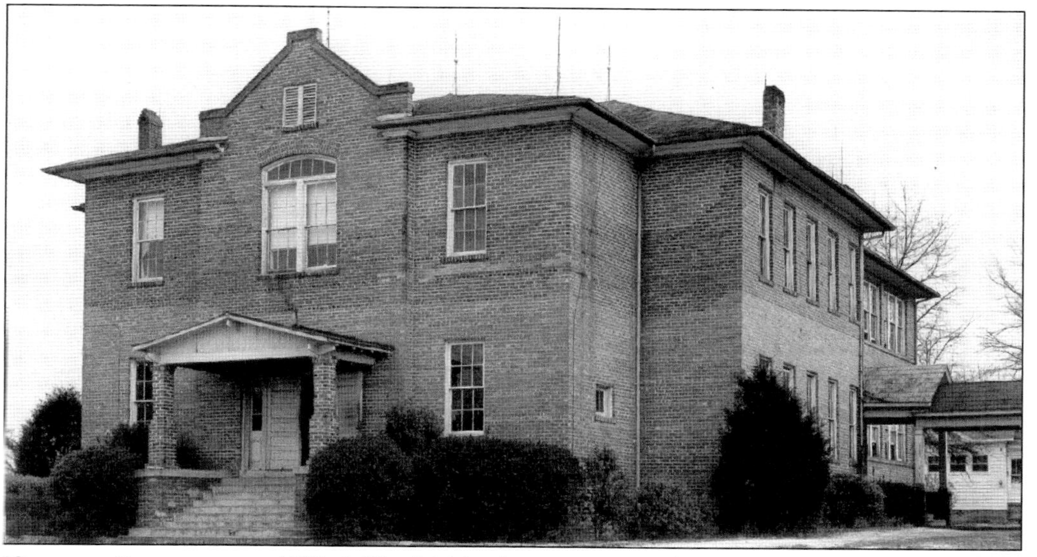

[School, Silverstreet, 1920s.] The initial private one-room frame school in 1901 had only six students. The town gave W.T. Livingston the bid for a brick building that was dedicated in 1913. Half of the original two-story design was constructed and contained two class rooms, a large auditorium, and library at a cost of $4,018, which was deemed sufficient for a few years. In 1920 the school had three teachers and 73 students. Silverstreet consolidated with Deadfall, Utopia, Ridge Spring, Burton, Trinity, and Reagin in 1924.

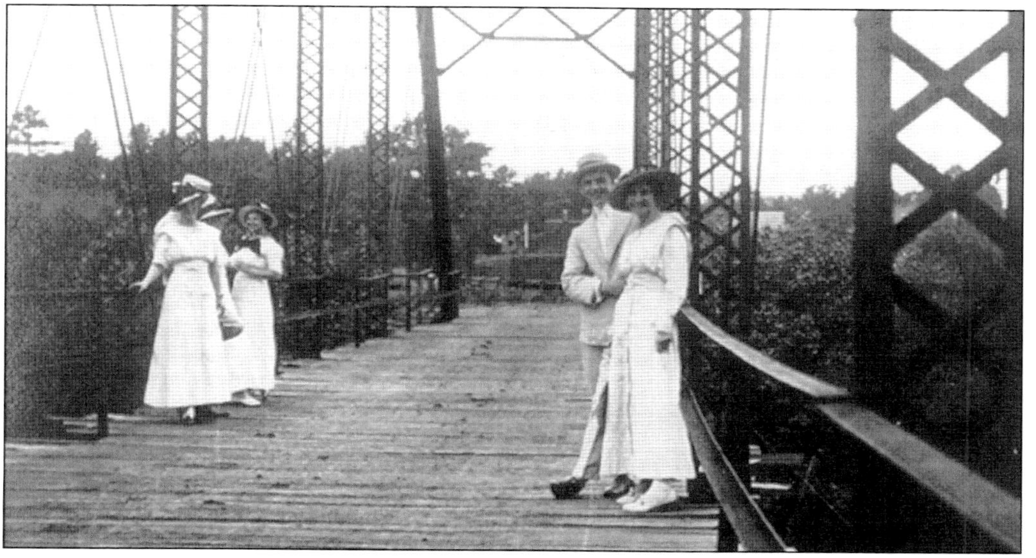

[Chappells' Bridge, c. 1930.] Thomas Chappells operated the first mule-driven ferry across the Saluda River. The first charter for this ferry was given to his son John who built the first store and later the first wooden single span (toll) bridge in 1845, which was washed away in the great flood of 1854. It was replaced and was the main crossing of the Saluda River in that area. This traffic brought customers up Main Street and past each store. The flood of 1928 prompted the building of a steel bridge a third of a mile upstream. The bridge's traffic bypassed the town, which diverted customers from the merchants and caused it to slowly die and become an overgrown ghost town.

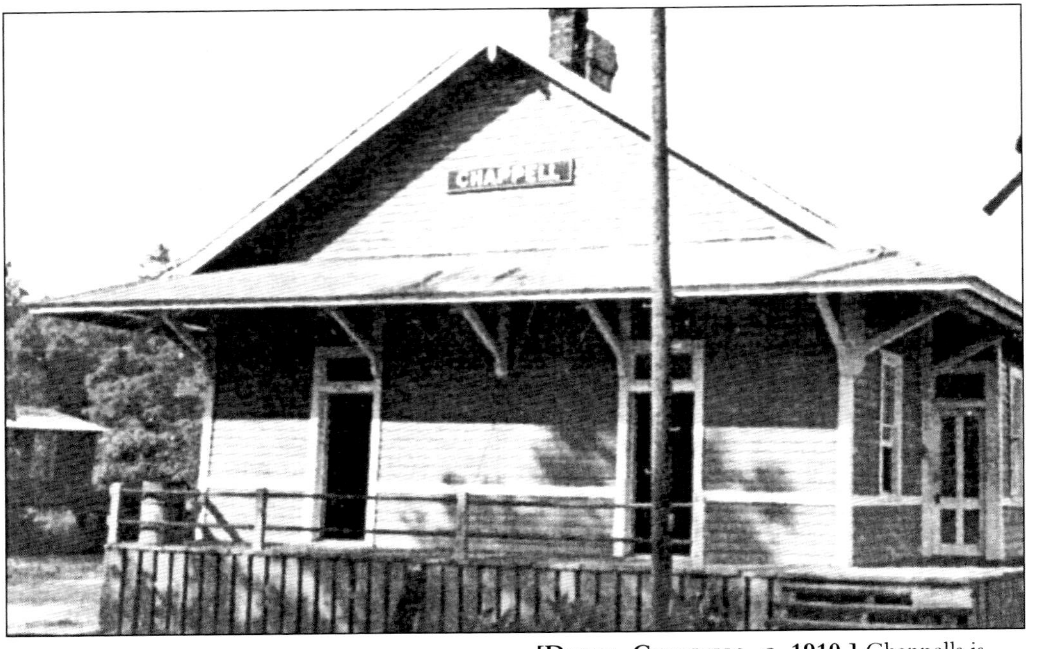

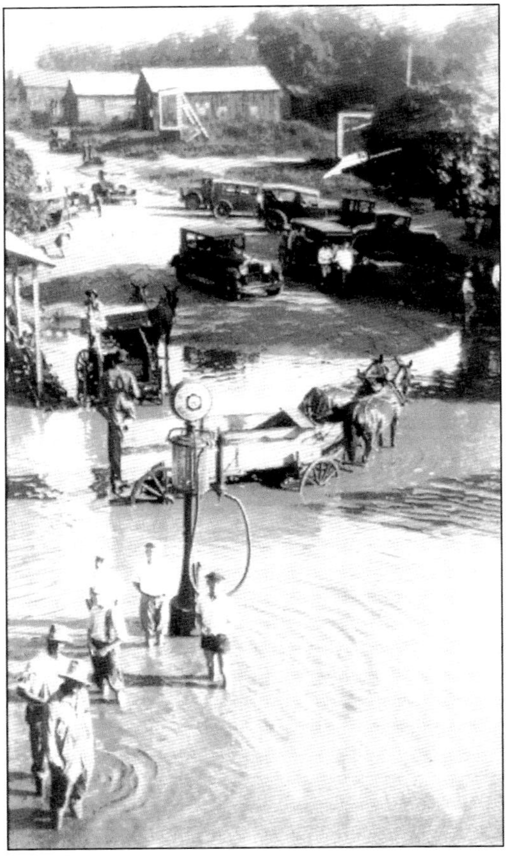

[Depot, Chappells, c. 1910.] Chappells is located 19 miles west of the courthouse on the lower end of the Saluda River elbow. The Greenville and Columbia Railroad (1852) which later merged into the Southern system, placed a depot at this significant hub. From 1880 to 1920 it was an affluent cotton market that by 1910 shipped an average of 8,500 bales of cotton annually. The town's block-long business district began near the depot and extended up the hill. It had hotels, banks, cotton brokerages, general stores, blacksmith shops, livery stables, doctors' offices, and a jail. The depot and buildings no longer stand.

[Chappells's Flood, 1928.] The Saluda River's flood of August 17, 1928 crested at 29 feet causing the waters to expand to a width of a half-mile and cover the Southern Railroad's tracks from three miles above the town to five miles below it. The water at the depot was ten feet deep. The force of the water washed away a 60-foot section of the wooden bridge. Flooded buildings included the depot, post office, cotton office of Coleman & Scurry, and stores of the Holloway Brothers and J.J. Amick.

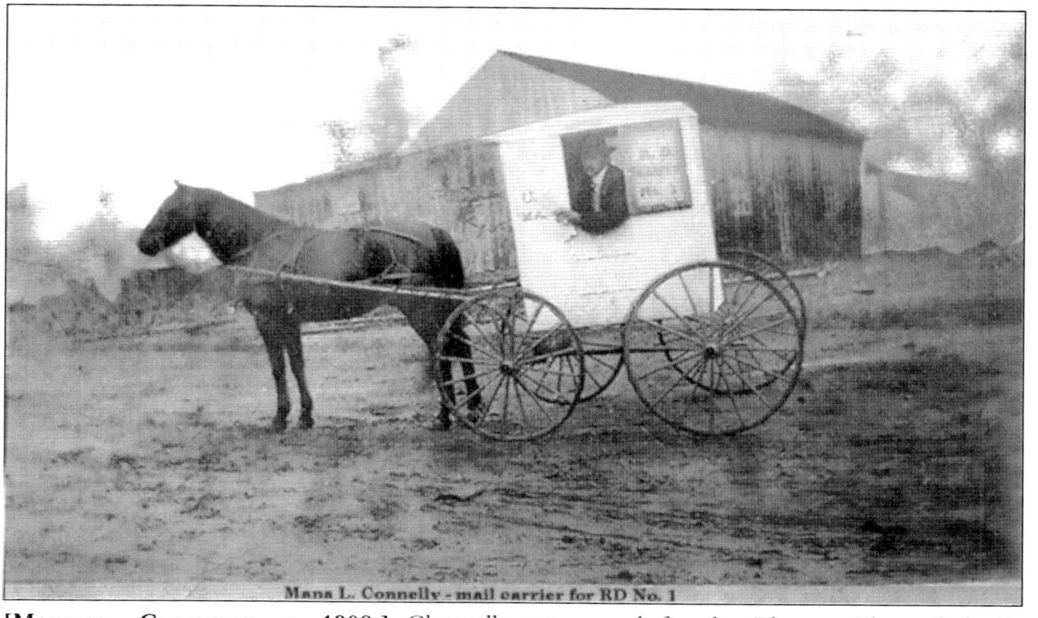

[Mailman, Chappells, c. 1908.] Chappells was named for the Thomas Chappell family in 1756. The first post office was called Chappells Ferry in 1820, then Chappells Bridge in 1851, and in 1881 Chappells. The town was incorporated in 1907. M.L. Connelly (1880–1949) was appointed a substitute rural mail carrier for Route 1 Chappells in 1905 and held that position until he retired in 1930.

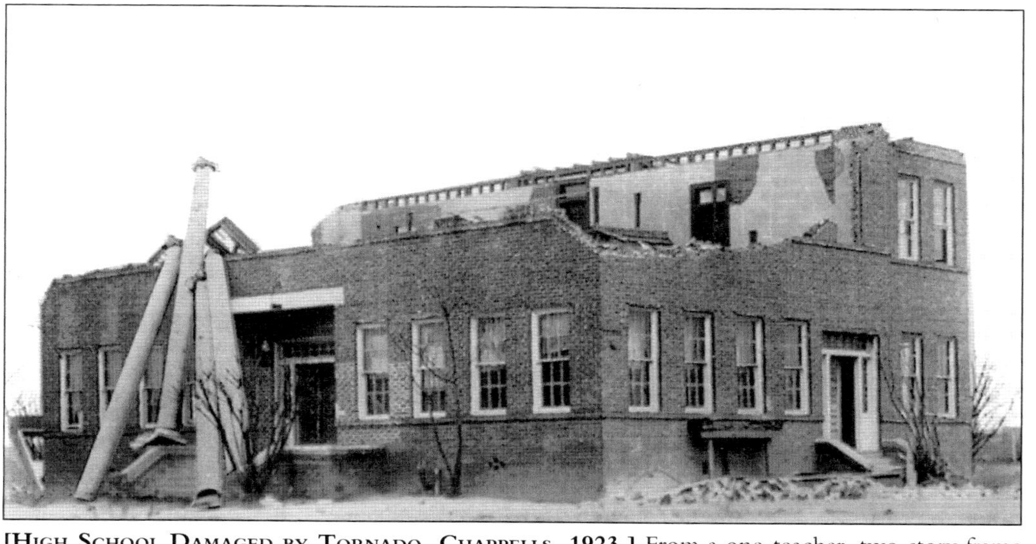

[High School Damaged by Tornado, Chappells, 1923.] From a one-teacher, two-story frame school for 57 students in 1900, a new two-story brick school with six classrooms and an auditorium was built in 1913 at a cost of $5,825. An April 1923 tornado blew the roof off the high school and into a nearby field and leveled the walls of the second floor auditorium. Fortunately, no one was hurt. The school term continued in a house across the street. The fall session began in the re-constructed school building with five teachers and it became an accredited high school. Later, three other small schools—Hope, Union, and Mudlic—were sent to Chappells along with a sixth teacher.

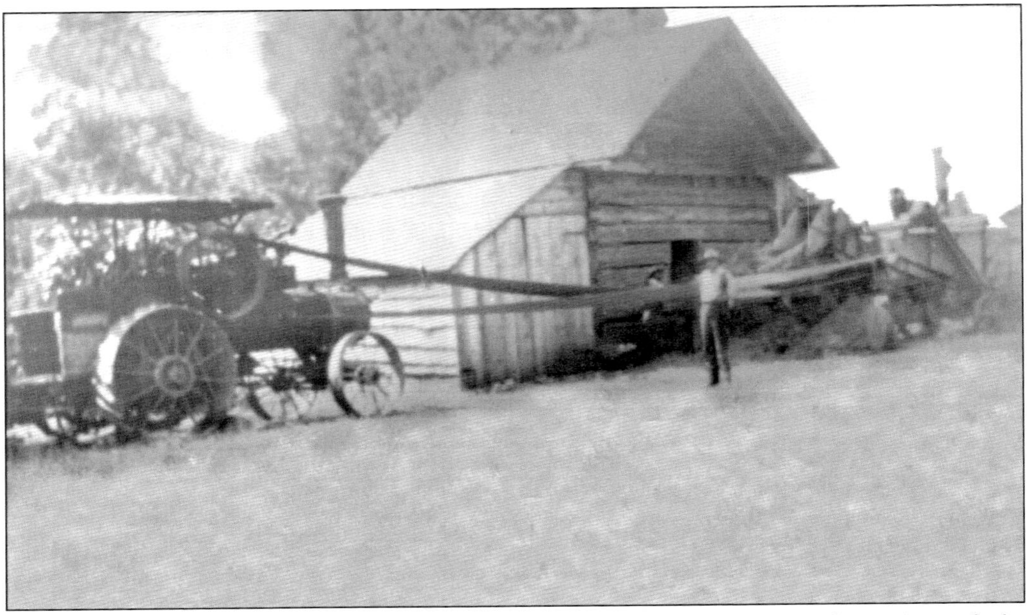

[MECHANIZED FARMING, C. 1915.] This view shows the evolving mechanization of the family farm where mules are being replaced by the early tractors. This steam-driven machine used wheels, pulleys, and long extended belts attached to a drive shaft, which, in turn had blades or devices positioned so that an agrarian activity could be more speedily and efficiently accomplished.

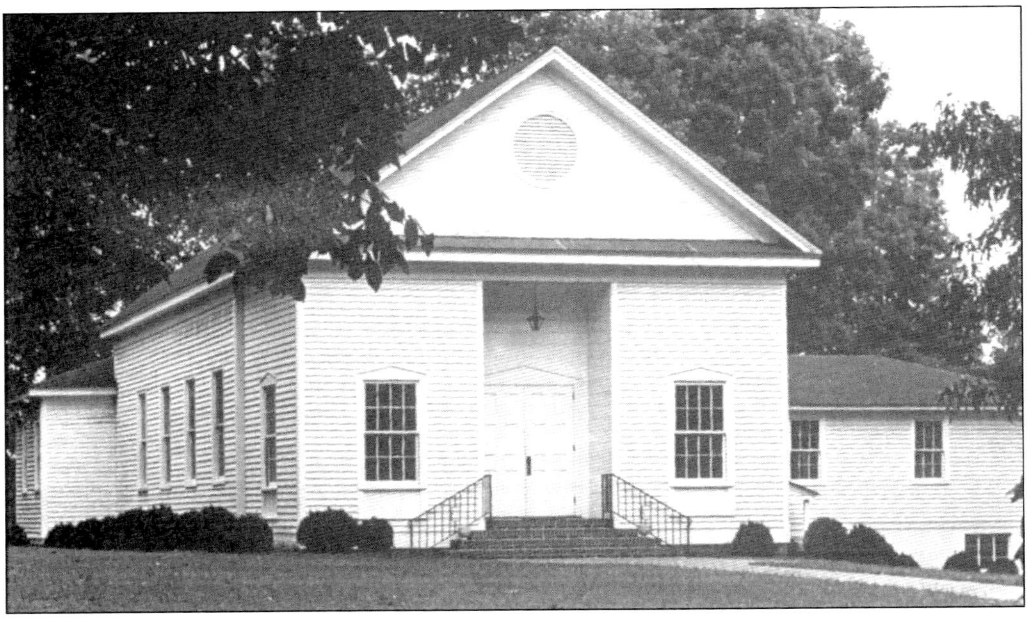

[EBENEZER METHODIST CHURCH, C. 1915.] This church, located a few miles south of Newberry village, was organized in 1814 and was first called Watson's Camp Grounds. J. Gantt sold the church lot near Ebenezer Church Road (2001) to the church's trustees. After this congregation had firmly established itself, it separated its ties with the Stoney Hill Church.

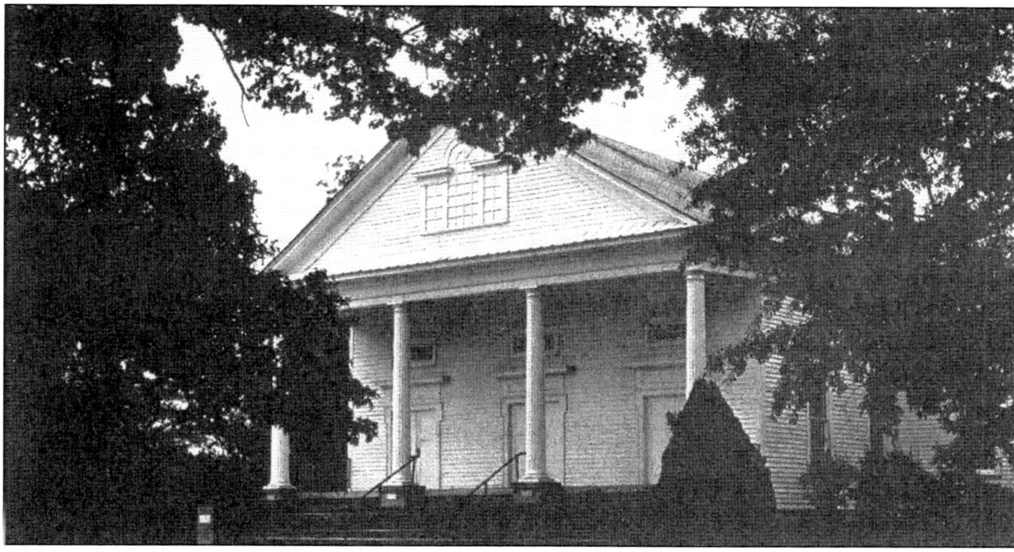

[Bush River Baptist Church, c. 1930.] The Bush River Baptist Church, 1771, is considered the pioneer Baptist Church in Newberry County. From this congregation sprang several local Baptist churches including the First Baptist Church in the courthouse village. The Bush River congregation remains a strong small community church. Its original structure is in excellent condition and is located on Bush River Road (2001).

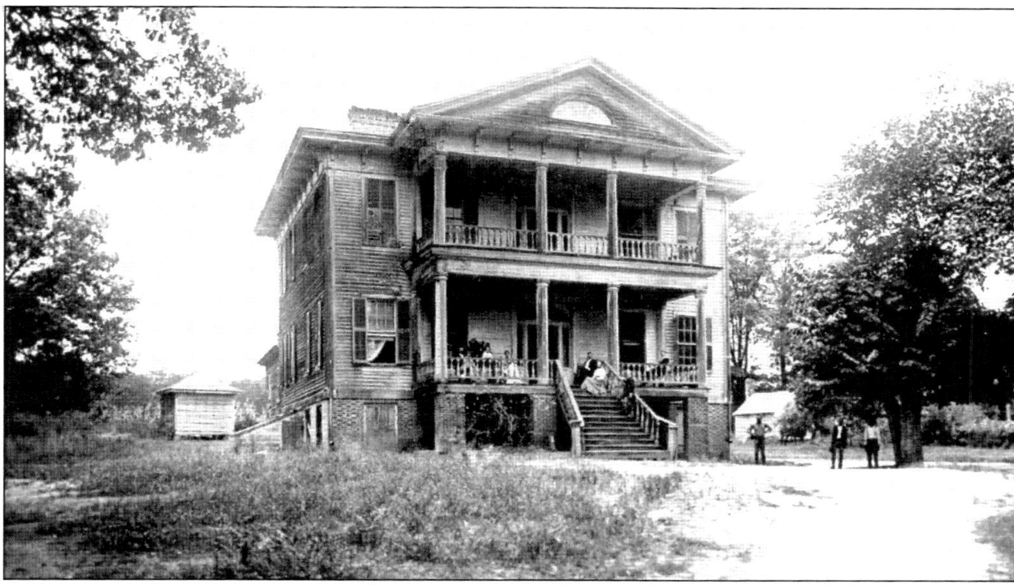

[Keitt House, c. 1910.] The Wadlington House, *c.* 1859, was built by Thomas B. Wadlington, who lived his later years at his plantation home and died in 1882. His sister Caroline J. (1831–1862) married Col. Ellison S. Keitt, who raised and commanded Keitt's Mounted Riflemen in the Civil War. He later served two terms as a Representative from Newberry in the State Legislature. Their son Thomas W. Keitt was a farmer and teacher who lived in the old Wadlington home, which became known as the Keitt house at Keitt Crossroads at the corner of Highways 34 and 176. It was destroyed by fire in the 1990s.

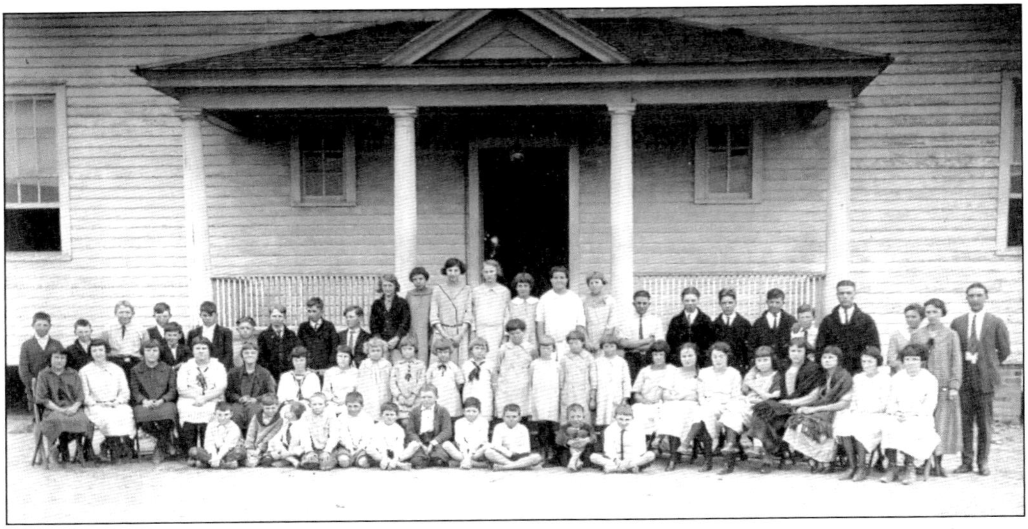

[**Mt. Bethel-Garmany School, 1920s.**] The Mt. Bethel Academy at George Lane Place on the Wendt farm was erected in 1877. The Methodists began establishing these classical schools in 1795 and they were located at several sites. Most became community schools after 1820. The school at this site lasted until 1919 when it was consolidated with the Garmany and McCreery schools and was called the Mt. Bethel-Garmany School with M. Cromer superintendent. The three teachers in 1920 taught 69 students divided by grade as follows: first grade, 13 students; second grade, 7; third grade, 6; fourth grade, 6; fifth grade, 9; sixth grade, 7; seventh grade, 5; eighth grade, 3; and ninth grade, 13.

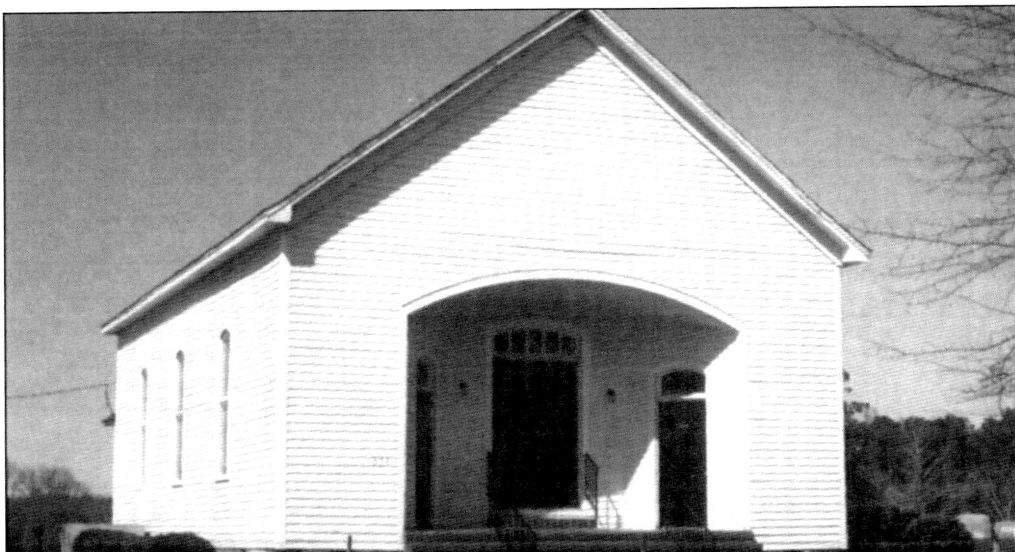

[**Clayton Memorial Universalist Church, *c.* 1910.**] This church was organized in 1907 and was named for Rev. D.B. Clayton; however, it was sometimes called the Halfacre Church. It was built on lands owned by D. Halfacre in 1881 from a track of one acre that was set aside for a family burial ground. This church is five miles east of the courthouse off road 219 on Clayton Memorial Church Road (2001).

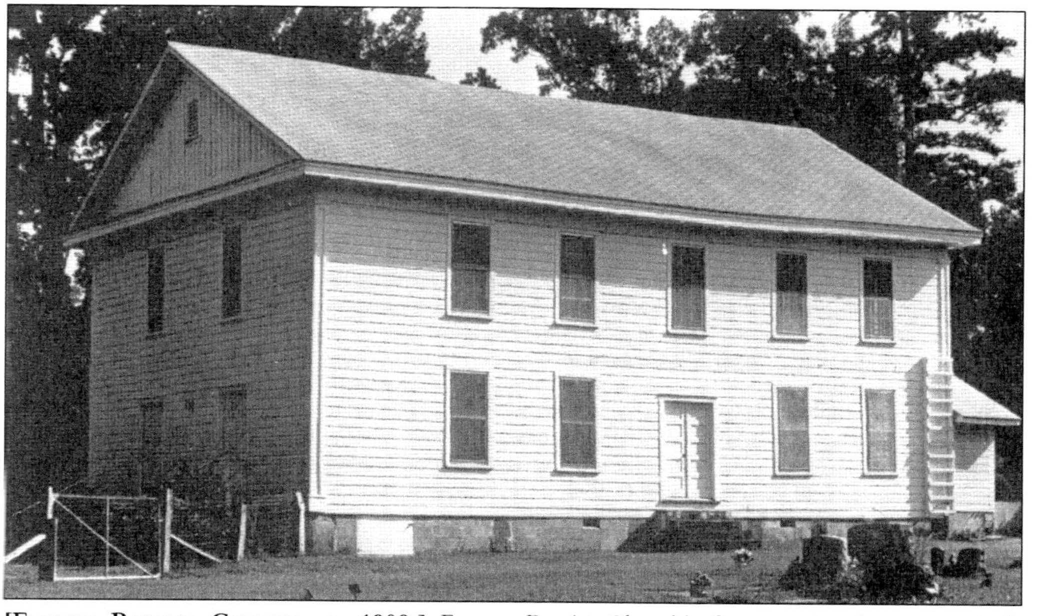

[Enoree Baptist Church, c. 1909.] Enoree Baptist Church's first meeting house was built in 1771 at Littleton's ferry by the Enoree River on Major Jesse Maybin's plantation. Later the congregation moved to a site near Keitt's Crossroads. The membership has remained below 100.

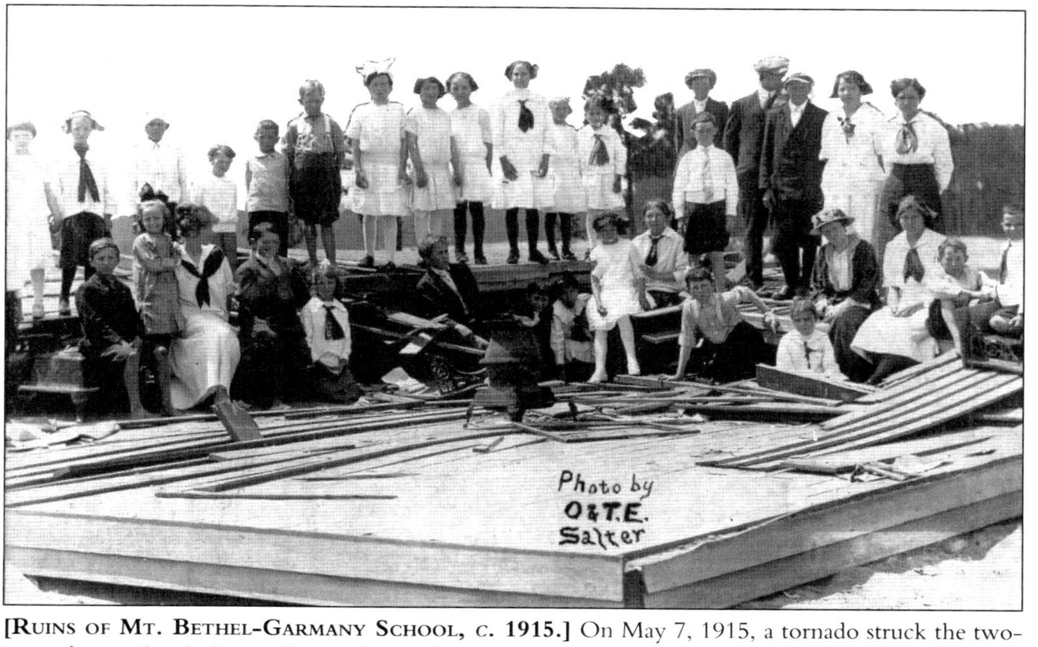

[Ruins of Mt. Bethel-Garmany School, c. 1915.] On May 7, 1915, a tornado struck the two-room frame school, three miles northeast of Newberry, at 1:30 p.m. and totally destroyed the building. The storm coming from the southwest knocked the structure six feet from its supporting pillars. The teachers, Margaret Barton and Mrs. Wilson Brown, and 35 children ducked below the desks as the walls collapsed inward and the roof smashed down. The broken desks created a small space for all to crawl out of the ruins. Fortunately, no one was killed or severely hurt.

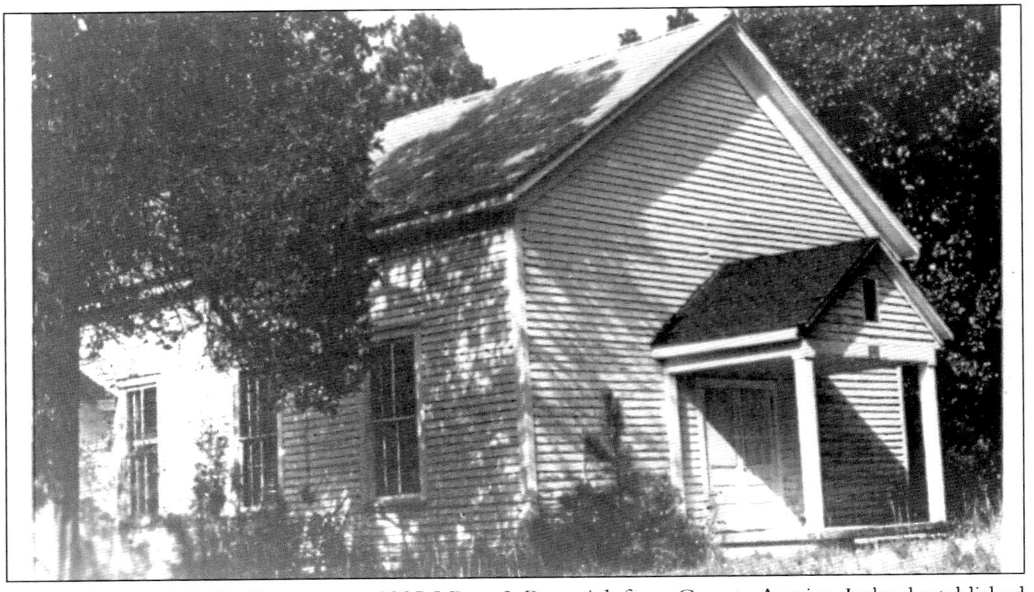

[KINGS CREEK A.R.P. CHURCH, c. 1805.] Rev. J. Renwick from County Antrim, Ireland established Kings Creek and Cannon's Creek Associate Reformed Synod churches in 1770. They became the mother churches of Newberry County, which at that time included Prosperity and Newberry. Renwick died in 1775 leaving these churches without a minister until Rev. J. Rogers of Scotland came in 1791.

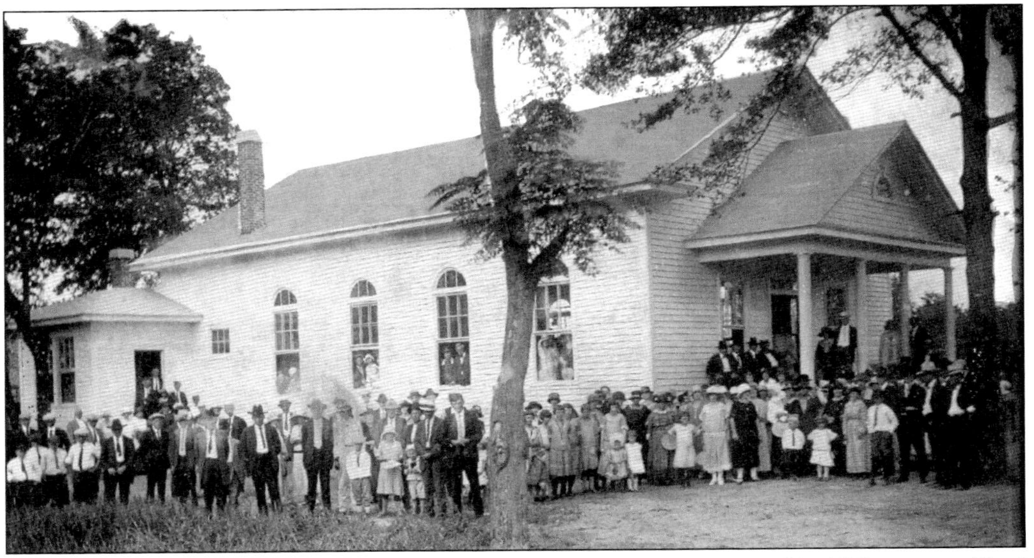

[LEBANON METHODIST CHURCH, c. 1925.] This congregation was organized in 1871, a tract of land was obtained, and the church built in 1873 in Caldwell Township. The frame structure had two doors; women and small children sat on the right side and the men sat on the left. Being one of a 17-church Newberry Circuit, services were held only when the circuit-rider pastor was present. The initial structure was in poor shape in 1923 so the second edifice on Mt. Bethel-Garmany Road was built at a cost of $4,250. The image above was likely taken on August 2, 1925 when the dedicatory sermon was given to an overflowing crowd.

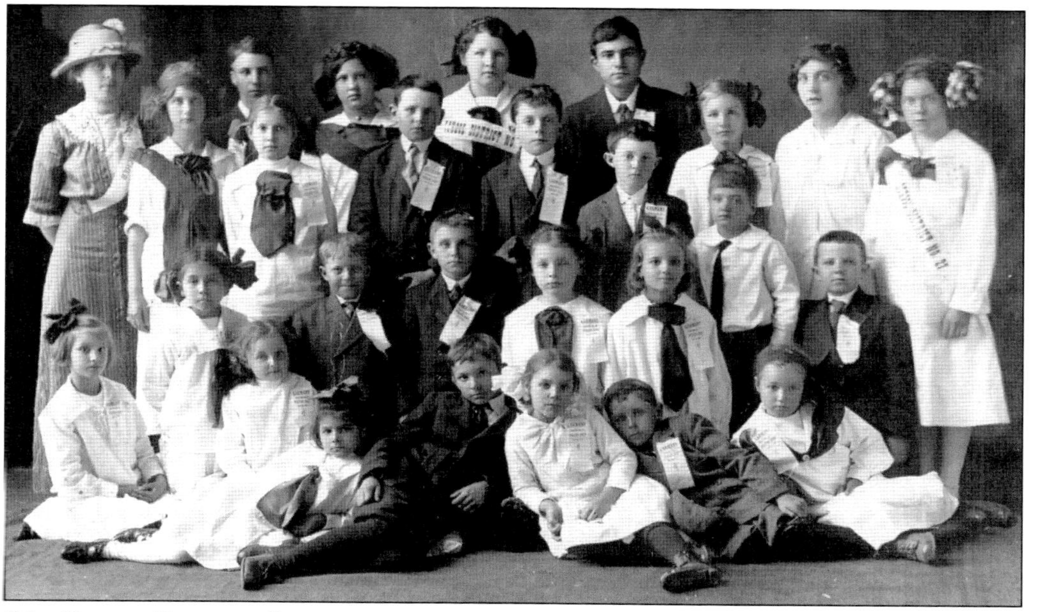

[Mt. Bethel-Garmany Schoolchildren, *c.* 1915.] In the 1915-era students of each school would go to the Newberry Fair and participate in the school day activities, including marching down Main Street and having their pictures taken. Each of the children wore banners and ribbons that related to their Fair activities. M. Cromer was the principal of the Mt. Bethel-Garmany School in 1920 and along with three teachers had a class enrollment of first grade, 13 children; second grade, 7; third grade, 6; fourth grade, 6; fifth grade, 9; sixth grade, 7; seventh grade, 5; eighth grade, 3; and ninth grade, 13, for a total of 69 students.

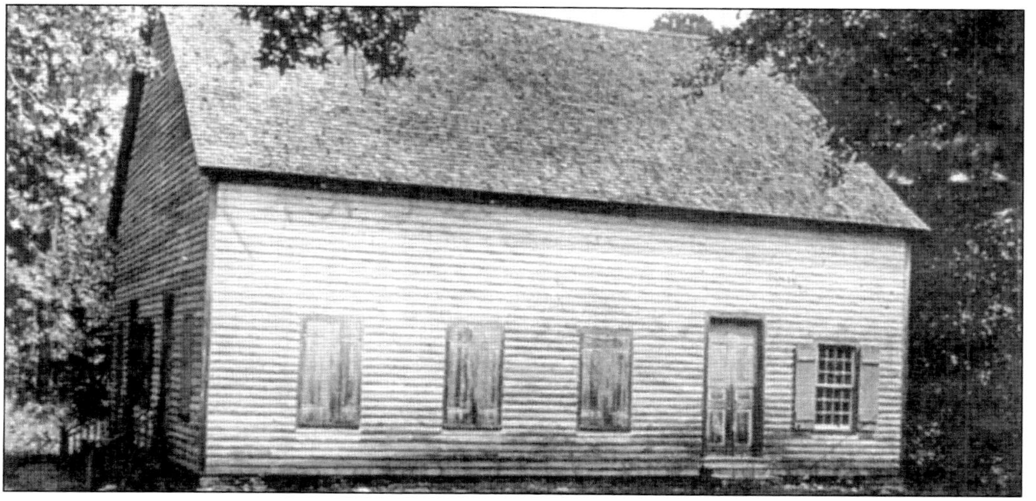

[Beth Eden Lutheran Church, *c.* 1910.] This church was organized by Rev. G.H. Brown, and the sanctuary was built in 1843 for a cost of $600 on a site five miles north of the courthouse. In 1858 the building was enlarged and remodeled at a cost of $1,300. The first log school house was sponsored by this church in the 1880s. By 1900 this one-teacher school had 53 students; it was replaced by a modern structure in 1908. During the 1930s this region was included in the Sumter National Forest and became sparsely settled.

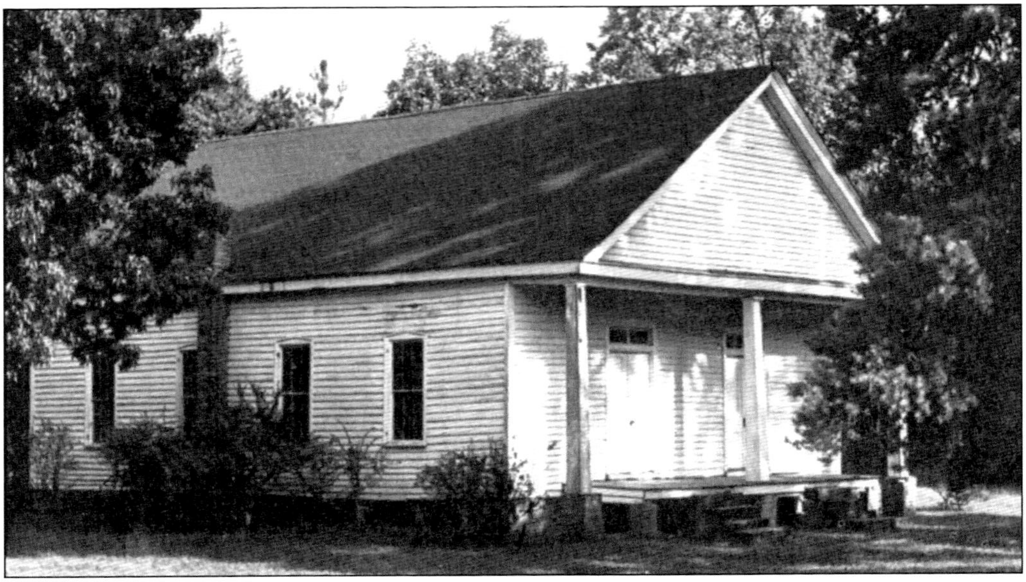

[Ebenezer Methodist Church, c. 1910.] This Maybinton Methodist congregation, the second Methodist Church established in the county, was organized *c.* 1785 and was located between the Enoree and the Tyger Rivers. The site of the initial structure is unidentified, while the second one was located near Casey's Branch. The third sanctuary, called Ebenezer, was built in 1848. Since no regular services were held during the middle of the 20th century, it was torn down in the 1970s.

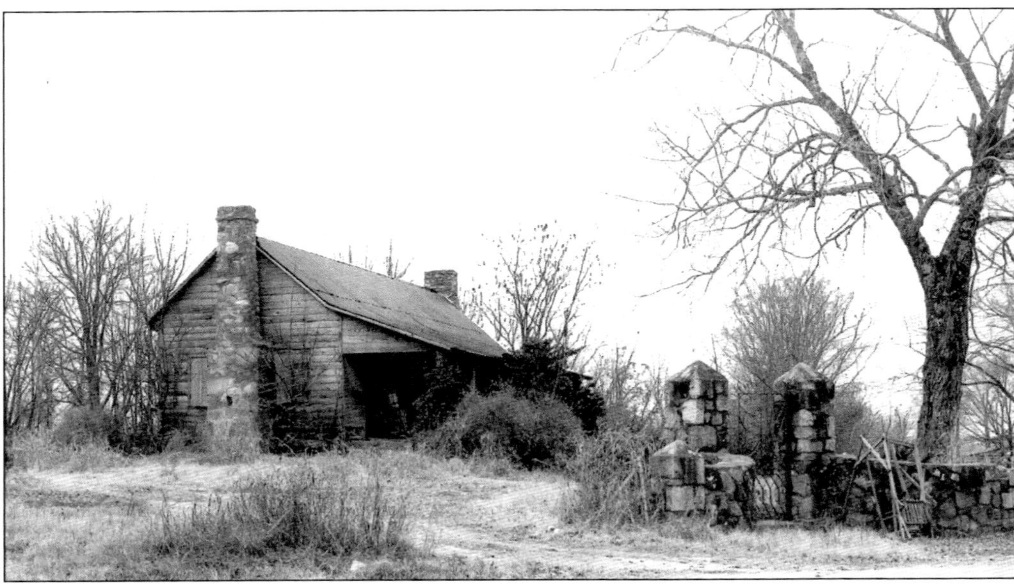

[Trading Post, c. 1900.] F. and P. Whitmire established a home at this site, which evolved into a trading post, tavern, and stagecoach stop. Its location, near the present-day Whitmire, was on the cross roads of the Old Buncombe Road, which ran from the mountains to the Atlantic Ocean, and the cross-county road known as the Old 96 Road from Fish Dam Ferry on the Broad River to the Old Star Fort at Ninety-Six. Whitmire's post office was established in 1852 with H. Whitmire (1811–1852) serving as its postmaster. A descendant of his married into the family of W.R. Hearst.

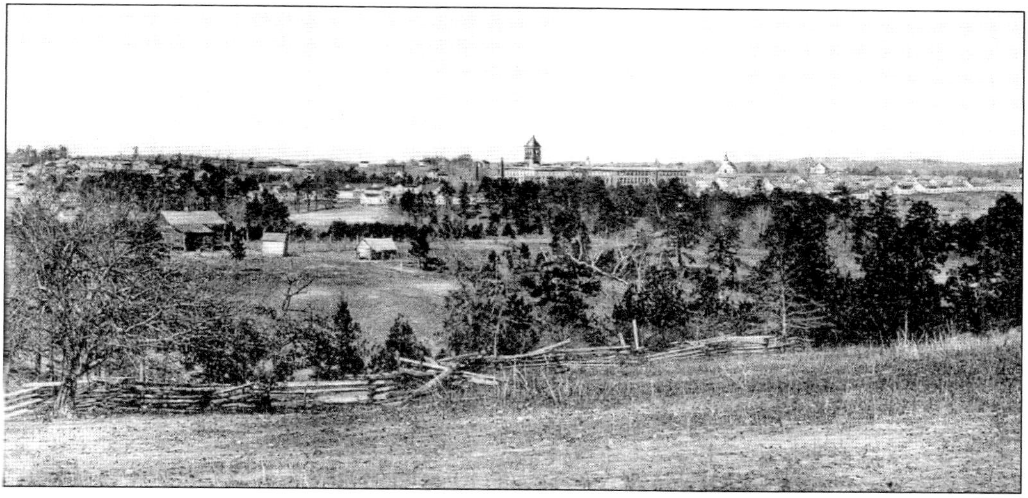

Bird's Eye View, Whitmire [c. 1908]. Whitmire, called the Pearl of the Piedmont, is situated between Duncan's Creek and the Enoree River in a rather rugged terrain of dense forest, wild shrubbery, grapes, plums, and berries. The water was clear, the land was fertile, and wild game roamed the forests. Whitmire was somewhat isolated with the nearest town being a distance of ten miles away. The people enjoyed sports of all types: fishing, hunting, and ball games.

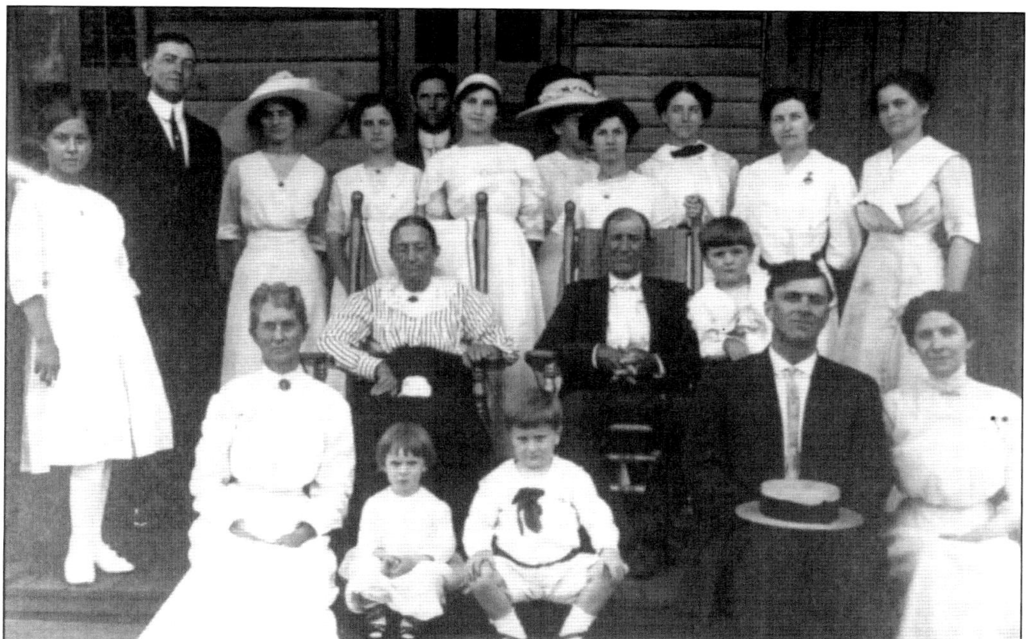

[Adams Family Reunion, c. 1905.] The J.T. Adams (1834–1919) family reunion portrait was taken on the front porch of their home near the Mt. Pleasant Road. The forefather of this family is seated in a rocker in the second row with his wife, E.M. Felker (1836–1914) seated at his left. The children, spouses, and grandchildren stand behind and in front of John and Malinda. John served in the Civil War and tended their farm near the Broad River and the Highway 34 bridge that crossed into Fairfield County. The family members were buried in the Mt. Pleasant Cemetery.

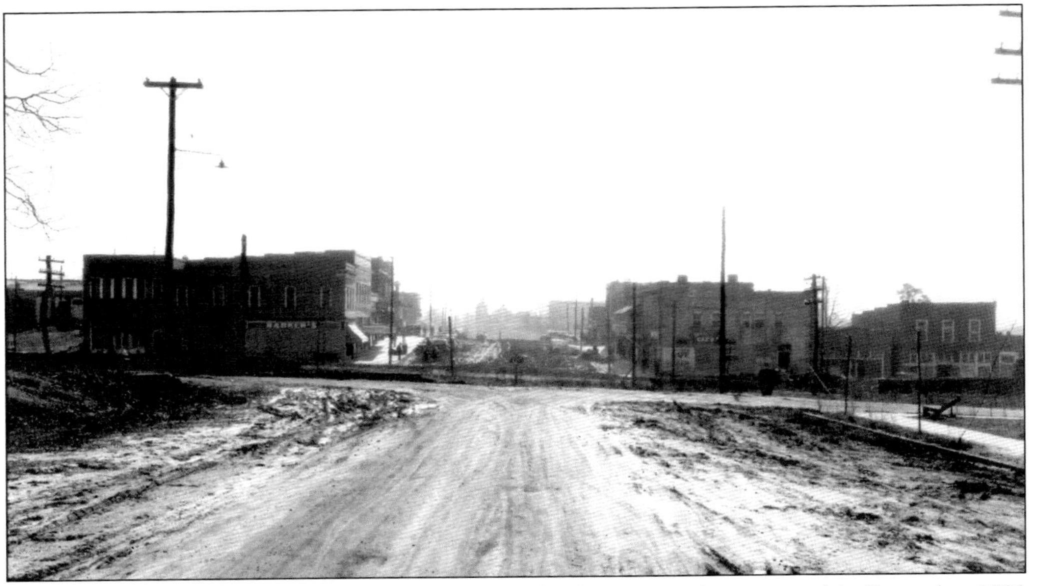

MAIN STREET, WHITMIRE [C. 1915]. The village of Whitmire was incorporated in December 1891 and had five stores and six houses. The first officials were Mayor S.A. Marchant and Aldermen Dr. R.R. Jeter, H.E. Todd, C. Tidmarsh, and B.F. Morrow. In 1890 the post office was removed from the old store at the Whitmire Place and relocated in the Spearman and Tidmarsh store with Spearman becoming the postmaster. The cotton mill operatives made Whitmire into the county's second largest town with a population of 2,500. The surrounding area had expanded to 5,000 by 1910.

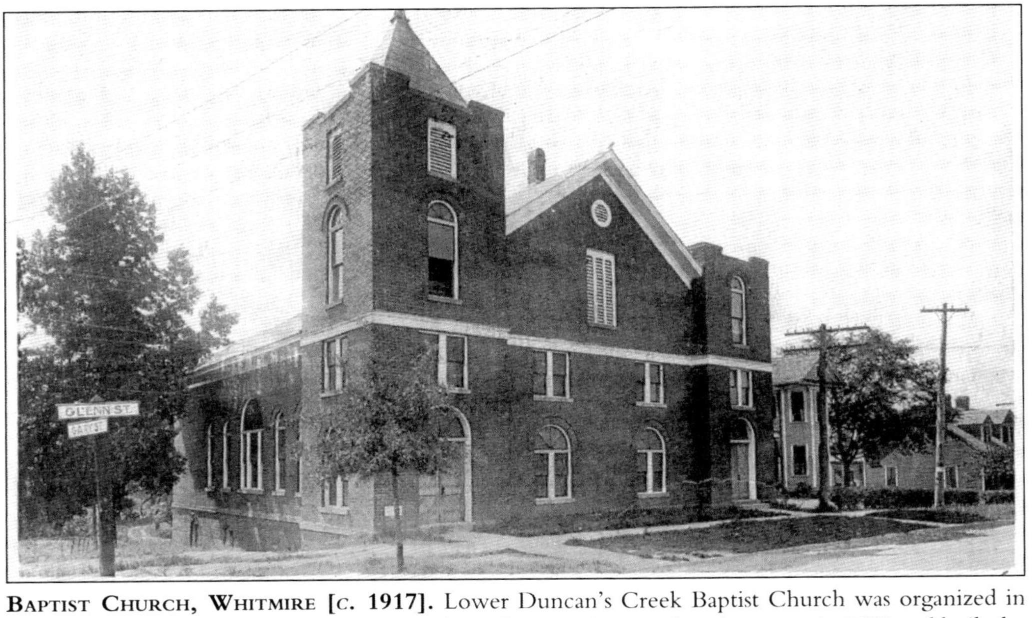

BAPTIST CHURCH, WHITMIRE [C. 1917]. Lower Duncan's Creek Baptist Church was organized in 1786 just a short distance from the present-day Whitmire. It moved to that town in 1893 and built the frame Baptist Church (seen on the right of the Coleman Avenue view), which was used for 23 years. In 1916–1917 the old structure was razed and a brick one built and renamed First Baptist Church, Whitmire. It became the second largest Baptist Church in the county during the 1904–1916 period.

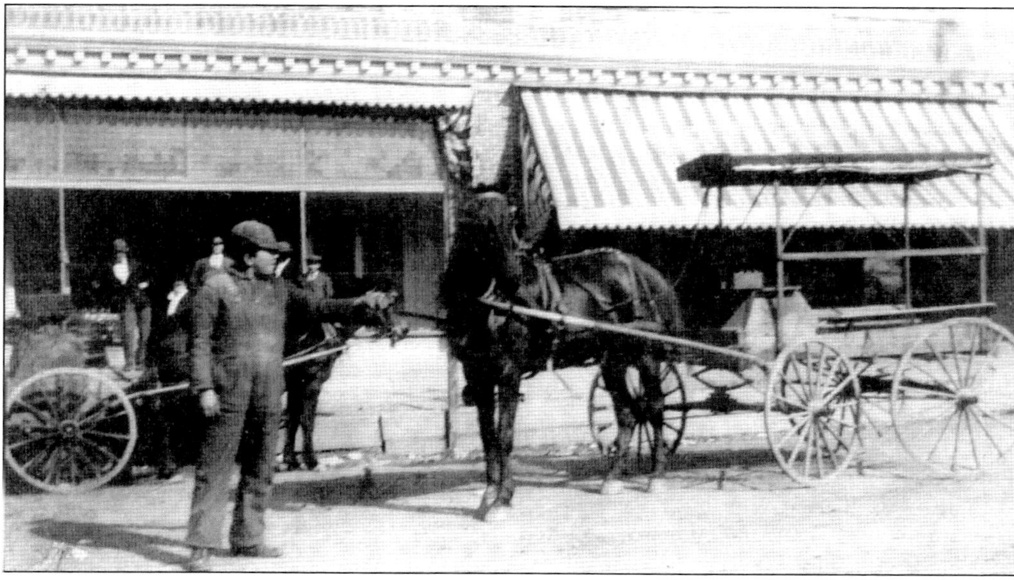

[Miller Brothers, Whitmire, c. 1915.] Miller's Brothers' hardware—with their delivery wagon shown above—sold a diverse range of goods from general merchandise to cars. In 1916 a major fire destroyed the main business section including the mill's Company Store, Miller's, Setzler's, a picture studio, and the theatre building.

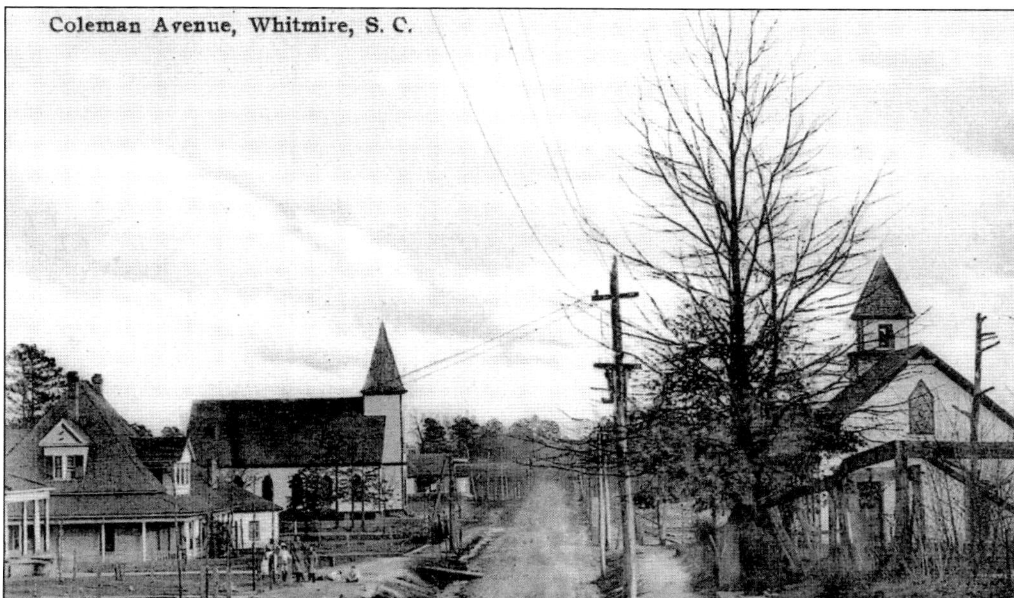

Coleman (Church) Avenue, Whitmire [c. 1900]. The Whitmire Methodist Church (right) was organized in 1892 with many members coming from the Mt. Tabor Church. It was the first church established after the town was incorporated in 1891. The congregation later moved to the center of the mill village and in 1904 exchanged that land and built a church facing Union Street. In 1920 a new brick edifice was built and has become the second largest Methodist Church in the county. The church on the right is the initial frame Baptist church.

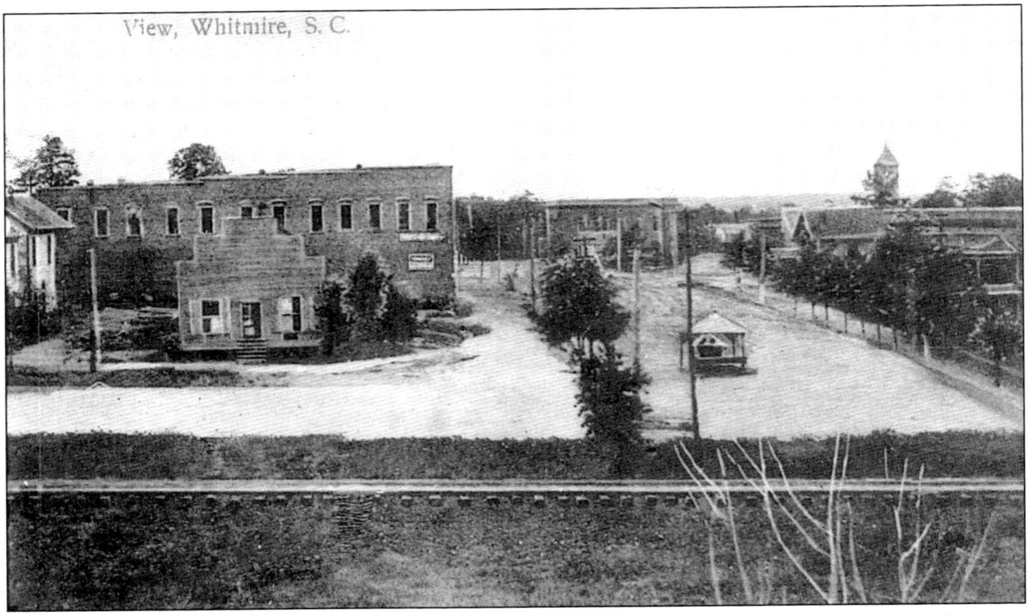

View of Public Square, Whitmire [*c.* 1910]. This view of the Public Square on Main Street at the railroad tracks shows the two-story Miller Brothers Store on the left, the First National Bank of Whitmire in the distant center, and the Morrow Hotel on the right mostly hidden behind a row of trees. The top of the mill's tower can be seen in the distance. In the center of the street stands the town pump that was mentioned in one of O. Henry's stories "The Rose of Dixie."

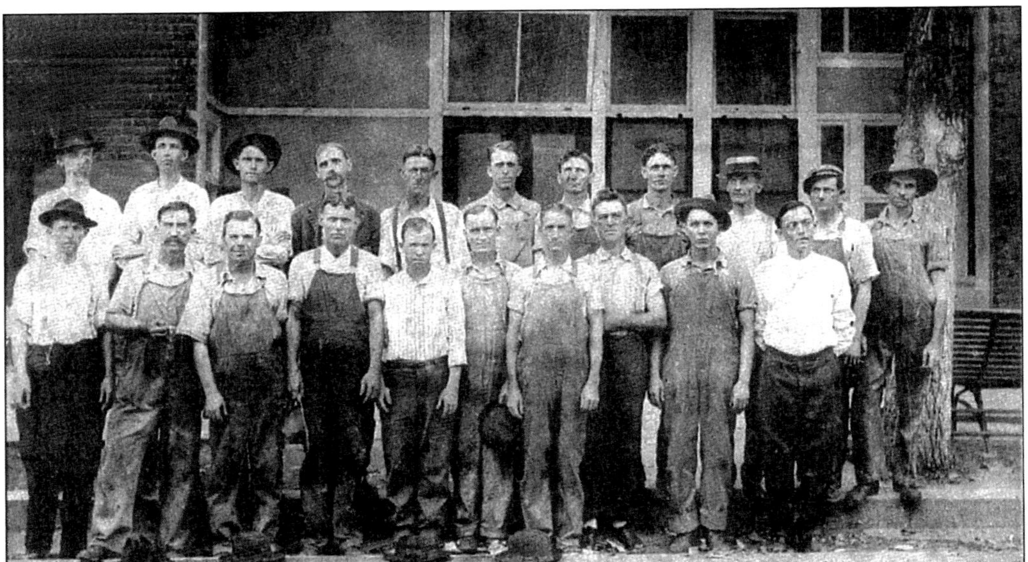

[Operatives in front of Glenn-Lowery Mill Store, *c.* 1912.] The mill began with 400 operatives, a village population of 1,000, and a payroll of $75,000. The average beginning pay levels were 72¢ carding, 60¢ spinning, 50¢ weaving, and $1.05 slashing per day. Their YMCA provided a skating rink, bowling alleys, pool rooms, gym, and auditorium where movies, musicals, and plays were given.

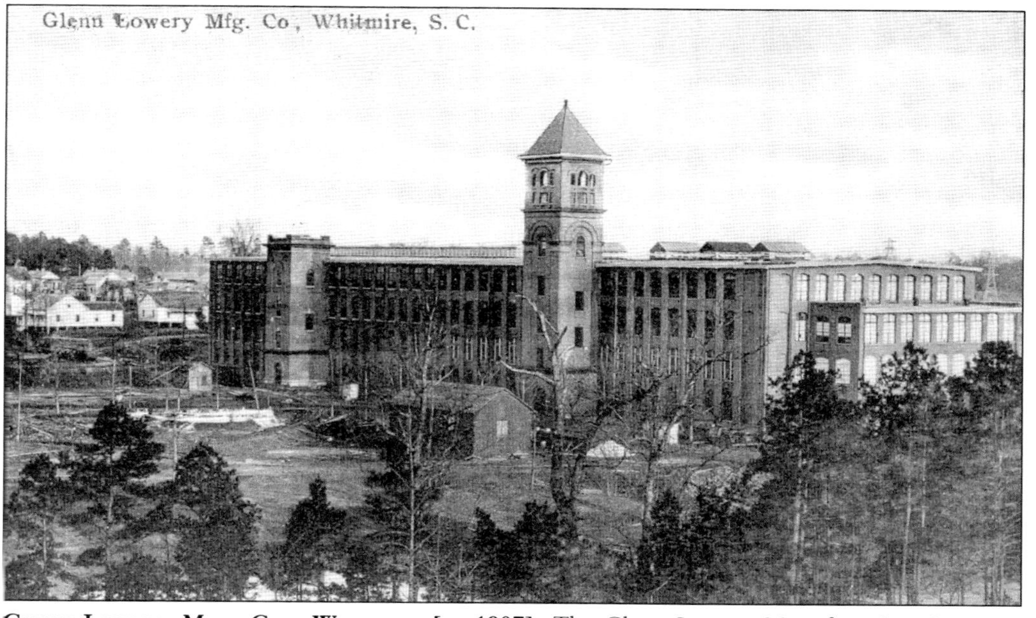

GLENN-LOWERY MFG. CO., WHITMIRE [*c.* 1907]. The Glenn-Lowery Manufacturing Company was established in 1902 with a capital stock of $75,000 and began with 400 operatives and a payroll of $75,000. The mill was housed in a four-story building with a basement and was powered by electricity that was generated in a powerhouse adjoining the mill. By 1905 it had 900 draper looms and 33,000 spindles, and it consumed 5,000 bales of cotton annually. Its initial product was brown shirting with a product value of $500,000. An expansion occurred in 1911, which added 1,000 automatic looms, 8,500 spindles, and 900 workers. In 1918 the mill further expanded to 71,000 spindles and 1,650 automatic looms.

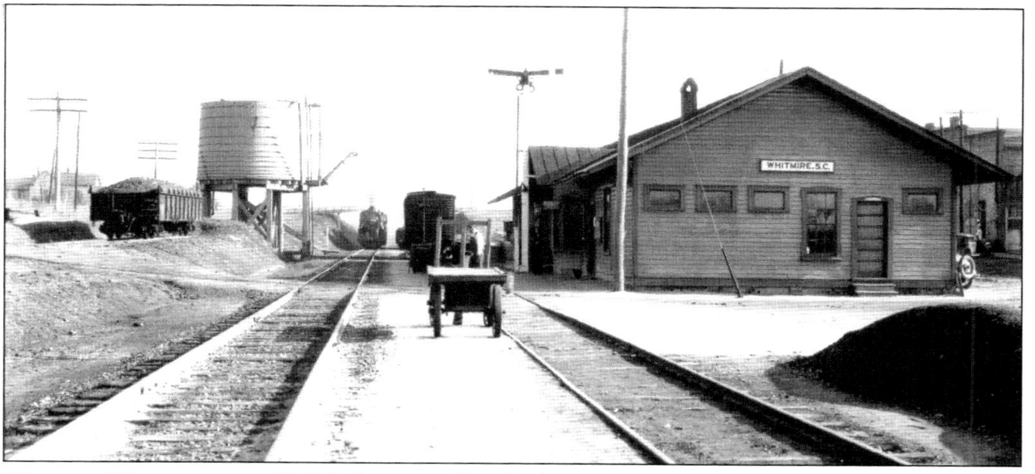

[DEPOT, WHITMIRE, *c.* 1910.] A new railroad, the Georgia-Carolina and Northern Railroad, built a line through this isolated area and placed a depot and fuel stop at Whitmire in 1890, opening up this portion of the county to the markets beyond. Later, it was absorbed by the Seaboard Airline Railways and became Seaboard's main line from New York to Atlanta stopping three-times a day in each direction. In January 1972 the depot was closed and moved to the backyard of Rev. B. Duckett.

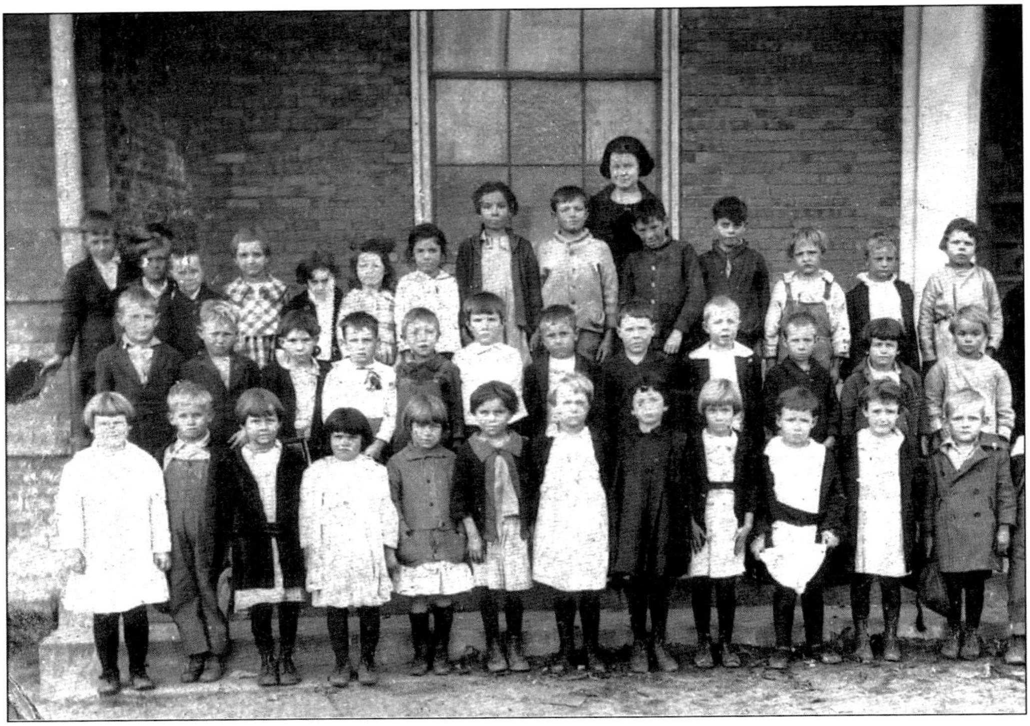

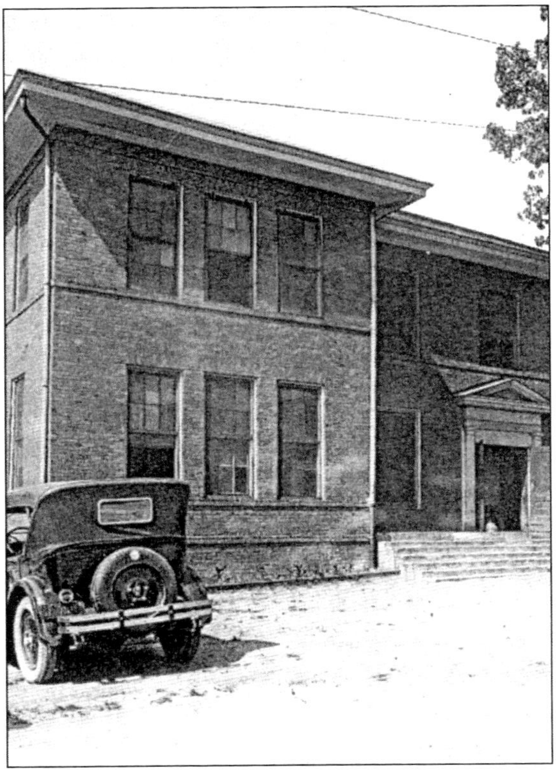

[FIRST GRADE STUDENTS, WHITMIRE, C. 1905.] In 1900 this village had two one-room frame school houses. The one built for the 41 white children had a single teacher and a 20-week session. The one-teacher building located near the black community housed 75 students for a 12-week term. Each school contained a mixture of ages that were predominantly grammar-level students. These first grade students are standing in front of the new Park Street school in 1905.

[PARK STREET SCHOOL, C. 1914.] The Park Street School, a two-story brick structure, was built in 1905 at a cost of $5,500. The Whitmire High School was organized in 1912 and was supported by a local levy of 12 mills. In 1913 a $10,000 brick school building was erected when C.B. Hanna was principal and Mrs. A. Lupo, Mrs. S.A. Jeter, Miss. L. Donnan, Miss. L. Coleman, Miss. W. Agnew, and Miss N. Fridy were teachers.

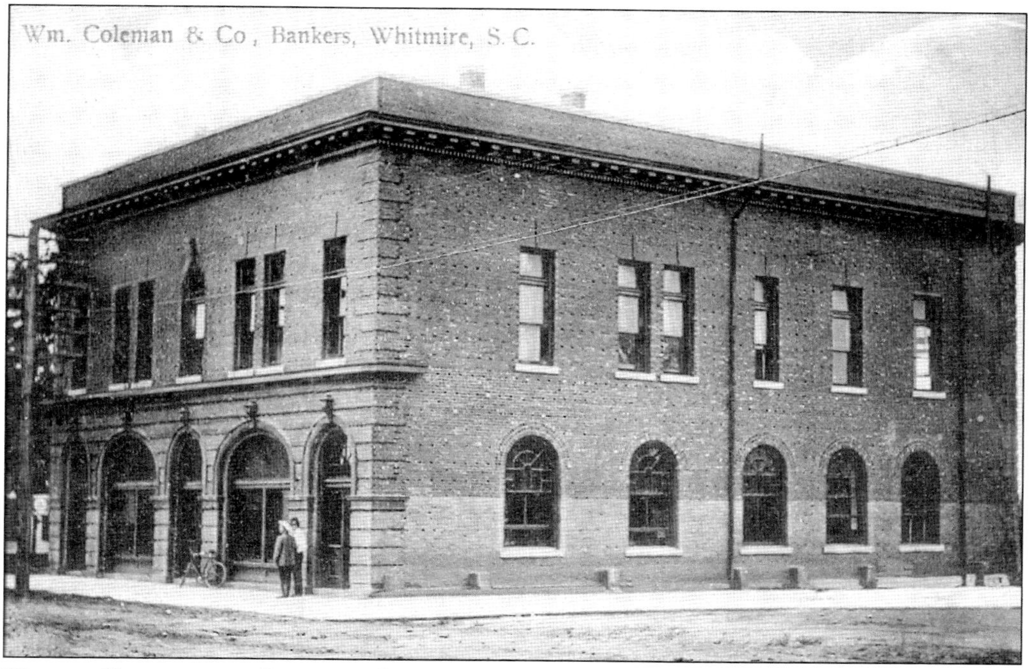

William Coleman and Company, Bankers, Whitmire [c. 1908]. In 1905 William Coleman had completed this handsome brick office building on the corner of Glenn and Main Streets. The street level housed the mill offices and the company bank (First National Bank of Whitmire, which failed in the 1920s). After the bank closed, the building served as a post office, school rooms, and the Whitmire Medical Center. The second floor was initially used as a Masonic Hall, central telephone office, and later doctors' offices.

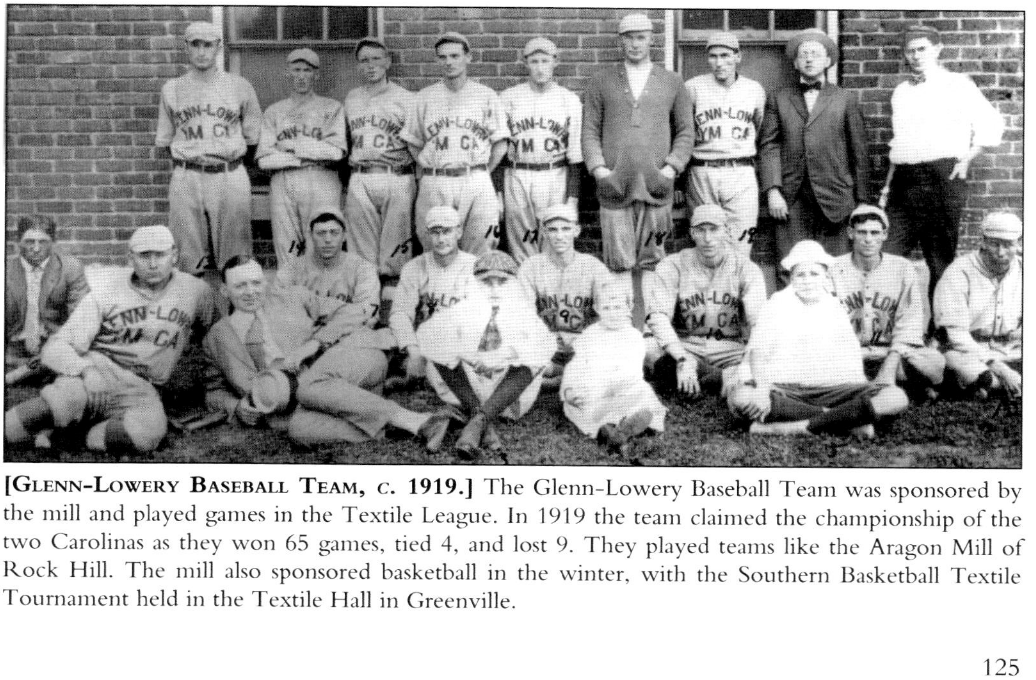

[Glenn-Lowery Baseball Team, c. 1919.] The Glenn-Lowery Baseball Team was sponsored by the mill and played games in the Textile League. In 1919 the team claimed the championship of the two Carolinas as they won 65 games, tied 4, and lost 9. They played teams like the Aragon Mill of Rock Hill. The mill also sponsored basketball in the winter, with the Southern Basketball Textile Tournament held in the Textile Hall in Greenville.

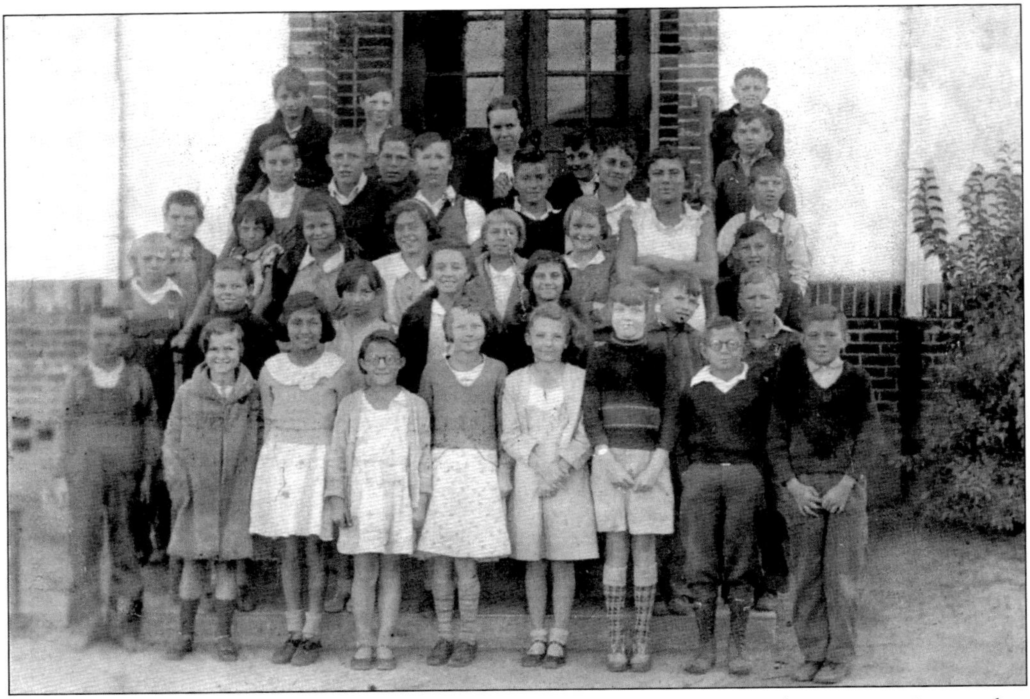

[Students, Whitmire, *c.* 1920]. In 1920 J.C. Brooks was the superintendent over a nine-teacher district. The enrollment by grades were as follows: first grade, 129 students; second grade, 56; third grade, 54; fourth grade, 51; fifth grade, 35; sixth grade, 13; seventh grade, 19; eighth grade, 10; ninth grade, 9; tenth grade, 6 students, for a total of 382. The State Department of Education standards for a four-year high school program were met in 1924 permitting this school to award state certified diplomas.

Acknowledgments

Many persons and institutions have contributed to the preparation of this book. I wish to express my gratitude to A. Stokes, T.L. Johnson, B. Bilderbeck, R. Copp, and T. Hayes of the South Caroliniana Library. A special recognition is due C. Martin for her contributions of images and caption data. Other essential contributions were made by J. Bergeran, P. Schumpert (Newberry County Historical Society), L. and J. Carbosco (Trader John's Antiques), P. Jeter, C.S. Prince, D.L. Woerner, E. Shealy (Newberry County Museum Association), and G. Henry (Newberry College). Sources for images included M. Addy, E.J. Boozer, Mrs. H.E. Brelmer, M. Connerly, M.J. Dyches, B. Fulmer, E. Greisser, M. Hawkins, M. Jayroe, D. Layton, E. Norris, D. Sease, R.S. Underwood, C.D. Wertz, and others at public meetings. Major historical references were from the following: Annual Report, State Superintendent of Education, 1900–1930; Newberry's *Herald and News* and *The Observer* newspapers, 1900–1935; *History of Newberry County, Volume 1 and 2*, T.H. Pope; *Newberry As It Was Book 1 and 2*, C. Martin; *Bicentennial History of Newberry County*, Newberry Historical Society; and *A History of the Lutheran Church in S.C.*

INDEX